THE FENRIS WOLF

Issue no. 11

Edited by
Carl Abrahamsson & Vanessa Sinclair

TRAPART*books*

The Fenris Wolf, issue no 11
Edited by Carl Abrahamsson & Vanessa Sinclair

Trapart Books, 2022

ISBN 978-91-987558-8-6 (paperback)
ISBN 978-91-987558-9-3 (hardback)
ISBN 978-91-987557-0-1 (e-book)

Trapart Books
P.O. Box 15
SE-598 21 Vimmerby
Sweden

info@trapart.net
www.trapart.net

The Fenris Wolf, issue no 11
Contents

Editors' Introduction

Welcome to the eleventh issue of *The Fenris Wolf* – as always a smörgåsbord of occulture and delightenment!

The ninth issue collected most of the papers and presentations from our conference "Psychoanalysis, Art, and the Occult," held in London in 2016. In 2019 it was time for "Re-writing the Future: 100 Years of Esoteric Modernism and Psychoanalysis," a symposium held in Merano, Italy. This current issue of *The Fenris Wolf* in a similar way collects material from that event.

In so many ways, this conference was remarkable. Not only because of its setting in lush and sunny Südtirol in Italy, but more specifically thanks to the actual locations: days one and two were held at lovely Schloss Pinzenau, and day three at the medieval Schloss Brunnenburg. This last location was extra relevant because of our loose theme that year: esoteric modernism.

Brunnenburg is the place to which American modernist poet Ezra Pound retired after having been released from his post WW2 sentence in the US. This timeless castle constituted a safe haven where Pound could collect his thoughts on life in general, and on his work with the massive *Cantos* project in particular. He was well taken care of by his daughter Mary and her husband, anthropologist Boris de Rachewiltz.

It was truly amazing to have Mary de Rachewiltz present for all of the last day of our conference. Not only did her son Siegfried "house" the event and present a paper himself; Mary was also active and asked questions, as well as answering those of others. It was a very special connection to history indeed.

In recent times, it has come to light that many revered artists, writers, poets, philosophers and performers have held esoteric world views or underpinnings. The innovative writing of T.S. Eliot, James Joyce, Ernest Hemingway; the poetry of H.D.; the automatic drawings of Austin Osman Spare; the spirit drawings of Georgiana Houghton; the accidental poems of Tristan Tzara; the noise concerts of Luigi Russolo; the collages of Hannah Höch; the montages of Man Ray; the expressionism of Wassily Kandinsky; and the early experimentation with film and photography. W.B. Yeats taught a young Ezra Pound Theosophy. Piet Mondrian studied Theosophy as well. The surrealists touted the theories of psychoanalysis, exploring dreamwork, automatic writing, synchronicity and chance.

Several recent art exhibitions worldwide have highlighted this conection: "Black Light" in Barcelona, retrospectives of Leonor Fini and Leonora Carrington in New York and Mexico City, respectively, "Mystical Symbolism and the Visionary Works of Hilma af Klint" at the Guggenheim... all in just the past years.

The field of psychoanalysis itself first began as an esoteric discipline – exploring previously uncharted territory with relatively few individuals meeting weekly at the home of Sigmund Freud. Some of Freud's occult explorations were quite overt, as he conducted thought experiments with his daughter Anna Freud and close colleague Sándor Ferenczi late into his life. Though Freud intentionally steered the public persona of psychoanalysis away from any occult leanings, his personal work with the esoteric went on well into his twilight years. Carl Jung also explored his own psyche in secret for decades as he created his masterpiece *The Red Book*, which was only discovered after his death and released publicly in recent years.

It is notable that so many cultural heavyweights, who are held in such high regard, deemed it necessary to keep their esoteric views and occult explorations hidden from the world. Clearly they felt these ideas would not be acceptable at that time. And they were probably right, as many of those figures who were more open about their views, were often shunned, denied or had aspects of their work ignored outright. It begs the question: why does society accept some aspects of the mind, but not others?

At our current moment of cultural crisis, it makes sense to look back over the past 100 years; to reflect on the cultural Zeitgeist before the First World War – the very same time period and cultural and intellectual epicentres that birthed the fields of psychoanalysis, the Dada movement and Der Blaue Reiter. Much like our times, upheaval and change were in the air. The arts and sciences were booming, as was philosophy, media and technology. Interest in Theosophy, Eastern philosophies, occult and esoteric belief systems was on the rise. Society's accepted values and consensus worldview were put into question; the status-quo challenged, refined and reformulated for a modern era.

This perspective of hindsight is useful for us when we look at our own times. Do we have similar explosive and provocative intersections between art and the esoteric? Are artists still drawing fodder and fuel from a magical attitude towards their own subconscious? These are all questions that can be helped by the free-flowing discipline of magico-anthropology that is housed within *The Fenris Wolf*.

Dissolving the rigid compartmentalization of the "magical" versus "unmagical" is necessary to be able to see the wealth of all kinds of important processes in history, whether they be called "magical," "creative," "subconscious," or simply "artistic."

The relationship between psychoanalysis and an ossified Western bourgeois attitude that could only find its redemption in two brutal world wars has been well documented. We can perhaps also regard the immense creative experimentations within "modernism" in the same way: as a safety valve that eventually popped and allowed for a volcanic stream to take new shapes of writing, painting, films, etc. A pure reaction to what Freud called the "death drive," and also an attempt at reformulating "givens" in general. Hence, a kind of survival strategy from within a culture that obviously had failed in its attempts to reach new levels of civilization, and punished itself by breaking down – in very similar ways as during a personal crisis.

By looking at history we learn, and seek new ways. It's not always necessary to burn everything down; constructive avenues are usually wiser and less violent. In this issue, for instance, we have pieces on grass roots attempts to intuitively formulate important concepts like "initiation," strivings to re-appreciate Chthonic contacts and currents, appreciating art and poetry as *nothing but* magical, an optimistic contemporary spirit in maintaining Nietzsche's "revaluation of all values," a critique of current clinical attitudes within psychiatry and psychology, and specific looks at key figures of modernist times such as Austin Osman Spare and Ezra Pound.[1]

There is a spirit in all of these creative people, poets, artists, and psychoanalysts that cherishes the individual path of exploration, which integrates intuition, inspiration, and an active acknowledgement of inner sources of information; i.e. a "gnostic" approach to behavior and expression. What we find inside ourselves always has value, and most often a considerably higher value than the rigid systems of any kind of functionality fetish collectivism.

As individuals we can swerve, trip, tremble, fall and possibly make "wrong" decisions and deductions along the way. That's simply how we learn, from childhood and onwards. As long as we carry on in a pure spirit of exploration, honesty and life-affirmation, we will, when looking back, have been true to ourselves.

Perhaps this is why the 20th century brought so much violence and extreme measures and attitudes. It was simply a reaction to a system so inert and repressed that it could only explode (rather than implode). And this is also why the attitudes of many key artists wouldn't make do with merely painting a picture or composing a poem or a piece of music.

The new eruptive freedom of form and content was simply so strong that it somehow needed to be anchored to something "outside" to be possibly understood. This can be seen as a healthy attempt to come to terms with what's going on – not least on the inside. One projects the emotional, aesthetic expression onto or into a "frame of reference" in order to evaluate its relevance. As the 20th century ended, however, this process of healthy intellectual or political anchoring had gone overboard in "postmodernism" and a fetish for extreme abstraction and aloofness, coupled with an ensuing inflation of hubristic self-reflection.

As we have now safely overcome this peculiar hurdle in (art) history, we can look both backward and forward in our attempt at understanding the drives of some extraordinarily creative people, and how their creativity connects to larger movements. Magico-anthropology presents a cluster of premises about that this openness has a lot to do with an overall species-level survival instinct. Whether we are grasping for emotional straws in a process of mass extinction, or perhaps – hopefully! – brain-storming/birthing new ideas for well-needed radical structural changes, we will do well to look at the people and ideas presented in this volume of *The Fenris Wolf*. They all left something behind, consciously or not, and it's our duty to evaluate and integrate what we find inspiring and useful in our own lives

---

1 For a specific comparison between Pound and Spare, please see Carl Abrahamsson's "Spare Me a Pound – An initial look at the Sui Genericism of Austin and Ezra" in Sinclair & Punzi (eds), *Outsider Inpatient – Reflections on Art as Therapy*, Trapart Books/University of Gothenburg, Stockholm, 2021.

and processes. If for nothing else, then at least to acknowledge that culture as such, as well as our views on magic, is *never* static; it *always* moves to strive to encompass, filter and express wisdoms that may as yet be "unvalidated" by the powers that be. But also to acknowledge that we all inherently – perhaps even instinctively – know that the ultimate arbiters and judges are always ourselves.

An editorial note: As the texts in this issue stem from various minds from various cultures, there are obviously some stylistic inconsistencies. We have chosen to keep these, including possible "magical" language quirks and experiments, in the name of heterogeneous and creative integrity. However, for any spelling or typographical errors, pure and simple, we assume full responsibility.

Finally, we would like to say that the views and values expressed in the various texts in this eclectic anthology are those of the respective authors, and do not necessarily represent our own views, those of Trapart Books, or any kind of general "Fenris Wolfean" perspective.

Vade Ultra!

Carl Abrahamsson & Vanessa Sinclair
Vimmerby, Summer Solstice, 2022

TRUE TO THE EARTH
AND A PAGAN CONCEPTION OF THE SELF

Kadmus

I would like to take the time to expand upon, and add justification to, some points I made in my book *True to the Earth: Pagan Political Theology* concerning pagan ideas of the nature of the self. In that book I attempt to reconstruct the metaphysics and theology that undergird the pagan or polytheist worldview. The argument, roughly, is that a culture tends to have a pagan worldview when it is an oral society and that writing introduces changes to human thinking and culture that distort, and eventually replace, pagan insights. In other words, despite important and rich differences, I argue that all oral cultures are pagan in the sense I intend and they share – to greater or lesser degrees – foundational metaphysical insights. Beyond this, I attempt to show the extent to which these lost pagan insights are needed in our world and often, in many senses, preferable to their monotheistic counterparts.

To present these ideas a bit schematically, oral cultures experience reality – both think and talk about it – in a specific way and literate societies in another way. The oral experience of reality is best identified with paganism. Literacy – which gives rise to abstract ideas and makes them central to its understanding and experience of reality – makes monotheism possible.

To offer a brief overview of the aspects of this metaphysics as presented in the book, in Chapter One I argue that a pagan metaphysics is committed to irreducible pluralism. This is a multiplicity without an overriding hierarchy and without one ultimate origin. Chapter Two presents oral pagan thought as constituted in terms of an associative relational or paratactic logic. There is a focus on active agents and actions over abstract concepts or stable entities. These actions and agents are constituted through the relationships they exist within and carry out. Chapter Three presents this focus on active agents as an understanding of all existing things as living. Here the associative relational logic was understood in terms of animism. One final aspect that ties the previous points together was offered in Chapter Four: *a pluralistic cosmos of relationally understood active bodies with agency is best described through an event ontology*. In other words, pagan metaphysics sees actions and events as fundamental, and rejects the fundamental nature, and indeed the existence, of substance whether that substance is understood as matter (which would include energy), or spirit (i.e. mind, consciousness, soul, etc.), or both.

Oral societies do not tend to have expressly developed studies of theology or metaphysics; instead we must excavate how these societies experienced reality indirectly from oral teachings that were later preserved in writing and records of the transition periods from oral to literacy during which we can trace specific changes in the thinking of the culture. This task is made more difficult – to an extent that is hard to over-state – because most transitions from orality to literacy have occurred via the mediums of colonialism, religious conversion, conquest, and generally the domination of oral cultures by literate ones. This leads, even in the case of much anthropological work, to a process of translating the thinking of an oral culture into the ideology of a literate one during which the unique aspects of oral culture are lost or concealed. For these reasons the transition from orality to literacy in Ancient Greece is particularly important as a paradigm case. Here literacy was developed primarily within the culture itself without foreign imposition or the complication of religious domination. To put it bluntly, the new ideas presented by the Pre-Socratic philosophers and by Socrates, Plato, and Aristotle can be understood as the first major manifestations of literacy's effect on the thinking of a culture. These ideas include that of an abstract perfect Good that is the origin of everything in existence, the view of the universe as an ordered and hierarchical totality, the idea of a substantial unified or singular soul that fully captures the individuality of a person, as well as the materialist theory of a fully physical universe made up of discrete types of matter or elements out of which everything is built and from which everything takes its nature. Each of these ideas is foreign and even unthinkable within an oral culture.

Here we will primarily be concerned with Homer and the characteristics of oral composition that Homeric literature epitomizes, with one brief exception. It is largely recognized that Homeric literature is primarily an oral artifact preserved at the birth of writing in Greece. I want to look specifically at what we can learn about the concept of selfhood found in a pagan context as captured in Homeric epithets, similes, and concrete descriptions of the interpenetration of divinities and humanity.

Allow me to offer some examples of the way the metaphysics of an oral society is preserved in its language. Oral language tends to have concrete words for events or actions that later become important abstract nouns in literate culture – indeed in most languages verbal variants of abstract nouns tend to be the older origin of those nouns. A key example in Homer is that there is no word for "nature" but only a verb form – "naturing" if you will. Classical period texts will have the abstract noun *phusis* for "nature" but the earlier Homer only uses to term *phue* which means something like "to grow". This is part of what I point to when I suggest that oral societies are working from an event ontology, one in which actions and events are what are ultimately real. Other abstract nouns, such as Goodness or Virtue, are only encountered in specific examples such as "good ships" or 'Achilles' virtue on the field of battle". They are relative terms defined by their context. This problem arises repeatedly in Plato's dialogues when Socrates asks his interlocutors for definitions of abstract concepts and inevitably receives concrete examples. When asking "What is courage?", for example, we are almost inevitably going to get a specific example of Achilles displaying courage in a given situation and so on rather than a general definition – much to Socrates' frustration. It was clear that the idea of abstract general definitions was very foreign and hard to grasp for Greek culture even several centuries after the dominance of writing.

When looking to oral texts, such as those of Homer, I tend to look first at the most definitive structural characteristics of oral composition since these are most distinctly of oral origination. The two most famous such structural characteristics are Homeric fixed epithets and Homeric simile so I will look at what these might tell us about the pagan understanding of the self first.

We usually think of epithets as brief descriptions that capture the nature of a thing. "The city that never sleeps" would be such an epithet for New York. In Homer there are so-called fixed epithets that provide essential elements to the meter of the poems. Some only appear applied to certain characters or things (such as "rosy-fingered" for the dawn and "polutropon" or "of many-turnings" which is usually translated as "clever" for Odysseus) while most others are applied to many different characters when the specifics of the situation are appropriate and the poetic meter allows or requires them ("godlike" is a good example here, though it is usually applied to characters of divine birth such as "godlike Achilles" "*dios achilleus*"). Let me draw on my one non-Homeric example to clarify the nature of epithet. In the *Greek Magical Papyri*, many of which either capture in writing chants previously passed down orally or maintain oral compositional characteristics even if not of oral origin, we find long lists of what seem like descriptions of the spirits or divinities one is attempting to contact. Here is an example:

"O child of Zeus,	"Διος τεκος,
Dart-shooter, Artemis, Persephone,	ιοχεαιρα, Αρτεμι, Περσεφονεια,
Shooter of deer, night-shining, triple-sounding,	
	ελαφηβολε, νυκτοφανεια, τρικτυπε,
Triple-voiced, triple-headed Selene,	τριφθοϒϒε, τρικαρανε, Σεληνη,
Triple-pointed, triple-faced, triple-necked,	θριωακαι, τριπροσωπε, τριαυχενε
And goddess of the triple ways…	και τριοδιτι…
Hail, goddess, and attend your epithets,	χαιρε, θεα, και σαισιν επωνυμιαις επακουσον,
O heavenly one, harbor goddess, who roam	ουρανια, λιμενιτι, οριπλανε
The mountains and are goddess of the crossroads;	
	εινοδια τε, νερτερια, βυθια, αιωνια
O nether one, goddess of depths, eternal,	σκοτια τε…"
Goddess of dark…"	

(PGM IV 2523-2528, 2561-2565)

What the English translation makes it hard to see is that most of these descriptions are single words and most of the lines of text are three words long. So "harbor goddess" is one word, as is "who roam the mountains" and "goddess of the crossroads". Look at the last three lines in Greek. They are literally just a list of singular words capturing each of these ideas alone. In English they are "O heavenly one, harbor goddess, who roam the mountains and are goddess of the crossroads; o nether one, goddess of depths, eternal, goddess of dark." So, this chant is just a list of epithets as the text mentions itself: "attend your epithets".

It is necessary to dig a bit into this idea of the "epithet" because the Archaic Greeks didn't understand it at all the way we do. This should become clear when you consider that what we identify as a given person or divinity's proper name was just as often an epithet to begin with. Patroclus, for example, is not just a name but means "glory of the father". Even the name Hekate, the goddess the previous chant likely calls, possibly derives from the epithet "far-sighted" or "far-shooter" which is often applied to Apollo as well. There is no clear line in Ancient Greece between epithet and name. Even in the, admittedly much later, chant from the *Greek Magical Papyri* the term for epithet is *eponumiais* which basically means "a name given to something or derived from something else" and is formed from the root word *onoma* meaning "name". The paradigmatic example here is something like *Peleiado*, an *eponumiais* for Achilles meaning "son of Peleus". Achilles here is "named from" his father. His father gives him his name. Similarly, Hekate is *Einodia*, named from her connection to the crossroads. But Patroclus is just as much named for his father's hope for glory.

If epithets are just names, what does our focus on pagan names tell us? First, names in a pagan context are unavoidably plural. Every one and thing has many names and, ultimately, there is no "one true name" which becomes an obsession in later monotheistic thought. Names are also shared; Hekate is not the only *Einodia* nor is Achilles the only "godlike" one. These names are all clearly relational, they derive from the relationships the named thing takes on or is found within and they weave interconnections with many things that share the same name. As so well demonstrated in the chant from the *Greek Magical Papyri*, names are also paratactic. *Parataxis* is the practice of listing things without an organizing hierarchical structure and is a major characteristic of oral poetry such as Homer's. The list of names of Hekate are not organized according to any prioritizing logic. None are more or less important than the other in and of themselves. This is a model of pluralism without totalizing organizing structure. Finally, names could be taken on and put off. Names were gained and lost.

There is a wealth of examples of dramatic changing of names especially in relation to the gods. The fearful Furies are renamed the *Eumenides*, or "kindly minded ones", in order to appease and calm their rage. Hekate becomes *Propolos* and *Opaon* of Persephone, or the one who goes before and follows after Persephone, because of her presence at both the abduction and return of Persephone. Perhaps most dramatically, in the *Homeric Hymn to Hermes*, we are told the story of how when Hermes was one day old he invented the musical instrument the lyre and stole Apollo's cattle. When found out he exchanges the lyre for Apollo's cattle. This is how Apollo becomes the god of music and the lyre, becoming the "leader of the Muses" (*Musagetes*), and how Hermes becomes *Epimelios* "the guardian of the flocks". The gods have exchanged names and in doing so become different than they were. Here we see that the selfhood of the gods themselves is fluid, open to changes based on the relationships they form or that are thrust upon them. Hermes changes Apollo's identity, and by doing so changes his own as well.

Let us turn to the consideration of Homeric simile. Homeric similes are extended comparisons of generally two contrasting and even conflicting views of life; for example the human and divine world with that of animals and nature. Internal linguistic clues have led to the conclusion that the similes are some of the oldest parts of the Homeric poems. More than just comparing the anthropomorphic and natural, the similes also contrast the heroic content of the poems with a more agrarian non-heroic form of life. In the similes, ships become horses and slain warriors become cattle slaughtered by farmers and so on. Allow me to offer one of the most striking of the Homeric similes as an example, found in *Iliad* book 16 lines 259-267. There the Myrmidons, newly allowed to join the battle by Achilles, pour with Patroclus from the ships and are compared to a swarm of wasps provoked by playful boys and randomly attacking anyone who passes by on the road:

> Straightway they poured forth like wasps
> by the roadside, which boys habitually provoke,
> always taunting them – wasps that have their homes by the road;
> thoughtless boys; they make a common evil for many people.
> Those wasps, if some traveler going by
> Unwittingly disturbs them, summon up all their defensive spirit
> And each one of them flies forth and fights in defense of his offspring.
> With heart and spirit like theirs the Myrmidons
> Poured then from among the ships.

The important point here is that the similes do not just offer a comparison based on some shared appearance but rather also capture surprising and even subversive shared temperaments and fates. The Myrmidons, this fierce group of great Greek warriors, are actually "a common evil for many people" destined to be killed as easily as small and fragile, if dangerous, insects. This is not just poetic but, I would argue, offers an insight into the nature and identity of the Greek warriors. The human and natural world – and the heroic and agrarian world – are not divided, but rather in the simile we see that they are ontologically interwoven and penetrating with these interconnections destabilizing the surface appearance of each side of the simile.

Before more explicitly stating my conclusion I want to look at some of the more overt content, rather than simply structural elements, of Homer's work. For this purpose let us consider Book 5 of the *Iliad*. This book features the near apotheosis of the Greek warrior Diomedes when Athena fills him with power and wrath. This book is fascinating because the gods are everywhere in it. They fight on the field of battle beside and with humans. Some are even injured, such as Aphrodite by

Diomedes himself. They whisk humans out of the battle to save them and appear to others to provide council. Book 5 represents the world of the gods and men at its highest level of mingling. What is most striking about this mingling is that for the careful reader it leaves profoundly unclear where gods end and humans begin.

Let us begin first with Diomedes himself. We are told that Athena temporarily granted him strength and rage, that she made fire blaze from him, that she made his limbs, feet, and hands lite. More than this, she repeatedly speaks to him, counseling him throughout the battle. At one point, a Trojan warrior seeing Diomedes on the field of battle states that his shield, helmet, and horses look like his but that "... it may be a god, I am not sure…not without god does he rage so, but some one of the immortals, mantling in mist his shoulders, stands close beside him…"[1] No more can we be sure, for Diomedes is so empowered and led by Athena – from his strength and appearance to his emotions and decisions – it is unclear if we would best say he is inspired, possessed, or replaced by her.

Throughout the book, and indeed Homeric literature, gods appear as specific mortals, speak as them and fight as them. Sometimes they are recognized in this, and sometimes not, but it is unclear when, or even if, we should conclude that there is a work of illusion going on and when instead the divinity and human have simply become one. This has led some ancient scholars to propose that the Archaic and Mycenaean Greeks may have seen all emotion and thought to be coming directly from the gods – a psychology via the divine. One thing is clear: as swiftly as the gods pop into and out of the battle, so too do they pop into and out of particular human forms. My contention is that the question of when we have a god appearing as a given human and when we have a human inspired-by a given god is an indiscernible and meaningless distinction that did not exist for the pagan Greeks. The gods lived in and through humans and humans lived in and through the gods in ever more complex interweavings. It is not, then, a question of illusion or replacement at all. This point becomes all the clearer when we investigate the etymologies of terms for virtue, which almost inevitably trace back to the idea of blazing with the fire or light of the gods. When Diomedes shines with his martial virtue, it is Athena who shines in and as him. He is virtuous to the extent that he is divine. At one point the ideas I have offered so far overlap, and Diomedes' empowerment by Athena is described in an extended simile connecting it to nature:

She spoke thus, grey-eyed Athena…
now the strong rage tripled took hold of him, as of a lion
whom the shepherd among his fleecy flocks in the wild lands
grazed as he leapt the fence of the fold, but has not killed him,
but only stirred up the lion's strength, and can no more fight him
off, but hides in the steading, and the frightened sheep are forsaken
and these are piled pell-mell on each other in heaps, while the lion
raging still leaps out again over the fence of the deep yard;

---

1 *Iliad* Book 5, lines 183-186

such was the rage of strong Diomedes as he closed with the Trojans."[2]

Here is Diomedes: lion, Athena, and mortal man. This is, in this moment, his identity.

The dominance of abstract monotheistic metaphysics has led to the idea that the self is something singular and, in some important respects, stable. It is, for example, a soul capable of eternal unchanging life in a Platonic, Cartesian, or religious sense. This idea, I would argue, is utterly foreign to oral cultures. Surely enough, there is something we might call the soul in Archaic Greece, but it is defined more by the way it most often loses its identity in death than the way it maintains that identity. Exceptions to this rule are achieved via ongoing relationships that go beyond any intrinsic capacities of the soul.

What is the self, then? It is a node in a web of relations marked out by names, epithets, and similes. It is an ongoing event of taking on these relationships, putting them off, being caught in them, having them thrust upon it, escaping them and so on. It is unstable and ever-changing. It is a subject in process, in contention, defined more by the shifting world around it than by internal characteristics. It is without essence. The relations that constitute the self are like a Venn diagram in which the human, the natural, and the divine shift in greater and lesser proportions. Ultimately, however, the real point is that the circles drawn around these terrains are themselves illusory and inconstant.

---

2 *Iliad* Book 5, lines 133-143

Spiritual Evolution
– For the Masses or for the Few?

Charlotte Rodgers

As much as we would like to deny or ignore it, the behaviour of human beings as a mass tends to operate within repetitive patterns and loops. Just as the history of humanity can be seen to work within recurring cycles of behaviour, the practice of the esoteric over the centuries is dictated by the way that man operates within context of these patterns, either as a passive acceptor of the status quo or as an initiator of change.

The magician is a being who relates to the world of 'other' and changes their mundane actions in recognition of this relationship. Observing the workings of the earthly realm and relating them to our emotional and intellectual selves is part of our personal survival, and relating these things to our spiritual practise is a necessity of a deeper progression. Only those who are spiritually ill, or part of a race doomed to extinction, do not allow themselves to see the interaction of the worlds without and the worlds within.

Both the human survival instinct and their innate desire to strive and progress dictates that spirituality looks outward. I'm not talking about syncretism, although of course this is relevant here; I'm talking about progress on the evolutionary level.

Historically this is not the first time to have such enormous, global turmoil and scientific and technological advancement, however I would say that the closest past parallel to this era would be the late 19th to early 20th century.

Then, the exponential progress in rational thought was counterbalanced, as human beings naturally and instinctively do, with a surge forward in educated, creative occultism and an interest in various types of alternative spiritual explorations.

However, the climate of that era necessitated that various approaches towards magical spirituality were something that was kept very much silent.

Partially this was because magical and esoteric studies teaches silence as part of their basic tenets, but also because anything that steps outside the mainstream has always been considered a threat to the establishment, and when the masses turn, the weird or wyrd minority become the scapegoats.

Homosexuals, pacifists, bolsheviks, freaks, witches (to name just a few) have all been targeted throughout the ages, and especially so in the 20th Century. Thus, keeping one's views to oneself was not just part of an arcane tradition but also a method of survival.

It is also well worth bearing in mind that this necessary silence can heighten the glamour, creating an aura of being elite, elevated and superior in some way.

So now, in the 21st Century, all of these rules of spiritual behaviour have changed, although the behaviour of the humanity as a whole, seemingly has not. The world is a crazy and crazed place and once again technology and the rational plunge forward, and their time old counterbalance – magic and paganism – are running strongly beside it; two sides of the same coin whose shared goal is to be 'more than'.

What has also changed are the views about what constitutes a target, an outsider and a scapegoat.

There has, ostensibly, been an upheaval in attitudes towards race, gender and belief systems; the narrow minded are now pilloried and targeted and brought to task with the same vigorous aggression that those who lived on the fringes once were.

This time around, with the aid of social networking, magic has gone mainstream; it is talked about loudly and proudly brandished as a banner of power, and a way to bestow status.

Fashion conglomerates use tarot as part of advertising campaigns, television programmes adopt figureheads of Satanic groups within their shows, and etsy stocks supplies for every type of modern magical practice with sales for tarot cards being the highest in 50 years and increasing all the time.

Now magic has always, of course, been about power.

On a base level this power has been over illness, enemies, financial impoverishment and love and on a higher level, power over the elements and human nature. To the onlooker this working with power, depending on the perspective, appears either amoral and horrifying, or glamorously mysterious, stimulating and enticing.

Now power is a huge draw card for all human beings, especially if one feels a lack of it, but it is also necessarily attractive to the corporate world, as power and money are the gods and the goals of these structures; so it's natural that magic holds an attraction to many operators within business environs, even if it is due to its 'gloss' and potential for spin, rather than its actuality.

I've seen surges of popularity in magickal expression and practice many times over the years, but never one that feels quite like the present magical revival… Probably because previous movements haven't had the benefit of social networking to push things into the focus of the public's vision.

There is a term called the 'Diffusion of innovation S Curve,' where a trend can be pushed to become a norm by the power of 'influencers:' people with enough charisma and power to create changes in perception on a wide scale. William Gibson had a term, 'cool hunter', for people who hunt down influencers that will work for them in the corporate world.

I recently wrote an article talking about the esoteric and magical as applied to contemporary fashion and the research for this was fascinating when analysed using the lens of the 'Diffusion of Innovation Curve'.

Of course part of magic's appeal is that it is replete with stimulating, evocative and very strong and inspirational imagery that lends itself beautifully to creative projects, but then most established and long standing religions also have such imagery; however unlike most standardised belief systems, magick has long has been epitomised by the Uber cool and the iconic; by people who generate waves that disturb the norm.

Generally these bright beings have remained on the fringes, or have been so obscure or niche as an original reference point, that although the effect of their stimulus is widely recognised the esoteric source isn't.

Icons such as Jack Parsons, Marjorie Cameron, William Burroughs, Anita Pallenberg, Gen P-Orridge, Austin Osman Spare, Kenneth Anger, Aleister Crowley... all were or are very, very cool beings who acted as a radar and inspiration to others who wanted to emulate, imitate and learn.

Although these people and their trappings hit the limelight many, many times, they faded again; until the power of social networking provided the impetus for them to become mainstream and in more recent trends, even adopted by Corporations as prime advertising fodder; one example being a campaign using Kenneth Anger advertising for Gucci.

Counter culture practices becoming the norm has been done many times before; just ask anyone who used to keep their tattoos and piercings, things some considered to be markings of their persona, place in society and life choices, hidden, and now find that every C list star and their grandmother has tattoos, piercings and a bit of BDSM gear in their closet.

Now one particular thing about this S curve of innovation is the after-effect: when the point is reached of critical mass, and the once obscure becomes accepted by the mainstream.

As I said earlier magical practice has assumed a fashionable status before, just never to this extent. Many such as myself are watching the rise of this phenomenon; some rather dryly, others perhaps trying to make a little money, sell a few more books or gain some extra notoriety whilst the esoteric star is high on the horizon, most of them thinking this too will pass.

I see television series, movies, fashion shows, fitness witches and stage shows referencing the esoteric groove, and though I still tend to think it will fade somewhat, I believe it is possible, this time around, that a magickal praxis will become an accepted approach.

In many ways this isn't a bad thing, and could even be a positive one if it indicates a move away from established corporate religion; although of course there is a possibility that pagan spirituality and magical practice could itself become a corporate run belief system.

I also believe that as there is presently a huge rise in change of attitudes towards materialism, there will need to be a change in attitude towards magical iconography; a detachment from object orientated spirituality. Seeing Austin Osman Spare's work, for instance, being used on £3000 handbags made me realise that proprietorial feelings one may have towards affiliated spiritual iconography is something that will need to be discarded in order to progress. The time for the material to represent the spiritual with accompanying territorial instincts, needs to be made redundant – otherwise ideas of ownership will come into the picture and pagans will be protesting and picketing with catholics outside movie theatres and Madonna concerts. I thought carefully around this issue as I create objects that can have spirits or god forms embedded into them, and I also come from a country where colonialists stole many spiritually imbued objects, and in doing so also undermined the fabric of the aboriginal existence. Whilst Gods and spirits can be embedded in objects however,they cannot be owned; they can be worked with, used to inspire and to focus, but not owned. If we do align our spirituality so completely with an object, and then we treat them as human beings have always treated the material, we will see our gods die along with part of ourselves.

"To Know, to Will, to Dare, to be Silent" could be also considered to be old hat and another outdated approach, though there is no denying that there is a level of necessary silence implicit in practice. Of course there are many levels of practice in every belief system, and even long established, widely accepted beliefs such as Buddhism have a higher level: a relatively arcane, esoteric and secret aspect.

One thing that is interesting about all of this isn't simply the ostensible growth in belief of pagan and magical theologies, but the huge amounts of individuals striving to master and interpret various esoteric systems.

Many cultures believe in magic, but often rely on a priest specific to their system. What I see at the moment is the rise of individual rather than group empowerment via a magickal approach. Of course modern society (western and increasingly eastern) is all about the nuclear family, non-Confucian ideals and a steadily growing cult of isolation, with its banner-head bedroom dwellers creating a new type of neurosis specific to this era (though admittedly there have always been outsider solitary magicians hidden away amongst their books in dusty rooms, it's a pretty archetypical image) although there is now a degree of connectivity of the various isolationist magickal alter egos online, and group workings do occur via this medium… such as the Trump workings, for example.

I'm a great believer in the power of the group to get things done magically but I must admit I haven't seen positive results to these global workings and I wonder why. Because definitions of magic have become so fluid and murky perhaps, and there is no clarity of working perimeters; because there are so many individual personas and no ability to properly join forces and channel power, or because there is simply no real core knowledge about what magic is all about?

Human beings are pack animals, and our natural instinct is to follow the herd. In the instance of widely consumed media imagery, the use of magickal and pagan approaches in expensive glossy spin utilises the thought of 'only the few;' generally these few being those with huge amounts of money. But this approach has filtered down on the wide scale, and many of those who are buying into the process are doing it on a budget, and rather than flag flying for a film franchise or a fashion house it is being used as an individually loud expression of 'other'… which is intriguing in that it is being obedient to online manipulations but also subversive in the way that information is practically interpreted.

Esoteric studies, paganism and magickal practice have always been fluid things based on the land and the culture. If you work with the spirits of the land and place, and the land changes, of course you must adapt. All of these approaches have cherry picked techniques that worked for them from experience, observation and often from other cultures, and with information becoming more accessible the stimulus for change has snowballed and I'm really not sure if practitioners have adapted on a deep level to all of this.

Accepted concepts of gender polarity and sexuality have changed immeasurably, the land and the sea have changed, our ancestors are still there but the values they communicate may well not be applicable, computers are the new altars and rituals that use golden toads will not work if the toad is extinct; however every man, woman and being is still a star and still has a shining trajectory.

I believe that a grass roots re-evaluation is necessary, starting with a definition of contemporary magickal spirituality and contemporary magickal practice, and that definition needs to acknowledge technology and trends and either integrate or separate itself from them. If need be we can slam that definition to pieces once we've made it, but in every beginning there is a word and that word needs to encapsulate… magick is change, and magick is progression, and magick works… and whilst it may well be on the way to being mainstream at this moment I'll tell you a secret: Magick may become a process believed in by many and it would be a great thing if it does, but practice of it isn't for everyone and never will be, because magick can also be painful, challenging and dangerous; under the glamour lies a process of insight and reevaluation, dissembling and reassembling that few choose to undertake. Israel Regardie said that anyone who is serious about undertaking a magickal path should also simultaneously undertake some form of psychotherapy, and though personally I'm a slam myself against the same brick wall a few times type of slow learner, I'd tend to agree.

What I do believe though, is when the mass of humanity are as willing to perform Chod as to buy an Austin Osman Spare emblazoned handbag, the world will be a better place. I'm not denying the fun and self empowerment of magickal spirituality or advocating some Christian process of emotional self flagellation; I'm just saying simply that until people are willing to go deeper, the magickal path will remain something that only a few will commit to.

SPACE AGE SPECTRES
– THE COMET IS COMING

Kasper Opstrup

In late 1973, the long-period comet Kohoutek passed close enough to Earth for the first time in c. 150,000 years to be observable to the naked eye. Historically, sightings of comets have been related to prophesies of the end of the world. We live on a planet characterised by change, upheavals and crises, but at least the heavens appear orderly.

When they are not, it must be a harbinger of doom.

In 1910, when Haley's comet appeared, the police stopped an Oklahoma religious group, the Sacred Followers, from sacrificing a virgin to ward off catastrophe. When Hale-Bopp appeared in 1997, it prompted the suicides of 39 members of the Heaven's Gate cult. According to historical witnesses, comets portended the fall of Jerusalem, the invasion of Gaul by Attila the Hun and the Norman invasion of the British Isles in 1066.

The sighting of Kohoutek was hyped in the media of the day as "the comet of the century." As people prepared to behold the wonder in the sky – scientists hoped it could provide answers to questions about the origins of the solar system – the comet's passage also stirred the imaginary of counter-culture luminaries like Robert Anton Wilson, Timothy Leary, John C. Lilly and Philip K. Dick. Independent of one another, they all began to receive transmissions from the outer fringes, channelling cosmist past and futures.

Leary had famously been sprung from a Californian low-security prison by the Weather Underground in 1970 – his crime was the possession of two marijuana cigarettes – resulting in President Nixon commanding an ultimately successful manhunt through Africa, Europe and Asia to bring him back to prison.

As the comet neared, Leary was imprisoned in solitary confinement in Folsom Prison alongside fellow inmates like Charles Manson, where he received a channelled "psy phi" text, telepathically transmitted from higher intelligences. Instead of seeing the comet as a cosmic emissary, warning of impending catastrophe, Leary saw in it the hope of a possible future:

The message of the Comet is this: From the vantage point of galactic society Intelligent Life cannot be considered intelligent until it has exchanged intelligent signals with extraplanetary beings. The comet is a humbling reminder, a signal to stimulate us to devote our central energies to start acting in an intelligent manner – communicating with the galactic society.[1]

Translating the transmissions into English, Leary eventually had them published as *Terra II... A Way Out* in 1974. *Terra II* proclaimed that it was time for earthlings to mutate and "come home in glory." The higher intelligences transmitted to us that it was time to leave the planetary womb and walk among the stars, as the goal of evolution was to produce a nervous system capable of communication with the "Galactic Network" where our interstellar parents await our return. Not only is it no longer necessary to die, but due to the deciphering of the genetic code we will discover the key to enhanced intelligence.

After the comet has reminded us to look to the stars, we must begin by sending the most intelligent, advanced and courageous members of our species in a "sperm ship [which] is the flower of terrestrial life" to an interstellar gathering.[2] Eventually, though, all life must come home. This voyage can only be made possible through total individual and collective freedom, responsibility to each other and our ecology, as well as living in a state of interspecies harmony where larval identities of race, culture and nationality have been transcended.

As soon as the voyage has begun, the most ancient prophecies will be fulfilled.

This text, part of what has become known as the 'Starseed Signals,' represents Leary's transhumanist turn towards a cosmic futurism, where he embraced technology, libertarianism, and the off-world goals soon summarised as S.M.I.²L.E. (Space Migration, Increased Intelligence, Life Extension). These themes are key to an expanded notion of cosmism – or cosmisms – treated as a cultural movement throughout the long 20th century.

These cosmisms share an idea about active or willed evolution and a vision of a new type of (post)humanity created by various inner and outer technologies. Today, we might also understand cosmisms as a kind of speculative fictions or theory-fictions concerned with another future. To get to that understanding, it is necessary to introduce some fundamental ideas. These are primarily drawn from the first two waves of Russian Cosmism, from the 1880s until the late 1930s, after which the ideas were suppressed by Soviet authorities.

SUMMON THE FIRE

In an age when paths not moving toward the cybernetic brutality of multinational capital appear to be exhausted, cosmism's various strands offer speculative paths uniquely relevant for re-opening other futures and utopian thought. The 20th century was full of unexpected encounters. Encounters that took off in more eschatological directions than we could have imagined. Underneath these developments, the cosmic themes of space migration, increased intelligence and life

---

1 Timothy Leary. *Terra II... A Way Out*. San Francisco: Imprinting Press, 1974, p. 11. The research presented in this article has been supported by the Novo Nordisk Foundation, NNF180C0054872.
2 Leary. *Terra*, p. 7.

extension were key concerns for scientists as well as many of the artists connected with the modernist avant-garde.

The drive behind much modernist art was to make projects instead of masterpieces. Projects of biological and social engineering would elaborate a vision of a future human type apt to exist under unprecedented conditions. Present wo/man was obsolete. What was needed was a plunge into the unknown. Liberal capitalism countered this utopianism by going from being a contingent project to becoming a reality principle where the map *is* the territory, where there no longer is an outside to the reality tunnels of hegemonic thought, not unlike what the cultural theorist Mark Fisher has called "capitalist realism." Since this capitalist realism has no offer of a better future, its default logic is one of anti-utopianism. The unknown can always be commodified and mapped onto the known. This politico-aesthetic double bind leaves us in a situation where the system is broken but there is no apparent alternative.

In the speculative fabulations of William Burroughs, Robert Anton Wilson, Timothy Leary and a host of other writers connected to the countercultural milieus of the 1960s and 70s, there is a consistent idea that we need to wilfully evolve the body in order to live in space, whether inner or outer. To survive, we must mutate and become more than what we are. This impetus can also be found among the earlier avant-garde and the idea can be traced back to (at least) the occult revival of the mid-19th century. It is closely connected to the themes and ideas of Russian Cosmism.

Like Leary, the Russian Cosmists – whose ranks included numerous philosophers, novelists, poets, avant-garde artists, scientists, medical doctors, activists, revolutionaries and so on – saw an attention to the heavens as heralding a new utopian age with a unified globe looking towards the stars. War, poverty, and dying would be a thing of the past. As such, it was a curious blend of occult anti-rationalism and rationalist technophilia.

Cosmism not only challenges the historicised trajectory of Western modernism by pointing to other types of modernisms and other ways to think about what it means to be modern; in its way of turning towards relegated knowledge and combining arts, politics and religion, it directly addresses some of the main tendencies in contemporary art from the past few years. For example, the resurgence of surrealist and animist tendencies – think ritual, witchcraft, transgression, meme magic – on the contemporary art scene. Occultism has always had its allure in counterculture. Like anarchism, it is a double-edged sword in that it spans the political spectrum.

At its most radical and illuminating, the turn towards the occult is a transgressive act. It challenges the power of institutions, degrades the psychic oppression of entrenched systems, and provides individuals with direct and unmediated access to an experiential way of being in the immediate now. In this sense, occultism is psychedelic, mystical and liberating all at once. But, as we are again seeing the rise of fascist forces and Strong Man politics around the world due to a peculiar contemporary overlap between myths, fictionalisations and lived reality, it might also be a timely reminder that many of the aesthetic concerns we discuss when talking about cosmism occurred for the first time around the rise of European fascism.

Initiated in the early 20th century with Nikolai Fedorov's posthumously published *What Is Man Created For? The Philosophy of the Common Task* (1906), Russian Cosmism was a kind of esoteric futurism, an avant-garde thinking in the borderland between art, mysticism, politics and science based on an idea about active evolution, that wo/man consciously can become more than what s/he is.

Drawing on ideas from Rosicrucianism and Theosophy, cosmism projected a vision of a future utopian society where both the human body and the human mind had evolved, a vision that would go on to influence the Russian Revolution in its search for a "New Man." In general terms, starting from Fedorov's speculative philosophy, the Russian Cosmists believed that the evolutionary development of humanity is far from complete and that our main task is to evolve further. This "Common Task" would involve a total reorganisation of social relations, productive forces, economy, and politics for one single goal: to achieve physical immortality and material resurrection so that all humans that had ever lived would live again, resurrected through advanced science and technology from what Fedorov called "ancestral dust." This should be gathered by travelling the spaceways in our very own 'Spaceship Earth.' Disintegration was the universal rule, reintegration was the human task.

The Cosmists wanted to rebel against death. They thought that if a solution to the problem of death can be found then solutions to all other problems will follow. Since the capacity of Earth would not be able to sustain this resurrected and immortal population they advocated the development of space travel and the colonisation of other planets. In order to survive in space, they proposed a metabolic reconstruction of the biological body in such a way that it could regenerate limbs and organs, exist without oxygen and derive energy directly from the sun as plants do. It should also become androgynous as the need for genders and sexual reproduction would end once immortality and the resurrection of all previous generations became real.

The main themes include the active role played in both human and cosmic evolution as well as the creation of new life forms, including a new level of humanity. That included serious scientific research into subjects long considered fit only for science fiction and occult literature.[3] At the same time, the insistence on transforming the given world is an example of an eschatological historiosophy that links cosmism of the nineteenth and twentieth centuries to the age old practice of magic and alchemy which in its Eastern practice always strove for immortality.

One of the key biocosmist thinkers, Vladimir Vernadsky, developed the theory of the *biosphere* (living matter) evolving into a *noosphere* (thinking matter).

---

3 Several of the cosmists' writings have been anthologised in Boris Groys (ed.). *Russian Cosmism*. Cambridge: The MIT Press, 2018.

According to Vernadsky, the noosphere will be the first time mankind becomes a major geological force. Today, it can be understood as a positive view on the anthropocene. As inhabitants first and foremost of the planet, human beings owe allegiance to the biosphere more than to any nation, ethnic entity, economic class, or system which makes cosmist thinking relevant today since it was built upon a notion of kinship where we put Earth first instead of humankind.

Like Fedorov, Vernadsky was convinced that one of the steps in wo/man's eventual evolution would take he/r through a stage where the depletion of resources in the biosphere will not permit humanity to continue to live as it now lives. In the future, humanity will have to change itself radically or perish in its degraded biosphere. The solution is through a speculative science involving the ability to alter the physical and chemical makeup of the human constitution. With the development of the noosphere, humanity has evolved to the point that death is no longer needed for future evolution.

Human desires, not biological necessity, will shape the future of humanity.

CHANNEL THE SPIRITS

Today, the configuration of the economy as a cybernetic information system has made the mind and its discipline as important as the discipline of the body was to modes of capital organised around industrial production. This suggests a further shift in focus from the body to the mind and the unconscious as needed locations for utopian investment.

While Fedorov developed Cosmism, the psychologist Richard Bucke published *Cosmic Consciousness: A Study in the Evolution of the Human Mind* in 1901. Bucke synthesised esoteric ideas but placed these concepts within a secular framework of psychology. This points forward towards Timothy Leary's multifaceted theory of cybernetic circuits of mind which he saw as a "navigational guide for piloting the evolution of the human."[4]

In collaboration with Robert Anton Wilson, Leary used his transmissions to develop the SMI²LE project. SMI²LE wanted to show that reality is mutable and that the future can be created through "reality tunnels" that will hack our brains. Wilson and Leary's futurism was concerned with the evolution of consciousness and points toward cyberculture and contemporary visions of an enhanced posthumanity, along the way blending elements of esoteric gnosis with alien communications, genre fictions, and psychedelic metaphysics.

Central to Wilson's concerns was what he called "Operation Mindfuck" which was based on the premise that who you are, and what you think you are, is a creation orchestrated and edited by your brain. The underlying thinking shares ideas with magic and positive thinking, specifically the belief that thoughts are

---

4 Timothy Leary. *Info-Psychology: A Manual for the Use of the Human Nervous System According to the Instructions of the Manufacturers, and a Navigational Guide for Piloting the Evolution of the Human Individual.* Las Vegas: New Falcon Publications, 1994.

causative; that what people think can have a transformative impact on reality. This led him to develop a series of brain-change games based on Polish philosopher Alfred Korzybski's general semantics, an optimistic mindset, and exercises in non-Aristotelian logic, what Wilson called maybe-logic. Among other methods, these games relied on Leary's Eight-Circuit Model of Consciousness, which stresses the role that crises play in producing change.

The Eight Circuit Model sketched eight periods and 24 stages of neurological evolution that Wilson and Leary used to explain both personal development and biological evolution. It stressed that evolution in consciousness would come in quantum states with energy levels and reality-dimensions lacking in the previous state and totally unpredictable from it. An example on the role of crises in development and evolution is Wilson's analysis of brain-washing techniques. In general, this is done by reducing the subject to a state of infancy which corresponds to vulnerability in the first circuit level, the so-called bio-survival circuit.[5] As Leary's prison mate, Charlie Manson, taught his Family: fear is the great teacher. The role of crisis is, in this perspective, to make us susceptible to be reprogrammed.

This interest in modelling consciousness and speculating in how to achieve higher states of it is related to a general concern for both cosmists and counterculture. It stresses that it is not enough to change society or simply mutate the body. Overcoming the category of the human necessarily also involves a new way of thinking. A kind of maybe-logic, or model agnosticism as Wilson also called it, which is closer to magical thinking than to scientific thinking, as it is not dependent on causal relations but on similarities, synchronicities, correspondences, associative leaps and image-thinking. Leary and Wilson rejected the finality of transcendence or apocalypse. Instead, they viewed the future as an open-ended, technologically driven transhumanist creation of potentially infinite extent.

The upper four circuits of Leary and Wilson's consciousness model were the 'stellar' circuits. While we all have evolved the first four circuits, the 'terrestrial' circuits, we now have to activate the upper ones which are coded into our DNA. Only a few persons – mystics, shamans, and so on – have throughout history had access to these levels of consciousness but in order to fulfil what is meant by our species-design, we all have to get there. So what will this future bring?

On the fifth level, the neurosomatic level, we begin to think asynchronically in gestalts. This circuit can be activated through hash or through yoga and tantra. It is imprinted on us through ecstatic experience and is similar to what Freud called the 'oceanic feeling.' This might have influenced Leary and Wilson's interpretation, as this circuit induces a kind of weightlessness which is meant to prepare us for living in space. We will become intelligent of our body.

Imprinting the sixth circuit, the neurogenetic, we will get access to what Theosophists called the Akashic records and Jung termed the collective unconscious. This can be activated through LSD or advanced forms of yoga and will develop abilities such as telepathy, meant to prepare us for interstellar communication. We

---

5 Robert Anton Wilson. *Prometheus Rising*. Las Vegas: New Falcon Publications, 1983.

will become intelligent of our brains.

The seventh circuit is a kind of cybernetic consciousness, where we will be able to metaprogram ourselves and all living things. It can be activated through entheogens and is operated by the logic from *Alice in Wonderland* (1865). We will become intelligent of our DNA.

Finally, the eight circuit is a non-local quantum circuit which can be imprinted through mescaline or near-death experiences. This is the circuit for full cosmic consciousness where one can both unify with the cosmos and go beyond time, space and the body. We will become intelligent of subatomic interactions.

Operation Mindfuck's various brain change games aimed specifically at getting access to these intelligences and cross the evolutionary threshold between the terrestrial and the stellar circuits in order to make it possible to leave the planet. Leary and Wilson imagined that this quest would grow into a social movement working on the realisation of Terra II, which becomes not only a cosmic destination but also the Earth transformed after we have imprinted our nervous systems to operate on higher circuits of consciousness.

While Wilson would later drift further towards ideas about longevity, Leary's plan for the colonisation of space varied greatly through the years. According to the initial plan, 5,000 of Earth's most virile and intelligent individuals would be launched on the vessel Starseed 1, equipped with luxury amenities in a move that can be seen as a precursor to not only Silicon Valley transhumanism but also memes about fully automated luxury communism in outer space. In the 1980s, Leary moved on to first embrace NASA scientist Gerard O'Neill's plans to construct giant Eden-like High Orbital Mini-Earths – which would use existing technology and raw materials from the Moon, orbital rock and obsolete satellites – before switching from space habitats to information habitats, from EXO-psychology to INFO-psychology, in a move that would align him with the bourgeoning cyberculture of the 1980s.

HAVE COURAGE, MOVE FORWARD

In hindsight, what the comet heralded turned out to be a new era of capitalism. 1973 – the year of the comet – was not only a year of cosmic transmissions and gnostic revelations. It was also the year a specific dream of the future, the counter-culture's dream about a world where we would all live in total freedom, became derailed by the military coup in Chile and the birth of neoliberalism as the end of ideology. Maybe that is why the year still haunts us, due to the interruption of its direction towards a future that never was, but could have been.

While they maintained a continuous conversation with speculative science, both Russian Cosmism and the SMI²LE project functioned analogously to magical systems that seek to use collective will and language to actualise a desired future, making them speak directly to contemporary discussions of the relation between futures and fictions. This discourse links to the neoliberal construction of subjectivity, but it also establishes a utopian rhetoric for the information age. However flawed, these theories are to be taken seriously if we are to understand contemporary notions of utopia.

Traditionally, when we talk about utopia and the future, we are thinking about the world to come as a question of organisation. But utopia is not only a place, it is also a method of imagining schemes, spaces, objects, that through the power of fantasy and desire, inspires change in the real world. The cosmic articulates a vision of utopia by projecting a particular configuration of technoscientific knowledge and ideological hopes into a specific program for action. Space was seen as the great outside, a place where utopia could be realised without any connections to the past.

What characterised both the cosmists and the SMI²LE project is that knowledge – whether spiritual or scientific – must be active. They wanted us to plan to overcome the natural, social, sexual, and other limitations of our species, thus creating an ever-expansive thinking that constructed a comprehensive worldview by combining science, art and faith to project a new society. They also shared a sense that the present state of knowledge is inadequate and that by searching through the past to find knowledge applicable to the future we may find that currently disparaged and currently unimagined sciences – alternative sciences, the 'parasciences' or 'pseudosciences,' magick – can assist or supplement what we need to know.

While this version of cosmism can seem like a relic from the space age, cosmist ideas are, at the same time, all around us. For example, when Barack Obama ratified the U.S. Commercial Space Launch Competitiveness Act in 2015, he helped give the right to private companies to make profits in space, thus giving American capitalism a new frontier, opening up the possibility for asteroid mining by companies like SpaceX. Today, it is the avant-garde of capitalism that have their eyes on outer space. The values have been reversed.

In 1973, it was all about evolving consciousness towards posthuman freedom. Today, it might be more a question of liberating the imagination so we collectively can picture other worlds and formulate alternatives. To speculate is arguably always a kind of thinking that carries a hope that a new idea will break into the established order and rearrange it. By speculating we get the possibility of confronting what we do not have words for. Speculative fictions are world-building, to use a term from science fiction.

World-building is a way of saying that one of the most effective way of treating the world today and/or the role of humanity in it, is to assume that everything is partly fiction. Empowerment is thus about gaining the opportunity to rewrite the script or actively produce new meaning. Myths and fictions – the stories we make to create meaning of the world – are one of the ways we are being controlled, but, at the same time, this terrain is also one of the places where it is possible to formulate alternatives and resist dominant narratives.

The contemporary interest in Cosmism – and by extension certain forms of science fiction, theory-fiction and other hybrid genres – points to the fact that our political and ecological situation are desperately calling for new stories, ones to be used for navigation on a planetary scale. Looking to the stars can result in not only media hyped events like the Comet Kohoutek whose name, due to lesser visibility than promised, for a period of time became synonymous to spectacular disappointment. It can also remind us that our cosmic existence is part of a bigger whole. A whole which we cannot explain but only apply speculative theories to in a pragmatic way and see what works. The discoveries of multiple pasts, such as Cosmism and its descendants, open up possibilities for thinking about multiple futures, maybe not as much in terms of cause and effect as in terms of similarities.

Futures we must imagine before they can move from the fantastic to the real.

Freud and H.D.
– Freedom of Thought and Speech

Elisabeth Punzi & Per Magnus Johansson

It has been estimated that Freud over the years had a total of 120 patients in analysis – more men than women, but the difference was marginal. The patients were in analysis in different ways. Some of them met Freud at only one or two occasions. Some had an analytic conversation with him during a walk, as in the case of Gustav Mahler. Other patients he met six times per week during a period that could last from a few months up to a couple of years. He also met patients who made several pauses during the analytic work. There were also patients who returned to him to take up the psychoanalytic work again.

Some analysands – as Freud called his patients – became public figures, after having been presented in so called case studies. One of them was Ida Bauer (married name Adler) (1882-1945), known as "Dora", who features in *Fragments of an Analysis of a Case of Hysteria* published in 1905. A major part of the text comprises a dream analysis, which is integrated into the therapeutic work.

Four years later, Freud wrote *Analysis of a Phobia in a Five-Year-Old Boy*, about Herbert Graf (1903-1973), known as "Little Hans", and later the same year he wrote *Notes upon a Case of Obsessional Neurosis*, about Ernst Lanzer (1878-1914), known as "The Ratman". Regarding "Little Hans", it was Herbert Graf's father, Max Graf (1873-1958) who led the analysis of Herbert Graf, although the father stood under Freud's supervision. In 1911, Freud published an analysis that concerned the Senate president Daniel Paul Schreber. The title of the book is *Psycho-Analytic Notes on an Autobiographical Account of a Case of Paranoia, (Dementia Paranoides)*. Daniel Paul Schreber (1842-1911) died the same year that Freud published his book. Freud never met him. He read what doctor Schreber had written. There is also the case study *From the History of an Infantile Neurosis*, about Sergei Konstantinovich Pankejeff (1887-1979), known as "The Wolfman", written in 1914 and published in 1918.

These five texts – of which three are based on Freud's direct experience of working with patients – have chiefly been written from theoretical points of departure and with theoretical aims. The case study of "Dora" was written to demonstrate the value of dream analysis in the therapeutic work; "Little Hans", to show that the so-called sexual theories could be confirmed in a child psychoanalysis; "The Rat Man" to illustrate how one could understand and analyse a new form of psychopathology: obsession neurosis, obsessive actions and obsessive thoughts. The case study of Schreber was written to show that even paranoid and psychotic states, which are often seen as severe and incomprehensible, are possible to understand using psychoanalytic theory. Moreover, psychoanalytic theory could contribute to an explanation of why the psychotic state had occurred. "The Wolf Man" was written to analyse and discuss how an original childhood neurosis can live on in the life of the adult man.

In a footnote written in 1923, in conjunction with a revision of the case study "Dora", Freud writes that the case studies were published with the patients' explicit permission, and in the case of "Little Hans" with the father's permission. Some of these patients commented on Freud's texts about them, and on their experience of psychoanalysis. This holds true for "Little Hans" and "The Wolf Man", but also, although to a lesser degree, for "Dora". This demands ethical reflection. What do we as researchers and clinicians do when we write about individuals?

There is a small group of patients, to which the poet Hilda Doolittle (1886-1961) belonged, who after Freud's death commented on their experiences of being in analysis with him. This group is relatively small. Those who never commented on their analytic experience with Freud make up a substantially larger group. Nor have their next of kin commented on the effect that being in analysis with Freud had on their relatives. Thus, in these cases there are no testimonies. Only the archival fragments remain.

H.D. AND FREUD

Hilda Doolittle, also known as H.D., a pen name suggested to her by Ezra Pound (1885-1972), expressed what her analytical work with Freud work meant to her, without using technical jargon. In *Tribute to Freud* (1956), she gives rich descriptions of her experiences and understandings of her analysis with Freud. Hilda Doolittle was born in 1886 in Bethlehem in Pennsylvania in USA and moved to London in 1911. Her father was a professor of astronomy, her mother had a deep and serious interest in music and was a music teacher (H.D., 1982). As a young woman, Hilda Doolittle was engaged to Ezra Pound. In 1913 she married Richard Aldington (1892-1962), another modernist author. They were married for a short time. She had a daughter, Perdita, born in 1919. Doolittle's lover, Cecil Gray (1895-1951) – a music critic, author, and composer, was the father. She lived in an unconventional relation with a woman, Annie Winfred Ellerman (1894-1983), known as Bryher, from 1918 to her death in 1961. Both of them had other lovers. And both were deeply involved in poetry and literature. Bryher was very wealthy, and married the author Robert McAlmon (1895-1956) in 1921. They divorced in 1927. After the divorce, Bryher married Kenneth Macpherson (1902-1971) and together with Doolittle, they travelled through Europe as a menagerie of three and established the film journal *Close up*. After the war, Hilda Doolittle and Bryher did not live together, but remained in contact with each other.

Hilda Doolittle had experienced several shocks and traumas and had also suffered from psychological distress and occasional breakdowns almost her whole life (Martin, 2008). In 1933, she traveled to Vienna to undergo analysis with Freud. She returned for another analysis in 1934. She had an interest in Freud's theories and read his works in the original German versions. Bryher supported the psychoanalytic movement and also took part in rescuing psychoanalysts from Nazi persecution.

Freud had a close relationship to Hilda Doolittle and communicated in a very personal way with her. In 1933, when Doolittle mentioned the last year of The Great War during an analytic hour, she wrote that Freud "said he had reason to remember the epidemic, as he lost his favorite daughter. She is here he said and he showed me a tiny locket that he wore, fastened to his watch-chain". Doolittle also had a relationship to Freud's family. He wrote to her in personal matters; "I am sorry you never saw our house and garden here in Grinzing"[1], he wrote to her in May 1935. Ernst Freud, Freud's son, and his family had settled in London, and Freud was gratified to hear that Hilda Doolittle, then living in London, was in touch with them (Gay, 1988, p. 609). She almost became part of his family; an intellectual woman with whom Freud could share experiences from psychoanalysis and from his reading. In his diary he writes about both Hilda Doolittle and Bryher. He supported H.D. and he was interested in her writing.

When Freud was seventy-seven, he could still impress Hilda Doolittle with his vitality. The professor told me, Doolittle noted in her journal, that if he lived another forty years, he would still be fascinated and curious about the impulses and the variations of the human mind or soul. He expressed his hopes and dreams to her. It is obvious that the contact between them was open when they discussed matters related to poetry, mythology, religion, personal distress, and how to find a place in a violent world.

It should be noted that Freud in his later years savored the companionship of many remarkable and accomplished women, like Hilda Doolittle. We could add Lou Andreas-Salome (1861-1937), Helene Deutsch (1884-1982), Joan Riviere (1882-1962), Jeanne Lampl-de Groot (1895-1987), Ruth Mack Brunswick (1897-1946), Marie Bonaparte (1882-1962), and, of course, his daughter Anna (1895-1982). There have certainly been strange perceptions of women in the psychoanalytic discipline. Nevertheless, women were, and are, a self-evident part of the psychoanalytic discipline and its development. The women mentioned here, and many more, left significant and inestimable marks on psychoanalysis. In 1910, when the members of the Vienna Psychoanalytic Society reviewed their bylaws, Isidor Sadger opposed to the admission of women. Freud firmly disagreed; he saw it as a serious faultiness if women were excluded by principle.

Freud lived in an age when political movements connected to the trade unions, feminism, and suffrage, were on the rise. The Jewish population gained access to universities and came closer to the public sphere (Beller, 1989). Within that structure, Freud gave both men and women access to a room in which they could think and speak freely about themselves and their deviances from the norm system

---

1 Grinzing is a village in the vicinity of Vienna, close to the Wienerwald.

that characterized the society they lived in. The deviances concerned both thoughts and behaviours. These deviances stimulated Freud to think actively, critically and freely. He is rarely afflicted with any kind of inhibition in his thinking and he does not express judgmental moralism. He understood that the human being is complicated and hard to understand fully.

Hilda Doolittle and Freud came from different backgrounds. She was raised in the context of the Moravian church. Freud had a Jewish background and the Jewish intellectual heritage was important for him. Yet, there were similarities. Freud came from Moravia, just as Hilda Doolittle's maternal ancestors. Moreover, their backgrounds were connected to spiritual and mystical traditions. In the Moravian church, mystical themes are present (Vogt, 2011). Freud's heritage was connected to the Jewish mystical tradition (Bakan, 1958; Berke, 2015). It should also be noted that *Tribute to Freud* is centered on mystical and religious themes and how these, and also Freud's collection of antiquities, became salient in the analysis. Both Doolittle and Freud abandoned the faith and traditions of their upbringing. Freud did not continue to celebrate Jewish Holidays or keep dietary laws. We do not however know whether his wife Martha continued to hold the traditions. It is known that Freud once expressed that he did not want her to light the Shabbat candles (Salberg, 2007), but we do not know how she responded to this. It is also known that Freud owned important pieces of Judaica and books about Jewish mysticism (Berke, 2015; Yerushalmi, 1991).

Freud declared himself Godless and was integrated in the majority society, but firmly identified as Jewish and had a close and a meaningful relationship to his Jewish heritage. He was the founder of psychoanalysis and responsible for its future. Hilda Doolittle abandoned her childhood religion and came to embody the lifestyle of modernity. She did not hide her bisexual and polyamorous relationships. Freud lived a steady family life. The differences did not hinder Freud from, according to Hilda Doolittle's own presentations, being able to listen, and speak to her in a way she could relate to. The unfamiliar was a point of departure for their mutual reflections.

Hilda Doolittle had suffered from writer's block. This was a reason for her analysis (Martz, 1983). During the analysis, she had an intense correspondence with Bryher (Friedman, 1992). She describes the analysis and her evolving relationship to Freud and his family. She for example writes about Freud's attachment to his dogs and how he out of concern for them once threw himself to the floor – keys and coins flying from his pockets. Freud wanted to give Doolittle and Bryher a puppy, but they were unable to care for it at that moment. Hilda Doolittle shows us a Freud who is open minded, supporting, and humorous, a much-needed counterweight to the widespread misperception of Freud as austere, judgemental, and conservative.

During the Second World War, Hilda Doolittle stayed in London and at the end of the war she went to Switzerland. Shortly after the war, she suffered a severe mental breakdown. She was in existential psychotherapy with Erich Heydt from 1953 to 1960. Heydt had met Ezra Pound, and the relationship between Heydt and

Hilda Doolittle had a semi-professional character. Her relationship to Ezra Pound, which she describes further in *End to torment* (H.D., 1979) was a substantial part of this analysis. She spent the rest of her life in Switzerland, but visited the United States in 1960 to collect an American Academy of Arts and letters medal. She suffered a stroke in July 1961 and died some months later, in the Klinik Hirslanden in Zürich. Her ashes were returned to the US and to Bethlehem, Pennsylvania. She was buried in the family tomb in the Nisky Hill Cemetery. Ezra Pound lived in Merano and Venice. They corresponded through letters but never met each other again.

Freud admired creative writers and seemed to have had a longing toward creative writing himself; balancing on the border of science and artistic expression. He praised creative writers such as Goethe and Shakespeare (Freud, 1917-1955; 1916-1957b) as well as the sculptor, artist, and scientist Leonardo da Vinci (Freud, 1910-1957a). In 1930, he received the prestigious Goethe Prize. In his acceptance speech, delivered by Anna Freud, he described that Goethe had insight in the importance of early emotional bonds, sexual desire and the repressive power of guilt; and thereby anticipated psychoanalysis.

THE WRITING ON THE WALL

In *Creative writers and day-dreaming*, Freud (1908-1959a) writes about fantasy and reality. As he expresses it, a certain knowledge concerning the source of creativity, and the constitution of the creative person, seems out of reach. Freud describes that the writer creates a fantasy world that is taken just as seriously as reality. In this manner, unsatisfying experiences can be transformed into creative work and ultimately into works of art. Simultaneously, Freud notes that overwhelming fantasies might also be a breeding ground for suffering and symptoms. He thus indicates that creativity and symptoms have commonalities. Yet the distinction between fantasy and reality must remain. In the creative state, the writer becomes absorbed to the extent that reality becomes irrelevant. On other occasions, the writer can reflect on what was created and the state in which it was created. If the individual however is absorbed by fantasy, he or she could develop difficulties in handling reality. Fantasies might become perceived as concrete, belonging to the reality, and the writer might become obsessed with himself or herself. Thus, the capacity for productive work as well as the capacity to communicate such work to others become diminished, or even lost. It should be noted that symptoms do not by definition exclude the production of creative work. However, if a delusional world gains prominence, the capacity to engage in productive and creative work, and communicate it to others is likely to be limited. Here, one must keep in mind that, from a psychoanalytic perspective, the ability to be productive is to some extent connected with overcoming and dealing with psychological distress and suffering. Freud used the term sublimation to capture how sexual impulses are channeled into productive and creative non-sexual goals, and he valued sublimations in the arts (Civitarese, 2017).

In 1920, Hilda Doolittle and Bryher stayed on the island of Corfu. One afternoon, Hilda Doolittle saw a figure on the wall of their hotel room; a head and shoulders – an illuminated template. Thereafter various figures appeared. She wanted to understand this experience, which she called *The writing on the wall.* She saw it as an example of spiritual realism. She expressed that she and Freud never argued about transcendental phenomena but rather immersed themselves in dialogues about myths, mysticism, and religion. However, she took up an opposing view to Freud's regarding *The writing on the wall.* He saw the experience as potentially dangerous. Hilda Doolittle (1956) writes that Freud had a materialistic side and strived toward rationalistic thinking.

On our part, we suggest that since the dialogues between Doolittle and Freud are centered on mystical and religious themes, the dialogues need to be understood with respect to their mystical and religious traditions. Here, we focus on Freud's refusal to see *The writing on the wall* as real, and we would like to nuance the description of him as exclusively rationalistic. We suggest that when he refuses to see the vision as real, he strives to draw H.D.'s attention to her creative work and we should remember that her writer's block was a reason for seeking out psychoanalysis. Doolittle (1956) describes that Freud encouraged her to write, to have confidence in herself and her writing. It is therefore reasonable to think that Freud wished that she would abandon her perception of the vision as real so that she would become less preoccupied with it and instead could engage in fantasy, creativity, and productive writing. Her writer's block was indeed solved. She became highly productive and among many works she wrote *Bid me to live* (H.D., 1960-2015), about her traumas from World War I, and her relationship to D.H. Lawrence – a work Freud encouraged her to write.

Our understanding of Freud's reaction to the *The writing on the wall* and his description of it as potentially dangerous, gains support if we acknowledge the view of creativity in the Jewish tradition. From this perspective, God and humanity are seen as co-creators of the world (Steinsaltz, 1999). In line with this, Madsen and Willert (1996) describe that in the Jewish narrative of creation, the creation of mankind is mentioned twice. The first time it is said that God created us equal to all in creation. This means that we are part of nature and everything that has to do with concrete survival. The second time the creation of mankind is mentioned, it is said that God created us in his image, which means as spiritual beings. As human beings we are nature and spirit, and the two elements need to work together. Mankind in turn creates the world and its organizations in its image. There is thus a connection between the Jewish view on humanity as co-creator of the world, and the emphasis on productivity in psychoanalysis. According to the Jewish tradition, we need to integrate the natural and the spiritual elements in ourselves and thus need to acknowledge that we are both connected to nature and to spiritual realms (Steinsaltz, 1999). If we become all natural, or "animal" in Berke's and Schneider's (2006) words, we lose our capacity for reflection, spirituality, and productivity.

We therefore suggest that when Freud counteracts H.D.'s perception of *The writing on the wall* as real, he strives to support H.D.'s capacity for reflection, productivity, and creative work, as well as her spirituality. In *Tribute to Freud*, H.D. describes how Freud encouraged her to write and to have confidence in herself and her creative work. We therefore find it reasonable to assume that Freud's description of H.D.'s experience in the hotel room as dangerous reflects an admiration of creativity and fantasy rather than a mere overvaluation of materialism and a positivistic world-view. To support her spirituality and creativity, he wishes for her to abandon her perception of *The writing on the wall* as concrete. He remained faithful to his psychoanalytical position and to his Jewish heritage. It should also be noted that H.D herself was ambivalent about her "real dreams" or "occult experiences", which could be distressing for her. In *Tribute to Freud*, she wrote that she had sought help but could not get rid of the experience by means of writing or talking.

We also suggest that Freud's resistance toward actually believing in an image could be understood with reference to the position of images in the Jewish tradition. The second commandment concerns idolatry and the absolute prohibition of producing and believing in religious images. Postman (1985) in his critique of contemporary western culture wrote that the second commandment underlines the importance of abstract thinking, speech, and words; phenomena that according to Steinsaltz (1999) are examples of human creativity. Moreover, Postman writes that images are powerful and thus might be used by individuals and organizations who want to exploit us. A word-centered culture needs to be sheltered from a powerful image-centered culture, and the Jewish position (which is shared by other traditions and religions) toward images reminds us of this need (Postman, 1985). In other words, culture needs to be protected against intrusive images. Both Freud and Postman were secular Jews. Yet they were obviously inspired by Judaism and reflected on the Jewish heritage. Postman acknowledges that the Jewish tradition invokes sensitivity and skepticism toward the power of intrusive images. Such sensitivity might have influenced Freud to describe *The writing on the wall* as dangerous. Such a perception might have strengthened his attempts to support H.D. to write, to create, so that she would not be caught up in, or overwhelmed by, fantasies.

CONCLUDING REMARKS

Our intention with this interpretation is to present the importance of acknowledging Sigmund Freud's Jewish heritage and how the Jewish tradition emphasizes certain prerequisites of culture and what it means to be human. We would finally stress the fact Sigmund Freud, a Jewish medical doctor, academically trained, married, father of six children, living almost his entire life in the same city, Vienna, met an analysand Hilda Doolittle, a woman, bisexual, who had an unconventional life-style, always in exile, moving from one place to another, from one country to another, without a stable home. But they found a mutual meeting point; they shared something. They met each other in dialogue, in the emergence of psychoanalysis, in the tension between similarities and differences, and in the right to talk about psychological distress, and to transcend it in writing. Freedom of thought and speech united them.

REFERENCES

Bakan, D. (1958). *Sigmund Freud and the Jewish mystical tradition*. Princeton: D. Van Nostrand Company.

Beller, S. (1989). *Vienna and the Jews 1867–1938: A cultural history*. Cambridge: Cambridge University Press.

Berke, J. H. (2015). *The hidden Freud: His Hassidic roots*. London: Karnac.

Berke, J.H., & Schneider, S. (2006). The self and the soul. *Mental Health, Religion & Culture, 9*, 333-354.

Civitarese, G. (2017). On sublimation. *International Journal of Psychoanalysis*, 97, 1369-1392.

Freud, S. (1953). Fragments of an Analysis of a Case of Hysteria. In J. Strachey (Ed. and Trans.), *The standard edition of the complete psychological works of Sigmund Freud.* (Vol. 7,. pp. 3-122.). London: The Hogarth Press and The institute of Psychoanalysis. (Original work published in 1905).

Freud, S. (1955). Analysis of a Phobia in a Five-Year-Old Boy. In J. Strachey (Ed. and Trans.), *The standard edition of the complete psychological works of Sigmund Freud.* (Vol. 10, pp. 3 – 1949). London: The Hogarth Press and The institute of Psychoanalysis. (Original work published in 1909).

Freud, S. (1955). Notes upon a Case of Obsessional Neurosis. In J. Strachey (Ed. and Trans.), *The standard edition of the complete psychological works of Sigmund Freud.* (Vol. 10, pp. 153-257) . London: The Hogarth Press and The institute of Psychoanalysis. (Original work published in 1909).

Freud, S. (1958). Psycho-Analytic Notes on an Autobiographical Account of a Case of Paranoia, (Dementia Paranoides). In J. Strachey (Ed. and Trans.), *The standard edition of the complete psychological works of Sigmund Freud* (Vol. 12, pp. 3-82). London: The Hogarth Press and The institute of Psychoanalysis. (Original work published in 1911).

Freud, S. (1955). From the History of an Infantile Neurosis. In J. Strachey (Ed. and Trans.), *The standard edition of the complete psychological works of Sigmund Freud* (Vol. 17, pp. 3-122). London: The Hogarth Press and The institute of Psychoanalysis. (Original work published in 1918).

Freud, S. (1955). The Psychogenesis of a Case of Female Homosexuality. In J. Strachey (Ed. and Trans.), *The standard edition of the complete psychological works of Sigmund Freud* (Vol. 18, pp. 145-172). London: The Hogarth Press and The institute of Psychoanalysis. (Original work published in 1920).

—ᴡ—Freud, S. (1955). A childhood recollection from "Dichtung und Wahrheit". In J. Strachey (Ed. and Trans.), *The standard edition of the complete psychological works of Sigmund Freud* (Vol. 17, pp. 145-156). London: The Hogarth Press and The institute of Psychoanalysis. (Original work published in 1917).

—ᴡ— Freud, S. (1959). Creative writers and daydreaming. In J. Strachey (Ed. and Trans.), *The standard edition of the complete psychological works of Sigmund Freud* (Vol. 9, pp. 141-153). London: The Hogarth Press and The institute of Psychoanalysis. (Original work published in 1908).

—ᴡ—Friedman, S.S. (2002). *Analyzing Freud. Letters of H.D., Bryher, and their circle.* New York: New directions.

—ᴡ— Gay, P. (1988). *A life of our time.* New York: W W Norton & Co.

—ᴡ— H.D. (1956). *Tribute to Freud.* New York: New Directions.

—ᴡ— H.D. (1979). *End to torment. A memoir of Ezra Pound.* New York: New Directions.

—ᴡ— H.D. (1982). *The gift.* New York: New Directions.

—ᴡ— H.D. (2015). *Bid me to live.* Edited by Caroline Zilboorg. Gainesville: University Press of Florida. (Original work published in 1960).

—ᴡ—Madsen, B., & Willert, S. (1996). *Survival in the organization: Gunnar Hjelholt looks back at the concentration camp from an organizational perspective.* Aarhus, DK: Aarhus University press.

—ᴡ— Martin, T. (2008). From cabinet to couch: Freud's clinical use of sculpture. *British Journal of Psychotherapy*, 24, 184-196.

—ᴡ— Martz, L. (1983). In *Collected Poems 1912-1944* by H.D. (pp. xi-xxxvi). New York: New Directions.

—ᴡ— Postman, N. (1985). *Amusing ourselves to death. Public discourses in the age of show business.* London: Penguin Books.

—ᴡ— Salberg, J. (2007). *Hidden in plain sight: Freud's Jewish identity revisited.* Psychoanalytic Dialogues, 17, 197-217.

—ᴡ— Steinsaltz, A. (1999). *Simple words. Thinking about what really matters in life.* New York: Simon & Schuster.

—ᴡ— Vogt, P. (2011). Zinzendorf's "Seventeens Points of Matrimony": A fundamental document on the Moravian understanding of marriage and sexuality. *Journal of Moravian History*, 10, 39-67.

—ᴡ— Yerushalmi, Y. H. (1991). *Sigmund Freud's Jewish heritage.* New York, NY: Research Foundation of State University of New York.

True Lies:
Towards (a Rehabilitation of) Mythic Thought

Hans-Peter Söder

Clearly, mythology is no toy for children.
– Joseph Campbell

Only the thinking that violates itself is strong enough to decipher the myths.
– Max Horkheimer/Theodor W. Adorno

There are two ways to study myths. One is as an anthropologist and/or genealogist, cum scientist, and the other is as an artist. Only the artist has the ability, and the necessary imaginative freedom, to deal with the irrational side of myth. Mythic thinking is dreaming, with eyes wide shut. It is symbolic thinking, a visualizing of the self in a world, where all the world is picture, a *world picture (Weltbild)*. Myths are always local. They are place bound. But in this enchanted sphere, the self is *not* at the center of this world, it is only a part of it (in contrast to the *experimentum medietatis* of the Renaissance, where mankind stood in the middle of the world and determined its center). In myth, there is no contradiction. Nothing is true, nothing false. All *is*, and all *is* incredibly credible. Myth can explain things that logic cannot. The heart has its reason of which reason knows nothing, noted Pascal the logician. Only through myth and the mythic can we come to appreciate the supreme power and the indomitable force of *eros*, the first god among *all* the gods (according to Parmenides).[1] According to Aphrodite, that is, the *personification* of desire, longing and passion cannot be explained in logical terms, because desire makes no sense. It can only be pictured in words and paint:

> Till now swift-circling a white foam arose
> From that immortal substance, and a nymph
> Was nourished in their midst. The wafting waves
> First bore her to Cythera the divine:
> To wave-encircled Cyprus came she then,
> And forth emerged a goddess in the charms
> Of awful beauty. / Where her delicate feet
> Had pressed the sands, green herbage flowering sprang.
>
> . . .

---

1 Diels/Kranz, *Fragmente der Vorsokratiker*, 28B: 13.

> Love tracked her steps, and beautiful Desire
> Pursued . . . [2]

When we concern ourselves with myth, what is called for is *inventive* and not logical thinking. It was Oscar Wilde and *not* Hegel or Kant who acknowledged that "Lying and poetry are arts…not unconnected with each other".[3] Myth is an *autopoietic* system that finds the means to create and recreate itself from within its particular world.[4] Only the literary artist is in a position to tackle both the irrational and the narrative aspect of myth. *Tief ist der Brunnen der Vergangenheit* (deep are the wells of the past) is how Thomas Mann begins *Joseph and his Brothers*, a work that would consume 17 years of his life to fill 1344 pages.[5] With this brilliant opening sentence Thomas Mann points not only to the necessarily murky bottom of the well, a substratum out of sight of reason, but also to its being a (cultural) reservoir, continuously supplying us with a life-sustaining stream of pictorial memories and image-creating myths. It is for reasons such as these, that I concern myself with myth as an artist, because only as an artist can I address such essential aspects of myth as enchantment, ecstasy, the erotic and the *mysterium tremendum* (the mystery that causes fear and trembling).

I am currently writing an epic, a mythic work, with the title *Dea ex machina*. It is to be a tetralogy that concerns itself with forms of communication regarding love and loving. The first book of the series is entitled *Helena at War* (2012). If we want to start at "the beginning," we must begin with this woman, because Helen is no ordinary beauty, not just another daughter of a god. Helen is the daughter of Leda and the swan. In this union, in this blending of man and beast, the mythic imagination draws up a narrative boundary, which is with us to this day. Helen is not only the *most beautiful* woman in the world, who blinds others with desire; she herself is blinded by desire. Helen embodies the mythic circle. It is Helen who makes us understand the need for Aphrodite. Without Helen, there would be no Achilles and no Odysseus. In Goethe's *Faust* there would be no Gretchen. Many other archetypes in the arts would also not exist. Thus we *must* begin our story with her.

The first part of the tetralogy is cast in the form of her myth. If we want to speak about the *logic* of modernity, we first have to come to terms with its myth(s). But what are we to understand by myth? Somehow, and this is the point of departure for my work, we all *know* in the heart of our hearts what myth is: it is a not-knowing "knowing". As we associate feeling with thinking, as we connect knowledge to ignorance, or join truth to falsehood, we are reaching back to mythic thought. This is the point of departure for the second book of the *Dea ex machina* project, entitled *Metalogicon: Eine Liebeserklärung an die Philosophie* (a declaration of love

---

2 James Davies, *Hesiod and Theognis* (Edinburgh: William Blackwood & Sons, 1881) 75.
3 Oscar Wilde, The Decay of Lying in: *Oscar Wilde: Selected Writings* (London: Oxford UP, 1961) 5.
4 Cf. N. Luhmann, "The Autopoiesis of Social Systems." In: F. Geyer and J. Van d. Zeuwen, eds., *Socio-cybernetic Paradoxes: Observation, Control and Evolution of Self-Steering Systems* (London: Sage) 172-92.
5 Cf. Thomas Mann *Joseph und seine Brüder* (Frankfurt/M.: Fischer Verlag, 2007).

for philosophy). Through its title, *Metalogicon* (2016), it already alludes to "metaphysics", the world *beyond* physics. Is such a world possible? If yes, what would such a world look like? And today, is it still a worthwhile endeavor to tell the story of how *logos* became *our* logic? Where does language begin, and where does it end? This is the question of the *Metalogicon*.

In the *Dea ex machina* I address two questions. Is myth merely the *Weltanschauung* of the *homo divinans*, the magical man? Are myths simply frameworks of primitive peoples? Or is myth and mythic thought something so universal that it still flickers in the collective unconscious of the *homo faber* and thereby still wields powers of influence? If myth were indeed a living *autopoietic* system, how could one reconnect with it? And why would one want to do this? In ancient Greek, say of that of the Homeric era, myth (μῦθος) is simply that which is being said or has been said. Myth not only belongs to the world of speech and talk, but *myth* itself is a self-contained world made of its own words and symbols. In Germanic languages this understanding of myth is already contained and explicitly spelled out in the word *saga* (that which is being said and talked about without knowing its origin and/or author). Thus one can say in German: "Die Sage" *sagt*, as opposed to English, where it would be "the myth *is* that...". But there is an *ontological* difference of quality here. *Saying* something and *being* something *is* not the same thing. This difference is brought out in the colloquial phrase: "I am just *talking*; I am not *saying* anything." Myth *is* not any "thing". It is *only* talk. But what *is* talk?

Talk is that, which is *not* written down. From all we read, the importance of oral tradition in pre-Homeric and Homeric Greece cannot be overestimated. We know very little about the content and import of these transient presentations. In Plato's *The Republic* and in his *Gorgias* we learn that children were told myths, as we tell, or *used to* tell, our children fairy tales (the relationship between *myth* and *fairy tale* is a subject in itself. It would be another tangent altogether to pursue the question regarding the consequences of the current trend of sparing our children the stories of burned witches and hearts being torn out of live bodies). Plato already noted that the myths told *to children* have a (potentially dangerous) afterlife (for the republic). But let us pose the questions differently: What are the consequences of an *absence* of myths? The importance of the (very few) observations on myth in the Platonic dialogues did not escape Nietzsche. In *The Birth of Tragedy from the Spirit of Music* (1872), Nietzsche came to the conclusion that the Greeks invented myth in order to conceal the Dionysian truth that there is no point to life. Myth, in other words, is a noble lie. In *The Birth of Tragedy from the Spirit of Music*, Nietzsche pointed out that *two* Greek worlds continue to exist to the present day: an Apollonian and a Dionysian world. We, however, terrified of death, of insignificance and nihilism, will only accept the Apollonian, the Aristotelian world of concrete existence and observable causality; and this, according to Nietzsche, has grave metaphysical consequences. Later, in *The Gay Science* (1882), Nietzsche argues that there *is* a *logos* to myth, but it cannot and should not *make* no sense. Myth, as Nietzsche contends, is not only *beyond* truth and falsity, it is also beyond good and evil. No judgments, no pronouncement can be made, or *should* even be attempted concerning the truth of *what* is being said in myth.

If it has not become clear at this point, let me say it directly. When I talk about myth and the mythic, I don't *know* what I am talking about, because myth is pre-verbal. Myth is horror. Myth is the original *horror vacui*. And siding with the grammarian Ludwig Wittgenstein, we all should leave it at that: "Whereof one cannot speak, thereof one *must* be silent." However, instead of silence regarding myth, we encounter *stupefying* loquaciousness. The literature on myth is extensive and wide-ranging, and surely, there are as many definitions, characterizations and classifications of myths as there are mythographers and mythologists. Why is that so? This is one of the questions that I would like to address.

No matter how one defines myth, all are in agreement that myths are *Ur-Geschichten*, originary narratives, from an olden time, where, and so begins the fairy tale *The Frog Prince* (and *Iron Henry*) of the Brothers Grimm, *wishing* still did some good: "In den alten Zeiten, wo das wünschen noch geholfen hat...". In myth is magic, but not in a demonic way. In *The Golden Bough: A Study in Magic and Religion* (1890), George Frazer calls it "sympathetic" magic. How are we to understand this kind of magic? The ethnographer Theodor-Wilhelm Danzel (1886 – 1954) came up with an astoundingly easy way to get a handle on this problematic term. He circumscribes magic (Zauber) by juxtaposing it to technology. Magic is *not* technical, and conversely, in all that is technical, there is no magic. Before technical man, before the *homo faber*, there was what Danzel calls the *homo divinans*: the magical man (der magische Mensch). The world of the homo divinans according to Danzel, was characterized by a uniform way of life (die Einheitlichkeit des Lebensstiles) and an overabundant wealth of symbolic forms (Reichtum der symbolischen Formen).[6] By a "uniform way of life" Danzel means that the *homo divinans* saw the world as a *symbolic place*, a place where magic happens without rhyme or reason. In the words of the geographer and explorer Eduard Pechuël-Loesche (1840 – 1913): "Dem Primitiven ist in allem Zauber" (for primitive man, in all dwells magic).[7]

If there is no cognition, as we understand it today, if there is no comprehension of objective causality, can one call "the magical appreciation of the world," *thinking*, especially if no rational knowledge is acquired? Yes, one can call it thinking, in the sense of "I *see* what you mean." It is for this reason, that *mythic thought* is *Weltanschauung* in the truest sense of the word. It is an acceptance of things in a *pictorial* way; it is a form of "thinking through" via symbols and symbolism. Claude Lévi-Strauss called this kind of archaic thinking *la sauvage pensée* (1962). Savage thought, however, according to Lévi-Strauss, has the same structure as modern thought. Albeit untamed, the savage mind "thinks" (through what Lévi-Strauss calls *bricolage*) by using whatever is *at hand* to come to a *Weltanschauung*. Whatever

---

6 Theodor-Wilhelm Danzel, *Kultur und Religion des primitiven Menschen* (Stuttgart: Strecker und Schröder, 1924) 2.
7 Ibid. 2

is at hand is that which "is around". In German we call "that which is around and around us" *Umwelt*, most often translated as "the environment". However, the German *Umwelt* refers to more than just that which wraps around the individual (cf. French *environ*). In *savage thinking* there is communication going on between the individual and the *Umwelt*. Lévi-Strauss' *structural anthropology* is one way, a logical way, to cope with the communicative structure of savage thinking. Is there a way that one could unite Lévi-Strauss' semiotics of *bricolage* with the three-dimensional concept of *Umwelt*? Yes, but this would be a mismatch; it would be another union of Leda and the swan. But this is precisely what the biologist Johann Jakob von Uexküll has achieved with his notion of *biosemiotics*.

The biologist and philosopher Johann Jakob von Uexküll (1864-1944) is chiefly known as the founder of ecology (as a science) and as a pioneer in the fields of cybernetics, theoretical biology and biosemiotics. With his introduction of the term *Umwelt* (in his book *Umwelt und Innenwelt der Tiere*, 1909), von Uexküll introduced a radically new kind of semiotics (capable of supporting Lévi-Strauss' notion of *savage thought*). For von Uexküll, *Umwelt* (environment world) is not the same as *Umgebung* (surroundings). The notion of *Umgebung* is a passive one. Objects and subjects blend together, and make up *the surroundings*. *Umwelt*, in contrast, is an active state of existence and being. The individual (and/or the organism) is part of the *Umwelt* and therefore actively shapes it. This idea of *Umwelt* is based on the realization that it is difficult to separate a being and/or an organism from its surroundings. Where does the organism end, and where do the surroundings begin? The perimeter of the organism, for one, is its outer shell, its skin, but it is also its very movements in both space and time. In a nutshell, for von Uexküll every animal has its own subjective time and its own subjective space, its *Umwelt*. With the concept of *Umwelt*(en), von Uexküll has thereby introduced a semiotics that differs fundamentally from the semiotics of de Saussure and Peirce. By including time in the production of signs and codes (because perception, in von Uexküll's *Umwelt*, happens in time) von Uexküll's semiotics not only adds another dimension to communication, it also (and this is more important for our purposes) is pre-linguistic. For this reason, von Uexküll's *biosemiotics* is better able to *situate* and localize mythic thinking than de Saussurean and Peircean semiotics is able to do.

Again, what makes it so difficult to comprehend myth and mythic thinking is that myth is outside (*the laws*) of written language. Myth is not only pre-verbal, it is *extra*-verbal. As it is separate from *objective* reality, myth is *not* history. Myth is only story. Myths *do* unfold in time, but not in historical time. Our habit of linking myth to historical time is necessary and essential, but is senseless. One mythographer, who is usually not seen as such, Augustine of Hippo, instinctively realized this in his attempts to come to terms with the founding myths in the *Book of Genesis*. "What then *is* time?" he kept asking himself (and the reader), "if no one asks me, so goes the celebrated phrase, I know what it is. If I wish to explain it to him who asks, I do not know." Because origin, catastrophe and eternity, are all *outside* the frame of *the historical* and outside of historical narrative, Augustine faced an impossible task in the *Confessions*. All of eternity, he finally concludes in one fell swoop, is wholly contained in the present. There is no past, there is no future, there *is* only the present. Time just "is" according to Augustine. More cannot be said. At this juncture we can ask already: Is Augustine's cutting the Gordian knot in Book 11 of the *Confessions* a true lie? We will answer this question later, for in Wittgensteinian terms, all we can say about myth *and* time is that myth *is* linked to time, in as much as myth tries to make sense of beginnings and ends in terms of origins and catastrophes.

The reason why myth is continually linked to history and the historical is that it is undeniably a child of *Chronos*. Myth is purely temporal. It lives only *in* the moment and *for* a moment. Myth *is*, ontologically speaking, only as far as it is *in* the action, *in* the ritualistic posture, *in* the split second of ecstasy. Myth lives in pure time, concurrently (and this adds another layer of complication) myth manifests itself in (cultural) space(s), especially in holy places, in shrines, and in sanctuaries of the self, the chief sanctuary being the body. In other words, myth is not *only* intimately tied to bodily experience(s), it occupies, and dwells in, the body. The body is not only a, or *our* cosmos, it is *the* mythic cosmos. In mythic thought then, there *is* no mind, only body. It is the body that thinks. How are we to understand this? D. H. Lawrence put this into words, as he spoke of "blood consciousness":

> When I take a woman, then the blood-percept is supreme, my blood-knowing is overwhelming. There is a transmission, I don't know of what, between her blood and mine, in the act of connection. So that afterwards, even if she goes away, the blood-consciousness persists between us, when the mental consciousness is suspended; and I am formed then by my blood consciousness, not by my mind or nerves at all. . . . . . now I am convinced of what I believed when I was about twenty – that there is another seat of consciousness than the brain and the nerve system: there is a blood-consciousness which exists in us independently of the ordinary mental consciousness, which depends on the eye as its source or connector. There is the blood-consciousness, with the sexual connection, holding the same relation as the eye, in seeing, holds to the mental consciousness. One lives, knows, and has one's being in the blood, without any reference to nerves and brain. This is one half of life, belonging to the darkness. And the tragedy of this our life, and of your life, is that the mental and nerve consciousness exerts a tyranny over the blood-consciousness, and that your will has gone completely over to the mental consciousness, and is engaged in the destruction of your blood being or blood-consciousness, the final liberating of the one, which is only death in result.[8]

Perhaps one way to understand mythic thought is that it is a *symbolic* way of life.

---

8 D.H Lawrence, *Apocalypse* (New York: Viking Press, 1966) 41-47.

Aby Warburg calls it a *Lebensform*. Symbols (in German *Sinnbild, sense*-pictures), of course, are notoriously challenging concepts. By their very representative nature, symbols and symbolic language are so basic and so pervasive that it seems almost futile to approach the cloudy mirrors of symbolism via logic and causality. But what makes symbols even more challenging is that they have an emotive power, in contrast to "just talk", that is, to rhetorical figures of speech. It is for this reason that Joseph Campbell defines symbol as: "A symbol is an *energy evoking*, and directing, agent."[9] It is there, in the ritual act, where body and soul become one, it is there where mythic thought survives to this day.[10]

Mythic thought is circular, unending and as I have shown, it is not only impossible, but it would also be bad form to speak on and of it in a logical, linear fashion. Therefore, I must return to a beginning, to Helen. The origin of the name Helen (Ἕλλην) is contested. That she is of the "Hellenes", that she is the most Greek of the Greeks, would make sense. But I am *not* trying to make sense of myth. I prefer the etymology offered up by the German philologist Ernst Curtius (1820 to 1885). Curtius traces the name *Helen* back to the goddess of the moon, Selene (Σελήνη). I prefer this etymology, because it further explains mythic thought:

> We have lost the cosmos, by coming out of responsive connection with it, and this is our chief tragedy... And we have lost the moon, the cool, bright, ever-varying moon. It is she who would caress our nerves, smooth them with the silky hand of her glowing, soothes them into serenity again with her cool presence. For the moon is the mistress and mother of our watery bodies, the pale body of our nervous consciousness and our moist flesh. Oh, the moon could soothe us and heal us like a cool great Artemis between her arms. But we have lost her, in our stupidity we ignore her, and angry she stares down on us and whips us with nervous whips. Oh, beware of the angry Artemis of the night heavens, beware of the spite of Cybele, beware of the vindictiveness of horned Astarte.[11]

---

9 Joseph Campbell, *Flight of the Wild Gander: The Symbol without Meaning* (California: New World Library, 2002) 143.

10 Of course, one cannot write or speak on "mythic thought" without referring to the German philosopher Ernst Cassirer (1874-1945). His main work, the three-volume *The Philosophy of Symbolic Forms* (1923-29) is not only *the* key work on mythic thought, it also continues to be one of the most important philosophical texts of the 20th century.

11 D. H. Lawrence, *Apocalypse*: 41 – 47.

The Occult and Psychological Healing in Iceland: Theological Explorations of the Potential Positive Psychological Implications of the Age of Fire, 1654-1683, in Iceland

Haukur Ingi Jónasson

The dedicated Netflix viewer who has watched all the seasons of the show *Vikings* might have become interested in the attempt of the pagan healer and magician Raven-Floki, to create a peaceful utopian society in the new found Iceland at around the year 825. But the story goes further back. A man named Pytheas of Massalia (Πυθέας ὁ Μασσαλιώτης) was a Greek geographer, explorer, and astronomer from the Greek colony of Massalia, now Marseille in France) who became famous for his explorations in northwestern Europe around 325 BC. Pythes was the first person to travel to the North-Atlantic, he came across an island he named Thule – later Ultima Thule, representing an island at the ultimate extreme, a land furthest away from human civilization. This became one of many imaginatively charged mythical islands rising from the depths of the North-Atlantic Ocean. Still, it has, ever since, been a mysterious place stimulating the imagination of all who hear about it.[1]

Both *Landnámabók* ("Book of Settlements"), written in the 1100s, and *Íslendingabók* dating from between 1122 and 1133, state that before the Irish monks, called Papar before Norse settlement and states that the monks left behind Irish books, bells, and crosiers, among other things. According to the same account, the Irish monks abandoned the country when the Norse arrived or had left before their arrival. The twelfth-century scholar, Ari Þorgilsson's *Íslendingabók*, reasserts that the settlers found items including bells corresponding to those used by Irish monks. No such artifacts have been discovered by archaeologists, however. Some Icelanders claimed descent from Cerball mac Dúnlainge, King of Osraige in southeastern Ireland, at the time of the *Landnámabók's* creation. According to this account, the Irish monk inhabitants left the island since they did not want to live with pagan Norsemen. One theory suggests that those monks were members of a Hiberno-Scottish mission; Irish and Scottish monks or hermits who spread Christianity during the Middle Ages.

Norse discovery

According to the *Landnámabók*, Iceland was discovered by Naddodd, a settler in

---

1 To name just a few: Descartes, Borges, Tolkien, Wells and Hugo all speculated about Iceland, this mysterious place of the sagas in their writing.

the Faroe Islands. The source claims that when sailing from Norway to the Faroes, he lost his way and drifted to the east coast of Iceland that Naddodd named Snæland (English: Snowland). Around 860 Garðar Svavarsson from Sweden also accidentally sailed to the coast of Iceland where he stayed for the winter at Garðarshólmi ("Garðar's Islet") and stayed for the winter at Húsavík.

The first Norseman who deliberately sailed to Garðarshólmi was Hrafna-Flóki Vilgerðarson. In 868, Flóki settled for one winter at Barðaströnd. After the cold winter passed, the summer came, and the whole island became green, which stunned Flóki. Realizing that this place was, in fact, habitable, despite the cold winter, and full of valuable resources, Flóki restocked his boat. He then returned east to Norway with resources and knowledge. The first permanent settler in Iceland is usually considered to have been a Norwegian chieftain named Ingólfur Arnarson and his wife, Hallveig Fróðadóttir. According to the *Landnámabók*, he threw two carved pillars (Öndvegissúlur) overboard as he neared land, vowing to settle wherever they landed.

Strange stories are told of the first explorers who came to Iceland. They found not only an uninhabited island but also a land inhabited by dragons, monsters, and giants, and some even turned into such beasts themselves. Some of these unknown pre-human inhabitants of the unknown inlands of the country were in human form.[2] On one occasion when Þórir was traveling south across the uninhabited central highlands of Iceland, he was approached there by a strange guy, a magician named Örn.[3]

The unknown territory of the unconscious is probably far too vast ever to be fully explored and made conscious, and to meander around it is not without danger. However, to ignore it can be even more dangerous because it can create impediments to growth or even cause a breakdown of the self when under the pressures of change. It is difficult to fall into the unknown land of the living God but even more dangerous to drop out of it. The settlers of Iceland were pagans and worshipped Norse gods, such as Óðin, Þór, Freyr, and Freyja.

CHRISTIANITY

In the tenth century, political pressure from Europe to convert to Christianity mounted. As the end of the first millennium drew near, many prominent Icelanders had accepted the new faith.

As civil war between the religious groups seemed likely, the year 1000 Alþing appointed one of the chieftains, Thorgeir Ljosvetningagodi, to decide the issue of religion by arbitration. He agreed that the country should convert to Christianity as a whole but that pagans would be allowed to worship privately. The first Icelandic bishop, Ísleifur Gissurarson, was consecrated by bishop Adalbert of Hamburg in 1056.

2 Some of these phenomena later found their way into the national symbol of the independent Iceland and became symbols of cultural transformation.
3 Davíð Erlíngsson, "Ormur, Marmennill, Nykur - Three Creatures of the Watery World" in *Islanders and Water-Dwellers* (Dublin: University College Dublin, 1996). 75.

With Christianity came a gradual transformation of the Icelandic culture that became more aligned with what was seen as appropriate by the new religious authorities. People still mainly relied on conventional wisdom regarding psychological issues and mental and emotional crises. However, with its promise of healing and its somewhat educated clergy and bishops, the new faith also started to play its role. Books on medieval healing practices influenced Icelandic society with this change and increased connections to continental culture. Even though the healing practices expanded somewhat, pagan remedies and curative dynamics based on primitive medical practices still flourished. People also deployed their common sense. Both individual and collective levels of the vital function of the healing imagination, with its call for a balance between the conscious mind and the sub currents of the unconscious, also influenced the Icelanders in their encounters with the healing potentialities; and that despite the dictation, help or appreciation of either religious or secular authorities.

As the connections with the European continent increased, more Icelanders would travel abroad for educational purposes. Upon return such individuals were often believed to have deeper insights and higher mental and spiritual powers than others, and thus more capable of dealing with the forces of the psyche and soul. One example was Sæmundur the Learned (1056-1133 A.D.).[4]

Once upon a time there existed somewhere in the world, nobody knows where, a school which was called the Black School. There the pupils learned witchcraft and all sorts of ancient arts. Wherever this school was, it was somewhere below ground, and was held in a strong room which, as it had no windows, was eternally dark and changeless. There was no teacher either, but everything was learnt from books with fiery letters, which could be read quite easily in the dark. The pupils were never allowed to go out into the open air or see the daylight during the whole time they stayed there, which was from five to seven years.

By then, they had gained a thorough and perfect knowledge of the sciences to be learned. A shaggy gray hand came through the wall every day with the pupils' meals, and when they had finished eating and drinking, taking back the horns and platters. But one rule of the school was that the owner should hold on to, for himself, the student who would be that last to leave the school every year. Considering that it was pretty well known among the pupils that the devil himself was the master, you may fancy what a scramble there was at each year's end, everybody doing his best to avoid being last to leave the school.

It happened once that three Icelanders went to this school, by the name of Saemundur the Learned, Kalfur Arnason, and Halfdan Eldjarnsson;

---

4 Sæmundur the Learned (1056-1133) was Iceland's earliest known scholar. Sæmundur was a chieftain and priest at Oddi after returning from Paris where he studied at the "Black School", the forerunner of *Sorbonne University.*

and as they all arrived at the same time, they were all supposed to leave at the same time. Sæmundur declared himself willing to be the last of them, at which the others were much lightened in mind. So he threw over himself a large mantle, leaving his sleeves loose and his fastenings free.

A staircase led from the school to the upper world, and when Sæmundur was about to mount this the devil grasped at him and said, "You are mine!" But Sæmundur slipped out of this mantle and made off with all speed, leaving the devil the empty cloak. However, just as he left the school the heavy iron door was slammed suddenly, and wounded Sæmundur on the heels. Then he said, "That was pretty close upon my heels," which words have since passed into a proverb.

Then Sæmundur contrived with his companions to escape scot-free from the Black School. Some people say that when Sæmundur came into the doorway, the sun shone upon him and threw his shadow onto the opposite wall. And as the devil stretched out his hand to grapple with him, Sæmundur said, "I am not the last. Do you not see who follows me?" So the devil seized the shadow, mistaking it for a man, and Sæmundur escaped with a blow on his heels from the iron door. But from that hour he was always shadowless, for whatever the devil took, he never gave back again.[5]

Even though it can psychologically be a genuinely frightening experience to surrender to the core of being that we often refer to as God, it can be even scarier, however tempting, to fall into the hands of the devil. The devil will be here defined as the reality—often symbolically portrayed—that is actualized through the narcissistic indulgence of our psychological shadow side. This is the bleaker part of us that we conventionally try to hide behind the mask of our persona and a reality that is commonly officially condemned by religious authorities. The paradox, however, is that even the harder the occult is condemned, the unhealthier and more damaging sprouts it spreads. When we are led by the shadow but pretend we are not, we tend to delude ourselves with the idea that our "motives are highly moral, while in fact, they are crude drives for power", and there is a tendency to mistake sophomoric aggressive and sexual phantasies as juvenile mystical wonders.[6]

Psychologically the story of the Black School can be interpreted as the journey through the sub-terrain of our inner psychological reality human. The Black School teaches you to gain insight into what is there to find, learn from, and master it. In the story, the 'shadowless' Sæmundur symbolizes the integrated self that can do without bearing the mask of the pretentious 'persona,' i.e., the shadow has been fully addressed. Nonetheless, such an intense educational experience can be psychologically exhausting and a life-threatening challenge.

---

5 Jón Arnason, *Icelandic Legends*, translated by George E. J. Powell and Eiríkur Magnússon (London: Richard Bentley, 1864). 226-228.
6 Von Franz, *The Interpretation of Fairy Tales*. 140.

However, the pupil who survives will be decorated with deep insights into the darker psychological actualities and procedures of the gloomier aspects of the human mind and the blemish of curiosity and survival.

There are many stories of Sæmundur's dealings with demonic forces and various assorted manifestations of the devil. On one such occasion, Sæmundur fools the devil, now in the form of a fly, into entering a bottle just to be locked up. This reflects a classic symbolic theme within the Christian tradition; the use of a 'bottle' for imprisoning some aspect of the psyche (often, in Jungian terms, the 'anima') to limit and hold back its explosive force.[7] In another tale, Sæmundur again fools the devil, who is now in the form of a seal, to take him across the North-Atlantic Ocean to Iceland. When close enough to the shore, Sæmundur pulled out a Bible and spouted its message at the devil to erode its powers. Upon arrival in Iceland, Sæmundur became a respected minister at the church at Oddi in Rangarvellir.

In Iceland, in the Middle Ages, especially in Catholic times (1000-1550), clergymen, especially bishops, and some kings, were commonly believed to possess sacred powers that enabled them to give divine counsel and even proclaim divine judgments. Their healing supremacy was mainly based on the patient's belief in their sacred authority. When such a laudable person would visit the house where the patients lay ill, that person was offered all the best the household had to offer, in the exchange and hope for good curative insights, advice and counsel. Though, it seems that the primary duty of the Icelandic clergy was, more than attempting cure or any type of pastoral care and counselling, to sustain faith, educate, baptize, offer the sacraments, even vaccinate, and educate.[8]

As said before, gradually, present-day books on medicine and healing were introduced to Iceland. Many of them were well known in Scandinavia; these books were usually translated from Latin.[9] They covered a wide variety of topics, most that seem to designate a strong belief—or at least sanguine hope—in the psychological healing potential of the human imagination. Curative remedies included healing advice, magical formulas, instructions on the use of plants and natural antidotes, the healing powers of stones and other inorganic things, prophecies, stories of the healing powers of holy men and saints, and more surgical and medically oriented remedies such as the drawing of blood, bathing, etc.[10]

All healing endeavors are, to an extent, based on principles that are akin to magic where the unconscious of the patient is affected or influenced either by the efforts of the healer or by the patient's unconscious strivings. Psychologically, the best therapists are the ones who are, despite their clinical orientation and skills, capable of allowing their subconscious to communicate directly to the subconscious of the other. This can, for instance, be done – but does not need to be done that way – by making referrals to something that the patient believes to be of transcendental and

---

7 Ibid. 146.

8 Jónas Jonasson: Íslenskir þjóðhættir (Reykjavik: Ísafoldarprentsmiðja, 1945). 381.

9 Bishop Brynjolfur Sveinsson is known to have owned a work by a French inquisitor Nicolas Remy, *Demonolatreiae* (1595).

10 Steffenssen, "Alþýðulækningar—Sjúkdómar".131.

sacred nature. Many psychological problems can be caused by a lack of insights into mental functioning and a sense of guilt and shame.

> A third woman was named Sigridur; she was with Thorlakur, who lived at Hallastadir. She sewed when others kept the holy hours before the feast of Magnus. Thorlakur asked why she worked so long, but she promised to stop. He came back and asked why she was so disobedient — and asked her to go away and not to work any longer. She said she was almost done sewing and kept on working until it turned dark. But when the men prepared to go to bed, she became mad; and they tied her up with ropes. Thorlakur defended her, however, and they tossed a coin to see if he should [as to cure her] promise a pilgrimage to Rome, to release a slave, or to give to the shrine of Earl Magnus. It turned out that he should give money to the shrine. Thorlakur brought her to Earl Magnus [presumably the shrine and not the person] and she became healthy.[11]

The workaholic Sigridur is conscient beyond what people around her regarded as standard. One potential underlying cause of obsessive-compulsive behavior, and the urge to act out her anxieties, could be the feelings of guilt or shame and the need to sublimate unacceptable feelings by undoing or compensation. As the behavior exhausts her, there seems to be, at the same time, an unconscious accumulation of conflicting subconscious ideas, some of them potentially associated with her views of the sacred and consequently packed with conscience-provoking contents. When bishop Thorlakur, a man related to sacral authority, takes a sheltering role, brings in his empathic attendance and indicates a willingness to take extreme personal measures to help, a curative transference is set in motion. Health returns as Thorlakur can mentally conveyance her mind and reconcile her rigid behavior and harsh standards of duty with a more helpful attitude. Another story from the same period is a tale of guilt.

> Two men broke a piece of gold from the shrine of the holy Earl Magnus; … [One] died in Pettland's fjord; his name was Gilli, but the other became mad and revealed in his madness what they had done; then a pledge was made that he would go south if he would become healthy from the shrine of Earl Magnus. He was taken there and became healthy.[12]

In Freudian terms, this is an example of a classic guilt complex. Two men go, potentially excited by the desire for gold, act against introjected social norms, steal a piece of gold, and of what object they believe is sacred. One dies—conceivably due to distraction caused by the feeling of a guilty conscience—forcing the other, who is

---

11 Finnbogi Guðmundsson, "Magnúss saga skemmri" in *Íslensk fornrit*, vol. XXXIV (Reykjavik, Hið íslenska bókmenntafélag, 1965). 329. (Transl. HIJ).
12 Ibid. 327.

now even more tormented by guilt, to interpret the other's death as a destined curse. His fear of ill-fated punishment has made him sick, and in a desperate attempt to get better, he speaks up and admits his perils. In repentance (literally meaning turning back), he attempts to make up for his doings by, psychologically speaking, 'regressing' back to the shrine where the hysteria originated. Once he is brought back—and noticeably, there is no mention of returning the piece of gold—he can reconcile and regain his mental health. Something of a similar nature is affecting the man mentioned in the following paragraph:

> A man is named Sigurdur; he was mad, so they put him into an animal skin (hide) and tied him up [in accordance with the law]; then he was taken to the holy Earl Magnus, and he became healthy.[13]

In this, it is most likely the suggestive power affiliated with the sacred king that allows for a healthy transformation and internal reconciliation of the mind of the insane man.[14]

It has been claimed that after the established church grew stronger in Iceland, the belief that demons caused mental disturbances also became more prevalent in the country. This had consequences, as in the 13th century, the clerical role of the *Exorcista* became one of the primary methods for dealing with the mentally ill.[15] It has also been argued that this caused mentally disturbed people to be even more stigmatized, ignored and poorly treated and, even further, it has been claimed that it was not until 1907, when the first mental hospital in Iceland was established, that things got somewhat better for the mentally ill.[16]

Perhaps this is true, but even though it may be difficult for modern people to comprehend, the curative impact of rituals and sacred symbols on the medieval mind—and even also on modern the modern mind—should not be underestimated. We can only imagine the profound impact that it must have had on the peasant to enter the church's sacred space, with images, symbols, and rituals that become a transformative realm in between the self and the sacred. Sublimated ideas, exotic paintings of the foreign lands of God, sacred stories, and wonderful colors all pointed to holy actualities that the Christian tradition had collectively tried out and spoke directly to the deeper layers of the psyche and the soul. Even today, Icelanders instinctively situate sacred signs both at prominent places and upsetting places (such as where car accidents have taken place) where special help is needed,

---

13 Ibid. 328.

14 See Ármann Jakobsson, Í leit að konungi: Konungsmynd íslenskra konungasagna (Reykjavik, Háskólaútgáfan, 1997). In the second section of his book "Konungur á jörðu og himni", or "King on Earth and Heaven" (89-154), Ármann examines among other things the sacral nature of the Norse kings, their appearances, their power and healing abilities. On Ármann's book in English see Elizabeth Ashman Rowe's article in *alvissmal* 9 (1999): 95-98 online at http://userpage.fu-berlin.de/~alvismal/9armann.pdf

15 Jón Steffenssen, "Alþýðulækningar—Sjúkdómar". 128.

16 Ibid. 125.

and particular respect develops around such places. [17]

A man was named Eldjarn and he was the son of Vardur; he had a wife and many children and lived in Kelduhverfi in the Northern part of the country. But during hard times he became very poor and sick, so he could not take care of himself; and he was so weak that he could not walk and had to be carried from place to place. It was in the spring, after Easter, that he was carried there Thursday, Friday and Saturday and he had no food. He arrived there at noon on Saturday, to the place where the priest lived, and stayed there during the night. And in the morning, when men went to sing prayers, he asked if he could be carried to the church. They brought him to the church. After the singing men went out in order to return later, and for the next hour of prayer, he lay outside, where they had arranged him. He was so weak that he was expected to die at any time. He thought of how fortunate he had been before and he wondered why the prayer he made had had such an impact on him, and he was deeply moved. He promised that he would fast for six days if God would give him some health; he promised to fast for both the feast of Olafur and of the feast of Magnus. When he had announced his promises, men went to prayers, and the priest sang a mass. When the Epistle was read, he fainted, and all that were present believed that he had died. In this unconscious state he had a vision; he felt that he saw a bright light in the end of the church and that it reached towards him. In the light he saw a handsome man, who spoke to him and said: "Eldjarn, is your will weak now?" He felt that he answered "that's how I feel, but it might not be so. But who are you?" He answered: "Here is the holy Magnus Erlendsson. Do you want to become healthy?" He answered: "I do."

"King Olafur, the holy heard your prayer and your promises that you gave us to regain your health. He has sent me to you to give you back your health, but he went to heal a woman in the fjords in the west because she had made her pledge to him." Then Magnus started to touch him, and he woke up when they were reading the gospel. He talked to the men that stood closest to him and asked them to help him get up. But they said "Why should we do that, when you are unable to stand?" He said "I believe that I am now healthy." They raised him up, and there he stood as the whole gospel was read and during the whole service. After the service he went to the priest and told him about the miracle and how God had restored his health. All praised God for the mercy that he had revealed through the holy Earl Magnus. [18]

---

17 Such symbols include, for instance, the large cross at Kaldadarnes, and the picture of Mary in the church at Hofstadir church, as well as the numerous crosses reminding travelers of fatal car crashes, along the roads in Iceland.

18 Finnbogi Guðmundsson, "Magnús saga skemmri" in *Íslensk fornrit*, Vol. XXXIV (Reykjavik, Hið íslenska bókmenntafélag, 1965). 330-332. (Transl. HIJ).

Within the history of healing, there has been an attempt to make a clear distinction between evidence-based healing and other healing therapies. In his book on the healing remedies of the common man in Iceland, Jon Steffenssen defines evidence-based healing as curative remedies that do not involve any 'higher powers' and do not depend on faith or belief but are based on the state of available technology within society.[19] On the other hand, he defines magical or mind healing as healing facilitated by "higher powers" and based on methods such as the signing of the cross, sacrifice, pledge, magic, and prayer.[20] Such healing is presumably on the healing abilities of the unconscious, whether described as psychic fluids, demons, gods, the divine, or the healing potentialities of the imagination. Jon also argues that the latter was better suited for healing mental disturbances. However, we now know that these two kinds of healing can be so intertwined that it becomes impossible to make a sharp distinction between them.[21]

REFORMATION

With the influence of the Lutheran reformation in Iceland in the 16th century, a slight change took place regarding the healing of mental disturbances. Whereas most of the healing remedies were the same as before, official belief in the healing powers of sanctified persons was disowned — even though the common man still relied occasionally on a belief in sacred places and saints. In a widely known Homiletic ("Húspostilla") of Bishop Guðbrandur Thorlaksson, written in 1597, there is mention of "the melancholia ("hugsýki") of disbelief by which one tortures oneself", which is explained as a lack of faith.[22] The reformation poet Hallgrimur Petursson, also aware of the possible impact of cognitive processes, speaks of guarding against cognitive and behavioral affairs that can cause mental disturbances and melancholia and says in Passion Hymn #36 from 1660, "Seek not the powers of this world's gain, Nor riches to augment. Wreck not the powers of mind and brain."

When we read Martin Luther (1483-1546), we notice that the Lutheran reformation was theological and psychological. Its psychological impact opened one of the doors for modernity, augmenting individuality and creating a more direct link between the individual and God. It encouraged the independent reading of the scripture, freed conscience from the authority of the church, and lessened its central authority regarding the sacred. In short, and at its best, it aimed at renewing the original message of Christ, freeing the imagination and fostering the natural process of individuation. It was a call to selfhood over and against the mass mentality and a protest against the surrender of our personal autonomy to external authorities.

The reformation thus encouraged increased psychological maturation of

---

19 Jón Steffenssen, "Alþýðulækningar—Sjúkdómar". 125. Transl. HIJ.
20 Ibid. 128.
21 Ibid. 128-129.
22 Dagný Kristjándóttir, "Hugsýki" in *Undirstraumar* (Reykjavik: Háskólaútgáfan, 1999). 326. 670 Ibid.

individuals and culture. But, all change is encumbered with ambiguity and easily inflicted with fantasies and fears. As the central religious authority of the church was drastically diminished in the course of the reformation, it became more and more the individual's responsibility to deal with relations between the self and God – making a private religion much more of an option than before. This created new possibilities, stimulating individual exploration of religious truths and the desire to create and experience something new, but also aggravating and encouraging those tendencies towards mental disturbance affiliated with a religion.

In former Catholic times, the Church in Iceland had, in accordance with Roman-Catholic custom, assumed the official role of the mediating and protective functions of the sacred in the relationship between the self and God. In doing this, it also tried to reserve to itself the right to decide whether a revelation — a transitional experience of the self regarding the sacred — was authentic or not.

In the Middle-Ages, according to Jung, it was a common notion that individuals should "model their entire lives and inner conduct on the life of Christ"; Protestantism, however, after having:

> ... pulled down so many walls carefully erected by the church, immediately begin to experience the disintegration and schismatic effects of individual revelation. As soon as the dogmatic fence was broken down and the ritual lost its authority, man had to face his inner experience without the protection and guidance of dogma and ritual, which are the very essence of Christian as well as pagan religious experience. Protestantism has, in the main, lost all the finer shades of traditional Christianity: The mass, confession, the greater part of the liturgy, and the vicarious function of priesthood.[23]

However, the unfortunate consequence of this indispensable cultural push for psychological self-alteration, maturation, and social reform was a psychological disintegration, where everyday psychological dynamics became feared and projected to a new extent. The imagination was not at all healing but, in fact, frightening. The sacred became scared. Just as a modern man may fear ill intentions of co-workers, colleges, etc., the common person in the 16th and 17th century Iceland feared ill-intended projections of others: "Magical-shots" ("galdraskot"), awakened corpses ("uppvakningar"), evil spirits sent by others ("sendingar"), mystical messengers ("dularsendlar"), attending spirits ("aðsóknarandar") and even God (not to mention the pagan gods) could inflict harm upon the self.[24] The outer and the inner fused, allowing infantile fantasy processes and projections upon others to surface.

Furthermore, in the same way as the dawn of the nuclear sciences created frequent reports of imaginative encounters with flying saucers, the cultural, theological, and

---

23 Jung, *Collected Works*, vol. 11. 14.
24 Einar G. Pétursson, *Eddurit Jóns Guðmundssonar lærða* (Reykjavik: Stofnun Árni Magnússonar, Iceland, 1998). 322.

psychological transformation of the Icelandic reformation indirectly led to the reporting of all kinds of strange psychic phenomena:

1595 - a beast in the Hvita-river next to Skalholt and signs in the sky [in the south];
1627 - an important dream took place in Akranes [in the west];
1628 - much revelation, visions, and dreams took place at Sida [in the East];
1631 - much dreaming was going on in Eyjafjördur (in the North);
1640 - wishing stone found close to Thingvallavatn.[25]

The official reaction of the authorities was typically skepticism and warnings against visions and revelations, a tendency that had prevailed since even before the reformation.[26] Such attempts show both the desire to inhibit or suppress the imaginary and the big concerns that the authorities had of not only the possible transformative powers of individual revelations on society but also their religious and political consequences. In a letter to Bishop Brynolfur, in the early 17th century, Jon the Learned writes:

> Now, in our times and century, if someone has a vision or receives revelation, then he will not dare to speak the Truth because he is threatened with torture or death.

During these actively anti-imagination times in Iceland, many priests came to view the elves as demons, not as descendants of Adam and Eve, and the tension between official theology and popular beliefs was widespread. Just as we might now debate the existence of God, in the 17th century in Iceland, the nature of the elves and hidden people was debated. The essential issue reflected by such debates concerning the acknowledgement of the imaginative as a part of the sacred. At that time, the harsh warnings against the introspective and imaginative – not unlike what we see today in the reductionist emphasis in biomedical chemistry, diagnosis, cognitive-behavioral approaches to therapy, and rigorous psychoanalysis, failed to take account of the possible harm the sacred can inflict upon the self if repressed. Then, just as now, the church seemed to dismiss and lose track of the importance of the inner experience, with the consequent withering of religious life. The soul, however, cannot be repressed: It finds its way and will, ultimately, triumph according to its sacred plan.

This hostility against the life of the psyche and the soul with its attendant condemnation of all imaginative revelations was almost certainly one of the factors that led to the official torture and execution of a considerable number of people accused of magic. These people had played with the powers of the imagination in accordance with a psychological necessity that was neither understood nor respected at the time by either themselves or by the authorities.

---

25 From Björn from Skarðsá, "Skarðársannáll".
26 Pétursson, *Eddurit Jóns Guðmundssonar lærða*. 384. 675 Ibid. 386.

The most ferocious attacks against the imagination, however, came from people who themselves were trapped and unable to free themselves from the overly vivid fantasy life. The Pilgrimage of Reverend Jon Magnusson (1610-1696) vividly illustrates how a troubled person can become frenzied by unconscious impulses and psychic dynamics. This strange clergy member, in a desperate attempt to externalize his fears, made others carry his burdens to lessen his own psychic pains.[27] Just as in the case with the European continent, the 17th century became the century when Iceland was characterized by its fear of sorcery and magic.[28]

MAGIC

Occultism in the form of sorcery—both black and white—was commonly practiced in Iceland up until the 17th century when it was forcefully attacked by religious and secular authorities in what was to become called the age of fire 1654-1683. During that time, more than two hundred people were charged with either practicing sorcery or possessing magical artefacts. This had some dreadful social consequences as, for instance, when someone had an accident or became ill, or it could be blamed on a person he did not like, who consequently had to prove beyond a shadow of a doubt that he was not a sorcerer. The supposed magical artefacts could be anything from pebbles, runic inscribed pieces of wood, or raven feathers. The owner could be promptly judged, and the heretic was carefully burnt *ad majorem glorium Dei*. What made this witch-hunting period in Iceland special was that out of the twenty people who were sentenced to death and burned at the stake only one of them was a woman.

If we can speculate that this anti-magic movement was some kind of a counterstrike against an opposing magic movement, we could say that the dynamics at play involved various factors that led both advocates and opponents from both camps to unleash and project their envy, greed and prejudices upon each other. What we would nowadays consider reasonable fears of everyday psychic dynamics among people turned into a psychic epidemic. In those times, fantasies literally went wild as people projected their shadows — primal phantasies, sexual desires and aggressive impulses — upon each other. Likewise, felt the projections of others as spells cast upon them. Persecution and executions, in the name of God, became feasts where archaic and sadistic impulses were granted uninhibited gratification in an isolated, simple and religiously motivated community.[29]

Magic is based on our natural wish to overcome and master the principles of nature by our imagination. The practitioner uses words or rituals to strengthen a wish in an attempt to force the wish into realization. Like the modern scientist,

---

27 Píslarsaga síra Jóns Magnússonar is a book he wrote to defend himself from accusations of injustly accusing others of magic. He writes about his sufferings and religious ecstasies, colored by his fear of magic and hell.

28 Jónas Jónasson, Íslenskir þjóðhættir (Reykjavik: Ísafoldarprentsmiðja, 1945). 370-380.

29 Matthías Viðar Sæmundsson, "Galdur og geðveiki" in *Píslarssaga séra Jóns Magnússonar* (Reykjavik: Mál og Menning, 2001). 391.

the magician plays with ultimate knowledge in an attempt to gain control of the unknown and has to calculate carefully the risks of doing so against his or her conscience, values and beliefs.[30] This dangerous self-alteration process can easily turn against the practitioner in the form of compulsions, obsessions, paranoia and fear of the sacred omnipresence. Struggling this way, on the very edge of our own morality, together with the associated encounters with all the unconscious features involved, can drive us insane. Ultimately, uninhibited fantasy inevitably leads to superstition, whereas contented imagination leads to authentic faith, the search for knowledge, and science.

We now recognize that magical thinking is characteristic in many mental disorders and exhibits itself in the belief that thoughts, words, and actions have the power to influence external events by means other than the culturally acknowledged laws of cause and effect. Associated with this is the fixated omnipotence of thought where we, as adults, regress to a childlike way of thinking, fusing our private needs and our external environment, and dwell in a primitive state of all-powerfulness with fantasies that have little or no bounds. Magical thinking is archaic, primitive, pre-logical thinking, such as is seen in the unconscious of neurotics, in small children, in normal persons under conditions of fatigue, as antecedents of thought in primitive man, and in schizophrenic thinking. The speech and thinking of the schizophrenic are frequently more concrete and active than normal, not yet capable of realistic abstractions, and more a symbolic equivalent of action.[31]

Moreover, magical thinking commonly manifests in beliefs such as the idea that bodily sickness is coming from the "outside" or in mundane rituals, such as the athlete who can only play in certain socks, etc. The psychology of everyday life shows a need to perform certain actions, in certain ways, to prevent misfortune, and in thoughts like "if only this, then everything would be better". Magical thinking is, in fact, a type of wishful thinking similar to that of those who take part in obsessive-compulsive thinking processes and behaviors, especially in all religious negotiations with God concerning destiny and the future. It easily surfaces in normal people under stressful conditions, when isolated, and after being traumatized, but it was more common among people in ancient times. The healing imagination uses magical thinking in the self's attempt to understand strange causal connections between people and events.

It may be possible to trace the origin of religion to magical thinking and envision a mental developmental process from magical thinking to religious thinking and, then, to more reality-based thinking. This would imply that humans used to be pre-logical and developed magic as a mistaken notion of causality due to similitude and analogy. In the life of the individual, clinical evidence shows a general tendency to magical thinking among young children and, in normal development, a gradual formation of more logical, reality-based thinking.

---

30 Jón Samsonarson, "Særingar og Forneskjubænir" in *Ljóðmál* (Reykjavik: Stofnun Árna Magnússonar, Reykjavík, 2002). 21.
31 Hinsie and Campell, *Psychiatric Dictionary*. 771. 374

To understand the healing implications of magical thinking in medieval Iceland, we need to understand the theoretical framework upon which it was based. A first-hand insight into this worldview can be found in *De Occulta Philosophia*, by the German Heinrich Cornelius Agrippa (1486-1535).[32] According to this book, all things are bound together by mystical connections called the sympathies, where sympathetic magic could join all animals, plants, humans, spirits, and matter in one secret, synchronizing network. The person with magical knowledge could tap into this secret and direct it to accomplish particular goals — just like the person with depth-psychological insights and experience with the dynamics of the psyche might be able to do today. This work was a major influence on and became a major resource for magicians and alchemists.[33]

This profound psychological insight, however, also fused with the superstitions of the age. No matter if the magicians are trying to heal their soul or their body; no reading will do, no rule, even if they mix God's words with it until this verse; *Sator Arepo tenet opera rotas*;[34] is used, but as soon as it is sung over a cure, then the reading gets power.[35]

This idea reverberates our endless need to believe that if we can just find the right formula, then we would then be able to activate the healing powers of some chemical, psychic, demonic, or divine force that exists just beyond our reaction. The danger of all such ideologies claiming the truth of its "correct" formulas that intersect with the imagination — be they magical, religious or biochemical — lies in their tendency to be overly literal.

Magic was used in Iceland for all kinds of tasks: to get attention and love (or should that fail, to curse the person), to kill foxes, for protection, to alter the weather, to gain strength, and to activate the healing imagination for cures and health. Black magic and curses manifested hatred, envy, the lust for glory, and the desire to control others. Black magic was believed to be based on some kind of pact with demonic forces and was used to perform evil deeds, whereas white magic was used to implement something purposeful, such as sharpening a knife, finding a wife, healing the sick, etc. (these terms were implemented as pre-politically correct ideas). Black magic was usually magic with a curse that one could defend oneself against by counter-magic, defense magic ("varnargaldur") or reaction magic ("víðsjá"). Psychologically, this implies the projection of an effect, and the receiving or fending off projections from others.

We see from this that magic, and the related magical worldview, served the purpose of manipulating the perception of the world in order to serve a psychological

---

32 See J. G. Frazer, *The Golden Bough, A Study in Magic and Religion,* 1955. 682 Also known as Agrippa von Nettesheim

33 Kathleen Stokker, "Narratives of Magic and Healing" in *Scandinavian Studies*, Vol. 73 no. 3, Fall 2001. 402. Examples from Iceland include Hugrás by Gudmundur Einarsson and Rev. Pall Bjornsson's Character Bestie.

34 This formula could be displayed in a quadrant for as where the word SATOR could be read in four different ways as: SATOR AREPO TENET OPERA ROTAS.

35 Pétursson, *Eddurit Jóns Guðmundssonar lærða.* 394.

purpose — it may possibly have also had a more extended social meaning, however, and have been an instrument for resistance in times when an open protest was impossible. The common person found refuge in his or her own world of mental images, in the practice of magic and by praising ancient divinities ... The desire to escape reality and oppression found itself an expression in dark hobbies that represented resistance against the harsh public law and oppressive religious ideas.[36]

Moreover, imagining oneself as possessing the knowledge to influence the cause-and-effect laws of nature gave the practitioner, just like a modern practitioner of scientific psychiatry, a sense of power. To regard the magic movement only as conscious propaganda, however, or as a tool for oppression used by the church and civil authorities may be too simplistic for explaining the complex psychological workings involved. It is better explained in terms of fears of the psyche, others, nature, and the sacred that got fused with the lust for power, greed, and with ill-willed proclaimings of the church itself, leading to a collective mental breakdown.

When the self breaks down, the unconscious takes over. Fantasies, illusions and hallucinations get confused with the direct revelation of the sacred and the absolute. In times of excessive repression, the magic movement represented a reaction against the control that the established church and worldly authorities had attempted to impose on the psyche. We can debate whether this was an untoward endeavor or not, but from both a psychological and a theological perspective, we should view it as a normal psychic reaction to an oppressed psychic life and an attempt to heal a repressed imagination. Impulses demanding gratification flooded the imagination and drowned it. Literalism, fixated fantasies and uncreative projections in the form of accusing, blaming, splitting, and scapegoating took over. Practitioners of magic gratified religious impulses by primitive art, and persecutors gratified aggressive impulses by executing others in the name of their absolute ideals.

The practice of magic signified unfulfilled longings and dreams and reflected an attempt to compensate for something missing in life. From this perspective, the Icelandic magical staves resemble "mandala" forms and point to an intuitive, though immature, effort to find something that was lacking within the psyche.

Jung saw the "mandala" like a geometric or pictorial design that symbolically represents harmony on a deeper level of the psyche. In Jungian psychology, they indicate the unconscious, saying, "this is a model of an order that your psyche lacks, this is your goal and you possess it within you — go and get it."[37] In therapy, unprompted drawings are valuable for getting conscious insight into the unconscious as they can reflect feelings or beliefs that lie deeper within the psyche.

It is possible to interpret some of the 17th-century magical staves (such as the ones here below) within the Icelandic heritage as unprompted manifestations of an underlying sacred aim unknowingly expressed in times of psychic oppression. In this period, the Icelandic psyche collapsed once again into a more archaic and

---

36 Sæmundsson, "Galdur og geðveiki". 391. Transl. HIJ 377.

37 Giorgi Geleishvili: "The Role of the Drawing in the Process of Psychotherapy", *Annals of Biomedical Research and Education*, 2003 July/September, volume 3.

undifferentiated life. The collective and imaginative individuation process normally encouraged by genuine Christianity came to halt for a while, not proceeding again until later.

Hulinhjálmshringur / Magic sign to make a person invisible. "To make yourself invisible, mix together three drops of blood from the index finger of your left hand, three drops from the ring finger of your right hand, two drops from your right nipple and two from your left one. Then mix it together with the blood from the heart of a living raven and boil it with the raven's brain and a man's bellyfat. Then use the ink to carve this sign on a piece of lignite and keep it in your hand."

Þjófastafur / Magic sign to find a thief. "If you want to know who has stolen from you, carve this sign on the bottom of a wooden bowl, fill it with clean water and sprinkle yarrow over it. Recite: I invoke the nature of the grass and the power of the sign to reveal who has stolen from me and others. In nomine domini amen. The thiefs face will appear in the bowl."

Magic sign to wake up the dead. "This magic sign can be used to wake from the dead, to exterminate a ghost, and it also has the power to drive away evil spirits; it must be carved on a piece of oak with a mixture of blood from the sorcerer's body."[38]

---

38 From a postcard published by Galdrasýning á ströndum, see futher at: http://www.vestfirdir.is/galdrasyning/magical_staves2.php Dec. 2005

QUESTIONS WE ASK OUR BODIES, THAT ARE ANSWERED BY OUR GODS. HYPNO-MIMESIS AND TRANSFORMATIONAL ALCHEMIES IN AVANT-GARDE PERFORMANCE AND THERAPEUTIC PRACTICE

Carlos Abler

THE BODY AS A SPACE OF ESOTERIC REVELATION

We gather here to share knowledge. Knowledge that not only reveals truths about our world—but transforms it. The therapeutic, yogic, mythical, magical, imaginal; these, are transformational modes of knowing. I now invite you to an exploration of a transformational mode of asking. Asking questions only the body can answer via a technique of intra-corporeal discourse which I shall call hypno-mimetic.

Hypno-mimetic techniques open the body as a space of esoteric revelation by combining the semi-involuntary ecstasy of the hypnotic, to affect a corporealized ingestion of the imaginal. Revealing knowledge perhaps not only from "within" the body, but also "outside" of it. Not simply from within the personal psyche, but from beyond, to the trans-personal psychic. These are questions answered by the body as a language of the universe itself.

If we hear such answers, what will become of us? Will they challenge our conception of what the body is? Of where it begins? Of where it ends? If it ends.

This is not an essay. It is a provocation. A call to action inviting you to draw from techniques and insights from religious history such as Taoist yoga, European renaissance mnemonic systems, Tantric Buddhism, Voodoo, Balinese Trance, and Christian Icons; theatrical traditions such as Butoh, Kabuki, Grotowskian dramaturgy, Modern Dance, Modern Mime; and therapeutic perspectives from Wilhelm Reich, Bioenergetics, Actualization, Dance and Drama Therapy.

Furthermore, we will explore cultural forces of corporeal and imaginal suppression including European Reformation, Counter-Reformation, and Puritanical Christianity, the suppression of rave culture, and other forces of decadence driven by the soul-less and sexless archonic bureaucrats who live to deprive us of the individual agency that would otherwise have us dancing as gods in the temple, rather than groveling before altars stripped of beauty, and begging to avoid the perils of authoritarian condemnation, for the forgiveness that never comes.

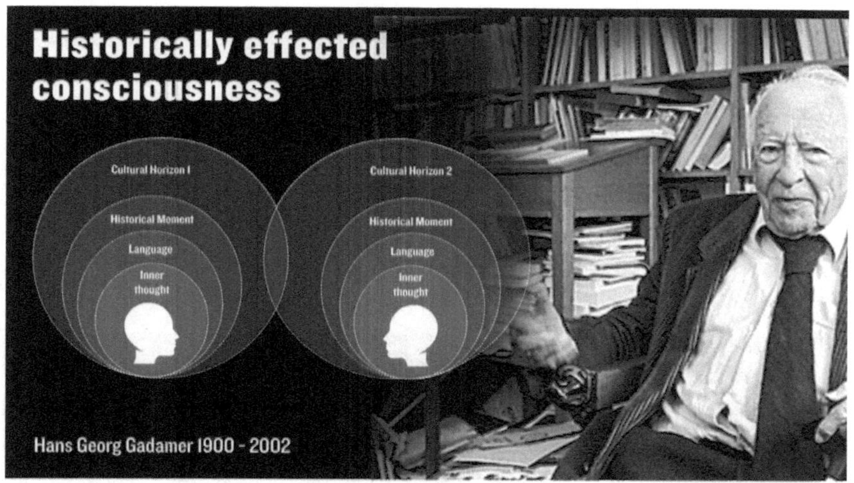

Our investigation will build upon an experiential and comparative anthropological approach inviting us to contemplate and enact worldviews and existential tools beyond what Hans Georg Gadamer might call our "Historically Effected Consciousness."

Historically Effected Consciousness speaks to the historical cultural conditioning that can impose limits upon what we can understand, thereby circumscribing the horizon of what we can see, conceptualize, express as language, and consequently know or make real.

Comparative anthropological cross-cultural engagement can help open this horizon by breaking the bubble of our historically conditioned limits via a confrontation with different, historically conditioned consciousness as manifest in disruptive language, knowledge, and action.

We will explore how hypno-mimesis specifically can break the enclosures of our epistemological prison, by liberating a more holistically integrated and competent body-mind. A body-mind liberated from the cosmological dogmas and methodologic limits that constrain our creative existential potential.

In the process, we will challenge the over-reduction of human experience and knowledge to hyper-rationalist, logo-centric, ego-centric, identity-centric, social-constructivitst, worldviews. We will perhaps restore an intra-animistic relational agency, as an other-than-human personhood is restored to the animal that is the body, and thereby expand the notion of what being human and animal actually are.

Insofar as this knowledge can be said to be esoteric, it is only because we have occulted our own inner knowledge from ourselves. The result of authoritarian societal control techniques that alienate us from some of our own most vital sources of knowing.

An organism which expends significant energy dissociating from the understandings produced by their bodies within themselves will be rendered a blunt instrument, ill-equipped to understand the world outside of itself. Perhaps, what you now call intuition will explode into a much richer faculty of knowledge and action as a result of hypno-mimetic cultivation. Perhaps your access to spirits, ancestors, truth, and life itself will become more full and immediate, as it has for me.

We will define hypno-mimesis in detail shortly, but first, a bit of back-story on the origins of the concept.

A BOY IN A MUSEUM CONTEMPLATES
THE CORPSE OF HIS PAST INCARNATION

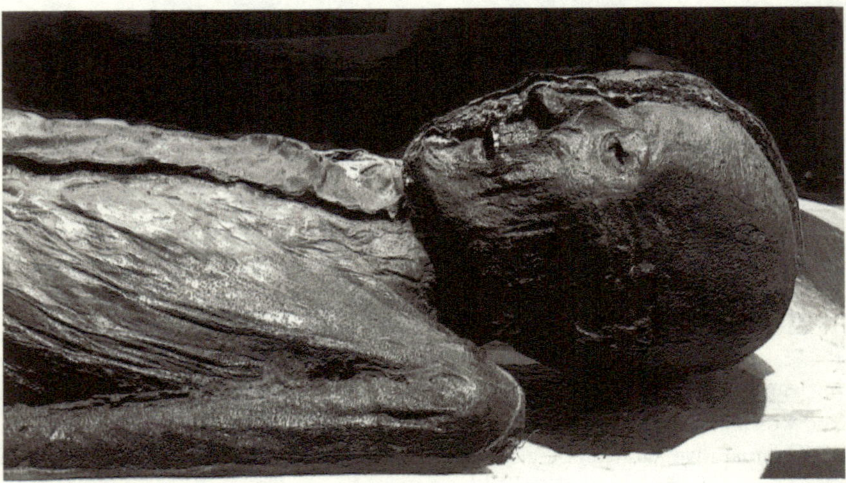

My journey into the body as a space of esoteric knowing began under the apprenticeship of a dead man.

At age 11 I joined a youth volunteer program at the Science Museum of Minnesota, working in the Egyptology section of the Hall of Anthropology. My mother worked there as an anthologist of crafts. In this place, I stood next to a 2,000-year-old mummy, explaining Egyptian funerary practices to thousands of people a year.

As my mother's agnostic rebellion spared me the torments and dogmas of her Catholic upbringing, Ancient Egypt provided the first conventional cosmological disruption to the infinity of my childhood imagination, in its reluctance to succumb to the mechanistic universe of atoms and epi-phenomena. And the Christian three-layer cake worldview was absent from my consciousness near entirely. At this time, I thought the devil was a cartoon character, never realizing that Christians actually took the Devil seriously. Rather, I was learning the cosmology of ancestral relations, that the heart, seat of the soul while the body lived, was mummified separately and returned to the corpse, and the brain, the junk yard of mundane earthly nonsense, was torn apart by a long silver hook and discarded as garbage. Something that made more intuitive sense to me than the holy trinity.

My body spent hundreds of hours in dialog near and with this dead man's body.

During this time, as my studies moved from Egyptology to Buddhism and Indian philosophy, I contemplated the concept of reincarnation with my mummified interlocutor.

I asked this dead man, "could your body have once been my own?"

"Does a transmigratory journey across the millennia re-unite us in this place in order to expand the cosmological potential of these museum visitors' relationships with their own bodies, and thereby find their souls?"

A LESSON IN SOULLESSNESS, TERROR, AND TRANSFORMATION FROM THE INUIT

Also, at this time in 1982, Tûkak' Teatret, an indigenous-focused theater company from Greenland/Denmark, was in residency at the museum. Emerging during the cultural identity crisis associated with 1970's Greenland's establishment of sovereignty from Denmark, Tûkak' Teatret was engaged in an existential confrontation of indigenous identity, development, and creative expression. They performed work blending Nordic and Inuit cosmologies, mythologies, and legends, with traditional performance themes that pushed audiences into a self-confrontation with the dynamics of soul and soullessness, toward a life-positive lust, nourished by existential terrors and interactions with other-than-human entities.

The play, "Inuit—The People", presented entities such as Amo, the black large-headed long-armed spirit seeks to help from the Sea Goddess Inunerup Arna, to help humanity recover its soul; and Toornaq Qaqqortoq who, driven by the obsession of progress for the sake of progress, represents forces that make man a stranger to his real self, living behind masks; and the foul and corrupting dog-headed spirit Ajumaq, who asked, quite understandably; "I wonder if a human being is the right place for a soul to reside?" (Nilsson, from Brask, Morgan 1992)

Of the several Tūkak' performances that I saw, one of the most moving moments occurred among hundreds of museum visitors on a busy Saturday afternoon, during a Uaajerneq (WHY-YER-NERK) performance. Uaajerneq is a tradition in which performers play grotesque and terrifying entities, used to help children develop mastery over the power of fear. "Imagine if you are out alone in your little kayak and you meet something and you freeze. You will drown. If you learn how to deal with that, you will become a very strong human being." – Makka Kleist (2015)

Even though the actors sat in front of the audience putting on their makeup as artistic director Reidar Nilsson discussed the meaning of their work, this seemed not to mitigate the horror the audience would experience as the figures stepped through the veil of trance to penetrate space with hissing contortions and boundary violating proximity. Sticks in their mouths created distorted drooling faces, fearsomely amplifying their bestial growls into a grotesque death rattle.

The stuff of nightmares. People in the audience actually ran in terror.

My 12-year-old body, witnessing and kinesthetically processing the power of actors transformed and entranced, scaring the shit out of a bunch of white people in a museum, was to have a permanent effect on me. A good one.

The primordial terrors and quests for soul recovery operated on me at a level entirely transcending the operational level of socio-political, colonization/de-colonization, identitarian, and other human territoriality-based power dynamics.

Instead, I was elevated to the spiritual realization of other-than-human relational-based dynamics.

I went to a space beyond the problematics of appropriating culture to the life-affirmative empowerment of being appropriated by culture, via the direct knowledge-manifestations of a the human body ecstatically unleashed by the penetration of the other-than-human, facilitated by hypno-mimetic trance.

WHAT IS HYPNO-MIMESIS?

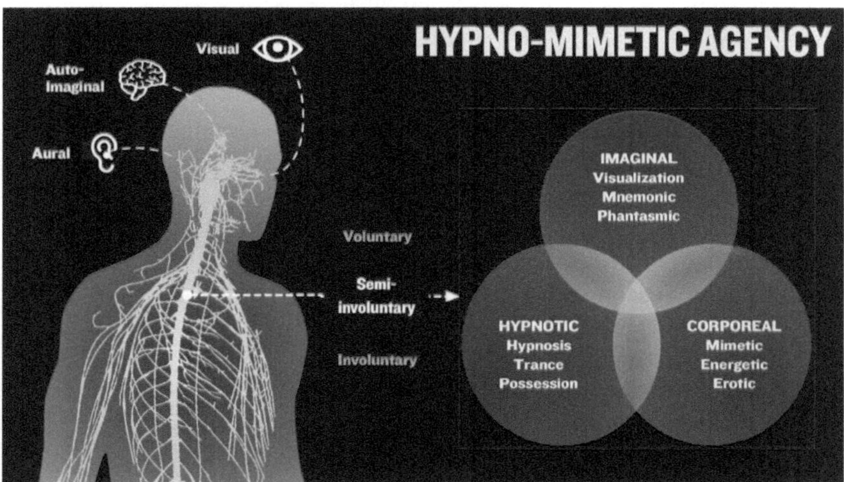

Hypno-mimesis can be viewed as a mechanism, a technique, and a competency, that combines elements of the imaginal, the hypnotic, and the corporeal, by which we become receptive to sensory stimuli and information largely bypassing rational linear thought.

—∾— The imaginal includes visualization, mnemonics, and phantasmic.

—∾— The hypnotic includes hypnosis, trance, and possession.

—∾— The corporeal includes the mimetic, energetic, erotic, and general sensual and supra-sensual experience.

Hypno-mimesis opens a space between the voluntary and the involuntary. A semi-voluntary interzone wherein we work with trance states and effects.

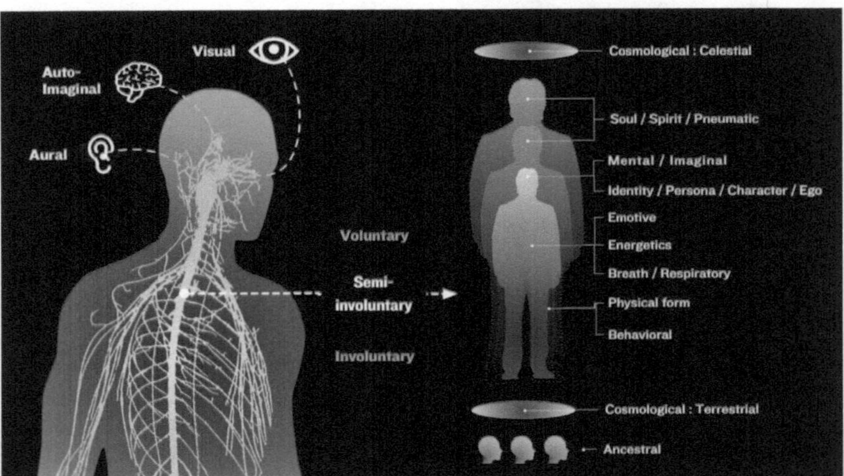

In a state of suggestive receptivity, you become hyper-impressionable to sensory inputs and auto-suggestive imaginings. Imaginal and sensual inputs, both realistic and surrealistic are then channeled as mimetic expressiveness across all dimensions of our being, from the densest aspect of our physical bodies, through the most etheric of subtle and phantasmal bodies.

As we shall see in forthcoming examples, this array of energy qualities, bodily articulations, psycho-emotional states, synesthetic sense blending, and reality shifting, will express themselves across dimensions of:

—∾— Physical forms, actions, and behaviors.

—∾— Respiratory, energetics, and emotions.

—∾— Ego, persona, character.

—∾— Mental and imaginal.

—∾— A subtle body structure often involving more than one type per 'physical body'.

—∾— A human-to-cosmic integration typically with celestial and terrestrial dimensions.

—∾— Ancestral, ghostly, and spirit, whether engaged in possession, or communication modalities.

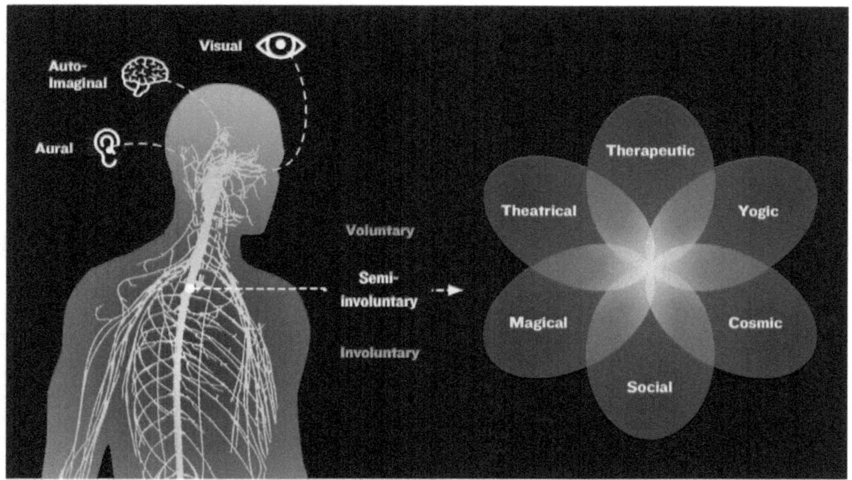

We are able to apply these hypno-mimetic expressions across an array of disciplinary applications, including the therapeutic, the yogic, cosmic or nature-focused integration, the magical, the social, and the theatrical.

Hypno-mimesis not only operates within these disciplines, but also in the creative synthesis between them. Indeed, as we shall see, this synthesis may manifest as a restoration of individual and cultural competencies that can become lost due to historical forces, such as the repression of imagination, sexuality, and ecstatic corporeal expression, such as are pandemic in post reformation and counter-reformation Western Christian societies.

To help us more fully understand what we mean by hypno-mimetics, let's dive deeper into the roles played by the constituent components of this neologism, the hypnotic, and the mimetic.

THE HYPNOTIC

As we enter the world of the hypno-mimetic we make a detour through the concept of trance. A concept which, like magic and Shamanism, present tremendous definitional challenges. Challenges due to multiple factors; the complexity of components involved, the intangibility of critical dimensions outside of the experience itself, and the fact that cultures interpret what we might call trance and various components using radically different ontological filters as applied to radically variant epistemological ends. Concepts like magic and shamanism are generally useful concepts in specific contexts, but often tearing them apart makes them even more problematic.

This definition from Judith Becker underscores all of this complexity at once: "I define trance as a state of mind characterized by intense focus, the loss of a strong sense of self and access to types of knowledge and experience that are inaccessible in non-trance states." Becker's definition embraces "meditative states, possession trance, shamanic trance, aesthetic trace, communal trance, and isolated moment of transcendence.

While many factors are shared in common, such as intense focus, loss of self and access to specialized knowledge, the diversity of applications is noteworthy as it includes meditative states, possession, shamanic trance, and transcendental states.

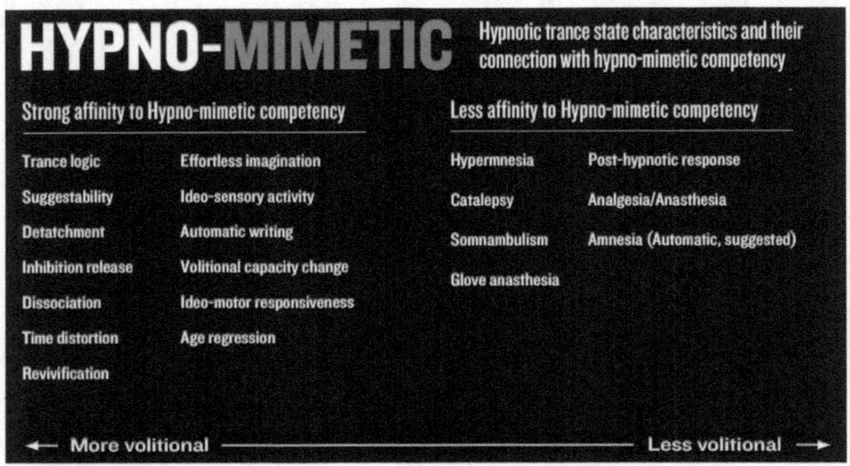

Crucial to note, is that what unites classical hypnotic effects, is some degree of involuntariness, the extreme end of which includes a complete loss of physical control or even consciousness.

On the more volitional end of the spectrum we have trance logic, suggestibility, detachment, inhibition release, time distortion, revivification, effortless imagination, ideo-sensory activity, automatic writing, volitional capacity change, ideo-motor responsiveness, and age regression.

On the less volitional end of the spectrum, we have hypermnesia, catalepsy, somnambulism, glove anesthesia, analgesia/anesthesia, and amnesia.

Hypno-mimesis has higher affinity to the more volitional states and effects of hypnosis. And insofar as we are considering hypno-mimesis in the context of yogic, magical, therapeutic or theatrical applications, we are concerned with developing a competency; therefore some level of volition is crucial. Even if potentially right up the point of losing it. Indeed, later, in the case of Butoh Dancer Akira Kasai, we will see how volitional hypno-mimetic expression can get pushed too far into a potentially pathological state of psycho-corporeal disintegration. Less polysyllabically known as madness.

While classic trance-state types and characteristics are not likely able to account for the entirety of Hypno-mimetic inputs or effects, they do provide useful constructs for investigation and experimentation.

Some trance states have a higher affinity for volitional creativity that others. For example, catalepsy is not terribly useful, as it's hard to do much in an unconscious state of physical rigidity.

More useful is trance-logic. Trance-logic supports parallel-reality processing; for example, a sense of being in the past and present simultaneously.

It's a bit limited to analyze volition at the categorical level. For even within a given state-effect there can be a range of expression providing for more or less healthful or creatively relevant application. Even for a category that has typically negative connotations when viewed only through a pathological lens, such as dissociation.

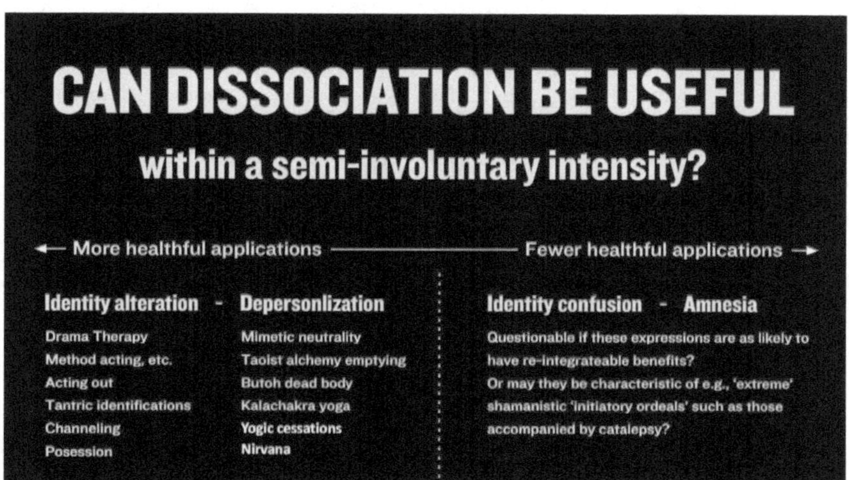

Dissociation is composed of four sub-categories; 1) Identify Alteration 2) Depersonalization, 3) Identify Confusion, and 4) Amnesia. Identity confusion and amnesia, are likely not so useful. However, identity alteration and depersonalization can have a positive role to play.

Identity alteration can play a productive role in:

—⁓— Drama therapy.
—⁓— Method acting.
—⁓— Tantric deity identification.
—⁓— Channeling and possession.

Depersonalization can play a productive role in:

—⁓— Techniques of mimetic neutrality; the empty vessel into which anything can be filled, or the zero-point of homeostatic pre-expressiveness.
—⁓— Taoist yogic exercises that involved emptying energetic residues from the organs and energy fields

—⁓— The butoh dead body

—⁓— Yogic cessations; from sense deprivation and withdrawal onto the ultimate idealized cessation of all fluctuations of the consciousness field as described in the Yoga Sutras of Patañjali.

—⁓— Assuming Indo-Buddhist cosmologies, the ultimate depersonalization in the form of attaining Nirvana, ceasing to reincarnate, exiting the personalization game altogether.

In these cases, depersonalization is not self-annihilating, but rather self-unlimiting, self-expanding, and otherwise positively transformational. Non-pathological depersonalizations do not resolve merely in depletion, they create space for other options.

For example, in the context of Haitian Vodoun trance possession, anthropologist and Avant-garde film maker Maya Deren comments:

> The ritualistic form treats the human being not as the source of the dramatic action, but as a somewhat depersonalized element in a dramatic whole. The intent of such depersonalization is not the destruction of the Individual; on the contrary, it enlarges him beyond the personal dimension and frees him from the specializations and confines of personality. He becomes part of a dynamic whole which, like all such creative relationships, in turn, endow its parts with a measure of its larger meaning.

> – Maya Deren; *An Anagram*, p .20

If hypnotic depersonalization is a gateway to an enlarged field of integrative potential, what cultural conditions enable it?

Psychotherapist and Balinese Mental Health workers Jensen and Suryani postulate that, "The strong sense of trust-belief in the Balinese personality, facilitates trance induction."

This culture-specific observation regarding individual trust-belief, as well as the community receptivity of trance as a positive attribute, underscores the need for an anthropologic approach to both understand conditions favoring hypnotic competencies and their cultural expressions, but also identifying cultural forces inimical to them. By using frames of reference dictated by the constraints of the Historically Effected Consciousness, entire categories of thinking may be unavailable, which can render disciplinary frameworks with significant blindspots.

A case in point is Wilhelm Reich's critique of the ethnocentrism of the European milieu of psychoanalysis among his contemporaries. The limited socio-cultural horizon in which psychoanalysis operated meant that its disease and health patterns were limited to that conditioned arena. Hence the risk to essentialize a socially constructed trait as a biologically determined trait. To avoid this myopic situation, psychoanalysis would have to look for socio-cultural contexts in which, for example, common European forms of sexual repression did not exist, in order to gain insight.

Citing Malinowski's work with the Trobriand Island society, which "knew… no sexual perversions, no functional psychosis, no psychoneuroses, no sex murder," Reich states Malinowski is correct to reject "the concept of the *biological* nature of the sexual child-parent conflict discovered by Freud," that "the child-parent relationships changes with social processes", and therefore such phenomena were of "a sociological and not a biological nature".

Even beyond 19th and early 20th century Europe, Reich believed that a non-distorted view of sexuality was impossible in Judeo-Christian Culture as a whole, where symptoms were endemic due to thousands of years of sexually repressive distortion of the human protoplasm.

Reich stated, "The moral and social evaluation of the most important biological human function was in the hands of sexually frustrated ladies and vegetatively dead professors."

Psychoanalysis simply had to move beyond the echo-chamber of its culturally-bound sample range.

THE MIMETIC

As for the mimetic, etymologically, mimesis stems from ancient Greek terms related to forms of imitation, such as acting. *Mīmēsis*, from *mīmeisthai*, "to imitate", from mimos, "imitator, actor". The term mimesis has a broad range of application across philosophy, and the arts, including mimicry, imitation, imitation, receptivity, artistic representation, and resemblance.

However, we will find that hypno-mimesis triggers unfamiliar revelations from corporeal territories for which no maps yet exist.

Or do they? Perhaps our maps have become lost, or we have just forgotten how to read them. As cultural forces have conspired to dull our capacity for love and pleasure (which, as Reich states, reduces our orgasmic potency), so have they conspired to dull our imaginal potency, rendering unconscious our hypno-mimetic abilities and fragmenting our practices. Scattered as the limbs of Osiris to the sands of an imaginal wasteland.

THE ICONOCLASTIC ATTACK UPON THE HYPNO-MIMETIC

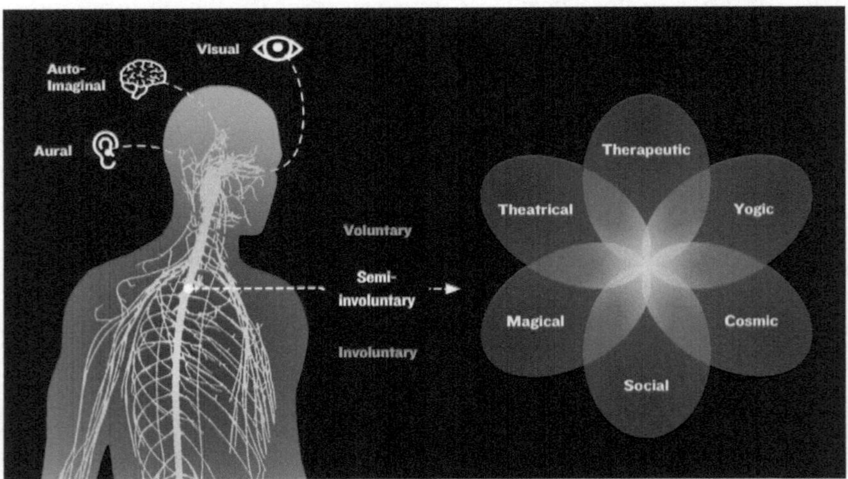

Forces such as Christianity's schizoid relationship between divinity and matter: On the one hand, Christianity offers rich opportunities for, as Patricia Cox Miller states, "the form of the human body" to be a "locus of spiritual presence." On the other, as we shall see, the iconoclasm and monotheistic remoteness may have shattered the experientially unified relationship between the transcendent and the immanent.

On the matter-positive enchanted world side, we have Jesus' incarnation as God's logos made flesh; the virgin birth from a woman's body; corporeal resurrection, the literal incorporation of the Eucharist's ritual cannibalism; the 4th to 7th centuries' zeitgeist via, "the cult of saints, the cult of relics, and the production of iconic art."

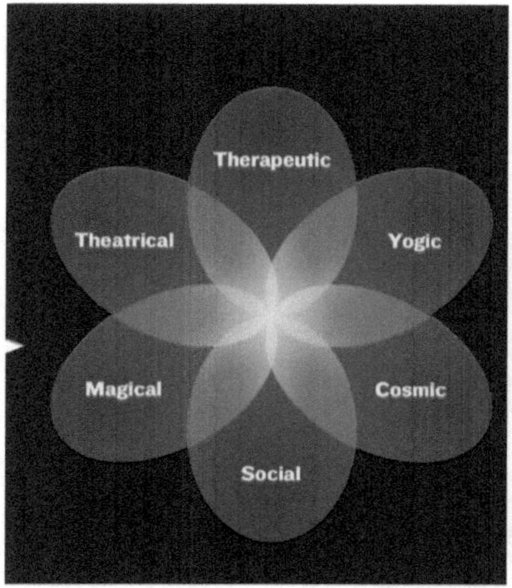
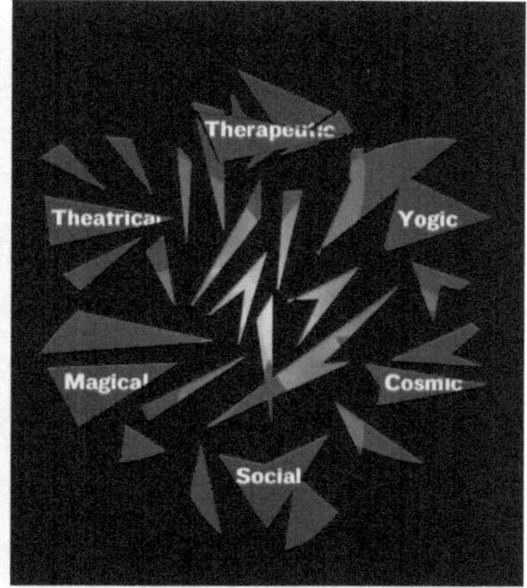

(Patricia Cox Miller The Corporeal Imagination, 2009).

The cult of Saints in particular, offering not only a context for spiritual physicalization, but also serving as syncretic refuge for indigenous god and goddess worship. However the simultaneously divine yet material manifestation of the Christ is the immanent in the transcendent par excellence. Though potentially at a schizoid cost.

Indeed, as Gauchet comments in the context of mono-theistic axial religion's disenchantment of the world via e.g., deistic remoteness, "The true originality of the relation to the world established by Christianity lay in this axiomatized ambiguity, which was a direct refraction of the union of two natures in Christ. It made the Christian into a being torn between a duty of belonging and of distancing, between forming an alliance with the world and being estranged from it." (Gauchet, 1985 p131)

However, the assault on the hypno-mimetic is full-frontal when various factions within Christian history used these iconoclasms as a pretext for persecution of their enemies, by invoking the commandment against idolatry; "Thou shalt not make unto thee any graven image or any likeness of anything" … "for I am a jealous God."

Enemies of the imaginal, these iconoclasts acted not merely to mitigate their God's jealousy, but to act as its agents, marauding our temples and visiting an arbitrary and vengeful austerity upon our senses. A trend that reached its climax in the era of the Prostestant Reformation wherein the vandalism of sacred objects evokes the more recent horrors of the Taliban smashing artefacts thousands of years in the making.

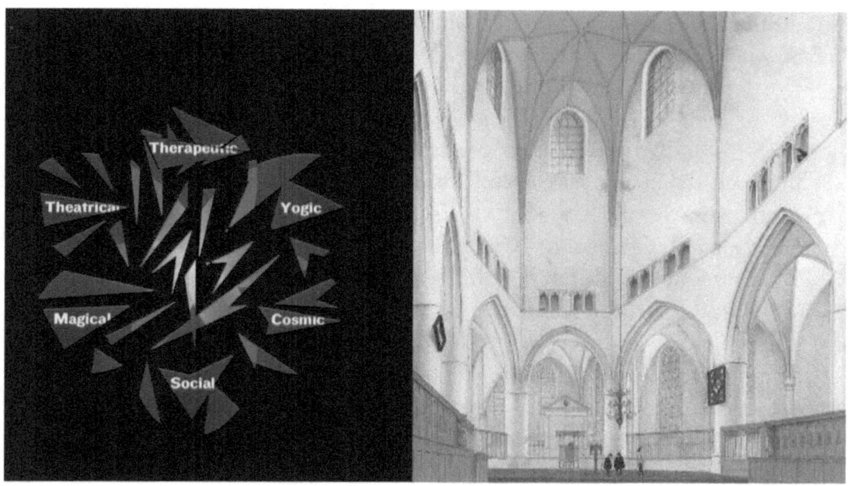

Paintings and sculptures looted and vandalized, churchwalls were rendered bare, by a Puritanical minimalist zealotry. One would think that perhaps a worshipper could take refuge in their personal imagination. That upon these barren walls one could project one's own ecstatically prayer-fueled visions of the divine upon them.

But one would be wrong. Unsatisfied with emptying the exterior world of the richness of vision, the reformation moved on to drain their interior worlds as well.

Such as was the case with their attack on Renaissance esoteric Memory systems, such as those practiced by Giordano Bruno in the 16th century which used mimesis at the phantasmal level as a structure for memorization.

A powerful enemy of this practice, Petrus Ramus, a 16th century pedagogue, attacked phantasmically based systems, and advocated replacing them with his arrangement of subjects in a dialectical schematic order devoid of the delicious imagery of occult memory techniques.

Authors such as Frances Yates, author of *The Art of Memory*, and Ioan Culianu, author of *Eros and Magic in the Renaissance*, cite Ramus' religious writings containing standard reformation condemnations of idolatry in connection with his attack on the imaginal as a mechanism or memory which were to be "replaced by an arrangement of the subject in 'dialectical order' memorizeable because of its 'natural' character." (Culianu, 1984, p.62)

Whether Ramus truly felt that the imagination was tantamount to idolatry or if he just leveraged the iconoclastic zeitgeist of the Reformation to argue favorably for his system I will leave for others to sort out. But one can speculate a combination of these motives. To be sure Ramus had many arguments against using memory systems as a less efficient means to accomplish the task.

Ramus "did not believe in the primacy of phantasm over speech, nor in the phantasmic essence of the intellect. The first condition for memory, conversion into a phantasm, was abolished. Thenceforth, gigantic construction of inner phantasm crumbled: they were replaced by an arrangement of the subject in 'dialectical order' memorizeable because of its 'natural' character."

Yates and Ioan Culianu are in agreement that, as Ioan Culianu wrote, "Ramus's main argument against inner phantasmagoria is…a religious one, the biblical decree not to worship images. The Art of Memory is condemned for its idolatrous nature." (Culianu 1984, p.62)

William Perkins, *A Warning Against The Idolatrie of the Last Times,* 1601

This anti-imaginal condemnation was repeated by William Perkins, one of the foremost leaders of the Puritan movement, and an attacker of Bruno's disciple Alexander Dicsone. In his *Warning Against the Idolatrie of the Last Times*, Perkins states; "A thing conceived in the mind by the imagination is an idol." Woah.

This sentiment is later echoed in 1647 by The Calvinist Westminster Larger

Catechism's interpretation of the commandment against idolatry. This document which generously supplies detail that God Himself left out of Moses' tablets, that idolatory could be effected "either inwardly in our mind, or outwardly in any kind of image or likeness of any creature." As Culianu states, this capacity for the imagination itself to be the ground of iconoclasm "gave the finishing touch to their external iconoclasm by means of an inner iconoclasm." (Culianu, 1984 p. 62)

Indeed, this inner iconoclasm may have given, for some, the finishing touch to the Christian religion entirely as a means of experiencing the sacred in an immanent form, whether everyday natural phenomena including the human body itself. For the connection to the imaginal plays a crucial role in seeing the world as something sacred; i.e., as something that is and means more than just a soulless mechanical clock of particles and epiphenomena. The imaginal supplies the enrichment required to fully metabolize the total experience and existential agency of a living, animate world, populated by always or sometimes invisible and intangible forces and beings. Forces and beings that are experienced to exist through signs, correlates, elevated states of consciousness, or the mind-boggling unexplainable, and that often cannot be reduced to our senses, attuned as they are to a limited band of the cosmic spectrum.

Marcel Gauchet posits that Christianity's role in the "Disenchantment of the World" began long before Reformation era iconoclasm, but stretches much farther back to monotheistic currents that led to a widening of the gap between the transcendent and the immanent due to the remoteness of God. Whereas "primitive religion", represented as not suffering the gap between the transcendent and the immanent, and Eastern religions, acknowledge the experience of fragmentation between perception and reality but try to overcome this gap—for example as Advaita Vedanta recognizing that the appearance of separateness of any kind is an illusion vis-à-vis the reality of a fundamental unity, Buddhism's dependent origination— "Western" religion widens this gap, fatally. Hence religion becomes the exit from religion, which "has 'inexorably' led to the vanishing of transcendence at the level of societal organization. It was precisely this disappearance of transcendence that gave Western modernity its specific form." (Cloots, Latré, Vanheeswijck, 2013)

As with any neurosis or psychosis-engendering repression of an inextricable natural human faculty, the repression of the imaginal and ecstatic faculties of the hypno-mimetic cannot but leave a fragmented relationship with the self in its wake.

Similarly, as alluded to above, Wilhelm Reich blamed millennia of patriarchal authoritarian culture for the sexual repression and subjugation of the subjective self-governing autonomy, emotions, pleasures, and vegetative currents of an inherently loving and orgastic human being, leading to the pandemic of neuroses.

We shall soon see potential hypno-mimetic pathways to transcending and transforming these neurotic social structures structures and ailments in the context of physically based psychotherapeutic techniques and Tantric Buddhism. But first, it behooves us to focus on the loss and recovery of the sacred as such.

THE RESURGENCE OF HYPNOMIMESIS
AND THE REDEMPTION OF A DE-SACRALIZED HUMAN WORLD
IN MIRCEA ELIADE AND CARL JUNG

Such authoritarian alienation – from the pscyho-emotional, sexual, religious, imaginal, and the ecstatic – made loss of Western society's hypno-mimetic capacity inevitable. A totalistic anti-ecstatic iconoclasm, later ossified by mechanistic materialism, deprived vast sectors of the post-reformation industrial West's birthright to walk as a divine being in a sacred world.

In order to resuscitate itself, in Jung's words, "Modern Man in Search of a Soul" endeavored to restore this capacity, directly and indirectly via artistic, therapeutic, religious, and academic modalities that included hypno-mimetic avant-gardes. As we shall see, the enhanced presence of hypno-mimesis not only benefitted from, but is fundamental to, many critical aims and beneficial outcomes of modernist creativity.

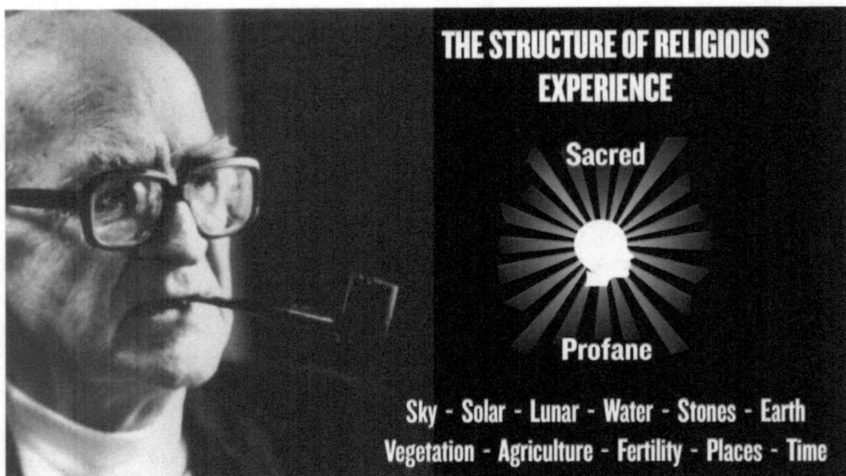

Helpful for those living in a de-sacralized world to recover a sense of the sacred, is to study the nature of the religious experience itself. And to do so in a manner free of the obligation to serve any particular dogma or reductive agenda. Mircea Eliade, who championed the History of Religions as an autonomous discipline, provided phenomenological, ontological, and interpretive frameworks for helping to describe the structure and qualities of religious experience which included a general definition of the sacred, as well as a taxonomy of their manifestations.

In *Patterns in Comparative Religion*, Mircea Eliade provided abundant evidence that throughout history, the sacred has always phenomenologically materialized in forms that also had a profane manifestation. Whether it's the sky and sky gods, the sun, moon, water, stones, earth, vegetation, agriculture, fertility, sacred spaces, food, animals, and time itself; the extraordinary always presents in forms that also materialize in the day-to-day ordinary.

This is the 'dialectic of the hierophany' as Eliade called it. The polarity of the sacred as revealed in profane or mundane instances of human experience, grounds divine revelation in the totality of the material world.

In the post-reformation and post-Christian West in particular, the remoteness of the sacred from day-to-day reality is so great for so many people, that it can be a surprising notion that the totality of religious history is one where the paradox of the transcendent materialized through the immanent was in fact not paradoxical, but normal.

By taking our cue from cultures or individuals capable of experiencing the transcendent in the immanent, the disenchanted materialists among us are invited to perform a hypno-mimetic cognitive alchemy in transforming the lead of their the de-sacralized worldview, into the gold of an animated living universe full of potent revelation and magical potential. We shall see, in the context of Taoist yoga, modern mime, and Butoh techniques, how an alchemical hypno-mimetic corporealization of these material entities can de-alienate the disenchanted from the source of spiritual genius.

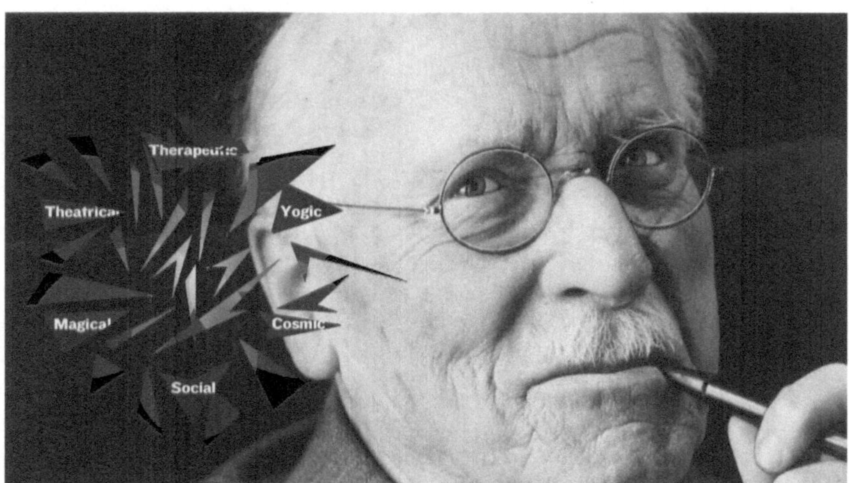

If Mircea Eliade is emblematic of the role comparative religions can provide in bridging the divide between a secular de-animated cosmos, to the sacred and alive cosmos, via our capacity to experientially and phenomenologically transform our perception of the external world, Carl Jung represents just such a bridge via the psychic and imaginal dimension of our internal world.

Using the concept of the psyche, a bio-physical concept more or less tolerable to hardened materialists, Jung posited that archetypes of the collective unconscious, dreams, imaginal contents, and other-than-conscious personalities constituted planes of truth that had their own objective validity, and that these psychic realities could yet exist in parallel with materialistic mechanistic truths. This functional mechanical psychologism provided the sleight of hand that leaves the hegemony of empiricism on its pedestal while providing a rationally acceptable means for the die-hard secular or religiously affiliated to reconstitute a deeply personal, unmediated relationship with religious experience. And, crucial for the concept of hypno-mimesis, a deep engagement with the imaginal that imputes to it the full ontological weight of the real.

As early as 1916, Jung postulated that the unconscious had two distinct structures: the personal unconscious and the impersonal unconscious, or collective psyche. Jung stated that there was risk in identifying the collective psyche as the personal. That one could experience "extreme states of superiority and inferiority." One was at risk of becoming "Godlike". The collective psyche was a space into which the personality could dissolve, "which resulted in the release of a stream of fantasies; 'All the treasures of mythological thinking and feeling are unlocked.' The difference between this state and insanity lay in the fact that it was intentional." (Jung, Shamdasani 2020)

Such intentional confrontation with the unconscious became a key focus for Jung. As has recently become publicly available via the publication of the *Black Books*, his imaginal diaries which fed into the *Liber Novus* or *Red Book*, Jung applied 'active imagination' techniques, 'switching off' the conscious mind to 'bore a hole' into his unconscious, to mine into psychic content, which he considered superior to dream content for supplementing the conscious attitude. (Jung, Shamdasani 2020)

While the extent of character of Jung's personal engagement with the imaginal was not public, he did publicly discuss guidelines for the creative expression of content accessed through hypnotic technique and affects. For the purpose of our focus on hypno-mimesis, the following examples constitutes a profound example of asking questions that the body can answer via an array of sensory modalities, suited to the inclinations of the individual.

> Visual types should concentrate on the expectation that an inner image will be produced. As a rule such a fantasy-image will actually appear – perhaps hypnogogically – and should be carefully noted down in writing. Audio-verbal types usually hear inner words, perhaps mere fragments or apparently meaningless sentences to begin with… Others at such times imply their 'other' voice… Still rarer, but equally valuable, is automatic writing, direct or with the planchette.
>
> (Jung *Collected Works* 8, p. 170-171, Shamdasani 2020)

In a 1917 dream book entry, Jung describes a multi-sensory experience of emergent psychic contents:

> Sometimes it was as if I heard with ears. Sometimes I felt it in the mouth, as if my tongue formulated words, and then it came, that I hear myself

whisper a word to myself. Under the threshold of consciousness everything was living."

(Jung, Shamdasani 2020)

Jung's mimesis on the psychological plane eventually attained the status of addressable independent identities – hypno-mimetic familiars. Early in his experiences of this he wrote, "Perhaps my unconscious is forming a personality that is not I but which is insisting on coming through to expression." And "I was in effect writing letters to my anima, that is part of myself with a different viewpoint from my own. I got remarks of a new character, I was in analysis with a ghost and a woman."

As the entities of Jung's imaginal world proliferated, so too did the extent of the elaboration of detail and dialog, developed in the *Red Book*. A pre-eminent example of which is the character Philemon, whom Jung beseeches for a magical apprenticeship, which at first leads to a deep interrogation of the relationship between reason, and unreason, vis-à-vis the incomprehensible. "Magic happens to be precisely everything that eludes comprehension" Philemon says. "But then how the devil is one to teach and learn magic?" Jung's I asks. Philemon goes on to say that magic cannot be taught. When Jung's I responds that "then magic is nothing but deception", Philemon warns "Watch out—you have started reasoning again". Jung's I says "it's difficult to exist without reason" to which Philemon replies "And that's exactly how difficult magic is." Jung comes to realize that "The practice of magic consists in making what is not understood understandable in an incomprehensible manner." And that while the rational one who suffices to live in a tidy explainable world has no need of magic, that "it is another thing for whoever has opened the chaos in himself. We need magic to be able to receive or invoke the messenger and the communication of the incomprehensible." And given that the incomprehensible cannot by definition be taught, that "One can teach the ways that lead to chaos but cannot teach magic." (Jung, *Liber Novus* p313-314).

If Giordano Bruno was the Reformation era martyr of the imaginal, Carl Jung is its post-Reformation vindication.

This elaboration on the nature of magic vis-à-vis the rational mind, has much structurally in common with Jung's use of the imaginal, and all other manifestations of hypno-mimesis that we shall continue to explore, with regard to the interrogation of the incomprehensible.

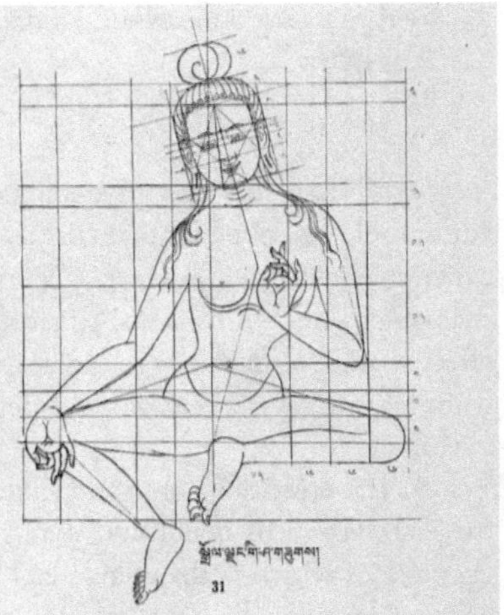

Is it any wonder that Euro-American survivors of the Christian Reformation's war on inner idolatry should find refuge in Tibet's Tantric Buddhism's practice of generative visualization? This imaginal skill effecting planes of consciousness and identification, underpins the Highest Yogas of Secret Mantra, by which one is said to be able to achieve transcendental attainment within a single lifetime. To quote Stephen Beyer:

> If contemplation is the heart of the ritual, then visualization is its living soul. Whether to prevent hailstorms or to gain enlightenment: it is the means by which the power of the deity can be directed and the force in the universe given shape. The ability to control 'appearances' is the affirmation of the practitioner's control of reality itself. (Beyer 1963)

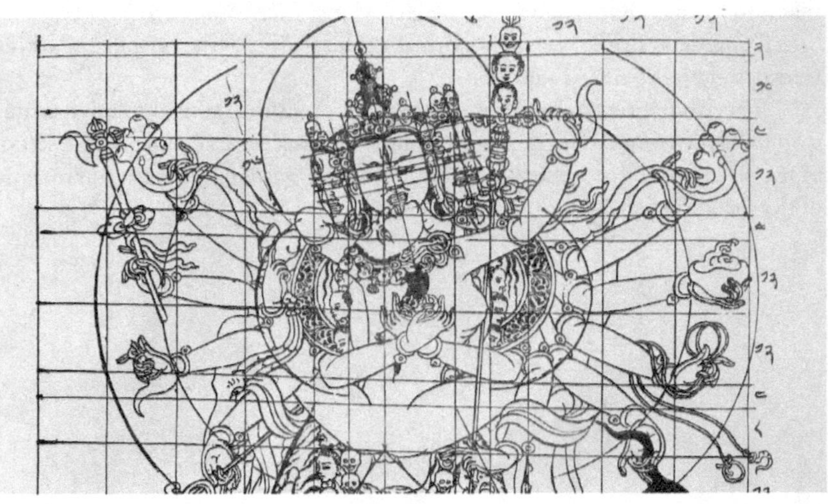

Not limited to the imaginal, this reality control technique is applied by Tantric magician artists, depicting Buddhas and Bodhisattvas via precise geometric formulas capable of transforming a painting or a sculpture into a living receptacle, or 'seat' for the person of the Buddhas themselves. If one were to bring such precise geometries into the mind itself, would the hypno-mimetic shaping of our cognitive landscape create such a seat in the space of intentional consciousness? Or does the application of these geometries to the density of the artist's medium facilitate an alignment of harnessing subtler frequencies in architectures that are already present on the mimetic plane of consciousness of the practitioner, if such structures could be mapped?

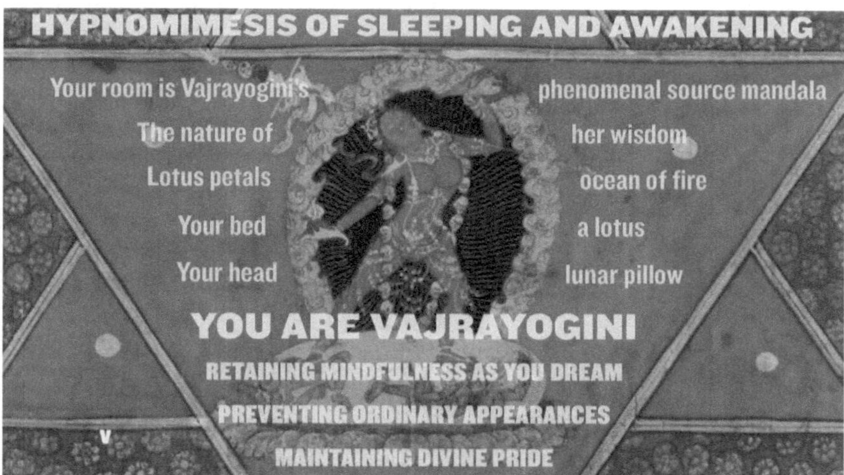

Through Secret Mantra techniques of the yoga of sleeping and waking, we bookend our consciousness with hypno-mimetic interventions that transform ordinary appearances into extraordinary realities, all the while maintaining lucidity while we dream.

> Your head on a pillow of the moon,
> you enter sleep,
> on a lotus bed,
> on a throne of jewels,
> in a room tranformed into Vajrayogini's phenomenal source mandala, in a land of Dakinis.

YOU ARE VAJRAYOGINI.

(Paraphrased from *Guide to Dakini Land*, Geshe Kelsan Gyatso, 1991)

Trading in your ego, you incorporate the divine pride of the goddess. Tantric Secret Mantra is perhaps singular in its application of a kind of salvific narcissism as a more expedient path to enlightenment; a divine self-regard that effects Eliade's sacralization of the mundane — I.e., the mundane identity — while also opening a creative space for synthesis between yoga, magic, drama therapy, actualization therapy, and others.

Interestingly, Secret Mantra doesn't just stop at a homeopathic ingestion of divine ego by which you annihilate your mundane selfhood; but for example, through the corporealization of the cosmic mandala, as it were, one unfolds one's entire being as so many lotus petals, to reveal the structure of the cosmos itself. You don't simply de-personalize yourself into the corpse-like emptiness we will encounter in Butoh or the zero point of neutrality in modern mime; you re-personalize with the entire cosmos. All directions, elements, and forms of knowledge realize themselves in the ground of your cosmologically corporealized consciousness.

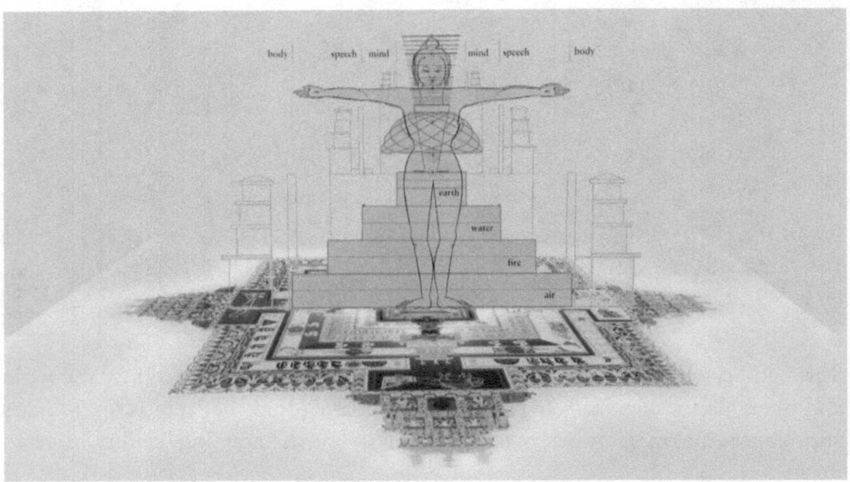

Olympic athletes of the imaginal, Tibetan yogins of the Kalachakra tradition build mental palaces, replete with 722 deities, all committed to memorization. The Kalachakra Mandala is composed of multiple nested mandala palaces. A mandala palace of body, impervious to blinding passions. A mandala palace of speech and its deity-invoking seed syllables. The mandala palace of mind that awakens, turning from nirvana to the samsara to help to heal and redeem others; awakening fully to the indestructible mind of pristine consciousness, until ultimately attaining the Supreme Lotus Bliss at the center of this grand phantasmic architecture.

In Supreme Lotus Bliss, your embodiment becomes the alchemical vessel, transmuting Male & Female, Semen & Blood, Lunar & Solar, into Empty Immutable Essence, via the erotic union of Compassion and Absolute Wisdom. (Crossman and Barou 1995)

Could there be a more elegant counterpoint to the puritanical henchmen that condemned the Renaissance magician's memory theaters to oblivion and their bodies to flames? Could we restore them all back to life, and then cleanse them in the redemptive flames of our enlightened sex?

What does your body say?

THE LOSS AND RECOVERY OF THE SEMANTIC BODY IN MODERN PERFORMANCE

If, in the context of spirituality, the erosion of the hypno-mimetic imaginal can be linked to a loss of the Divine Body capable of expressing the sacred; then in the context of performing arts, the erosion of the imaginal can be linked to the loss of the Semantic Body, capable of expressing dramatic meaning. In modern Euro-American theater disciplines, this hypno-mimetic fragmentation expresses itself as a metastasized split between acting and dancing.

In the case of acting, the decadence of mimetic technique reduces the performer to a talking head in service of the written word, rendering the body an inarticulate meat carcass transmitting ambiguous signals to the audience. In the case of dance, the absence of mimetic technique correlates to an emphasis on formal stylization that becomes increasingly remote from content, and/or ambiguous expressionism emptied of dramatic narrative significance.

As Eugenio Barba says in the *Dictionary of Theater Anthropology*: "The tendency to make a distinction between dance and theater, characteristic of our own culture, reveals a profound wound, a void with no tradition, which continuously risks drawing the actor toward the denial of the body, and the dancer toward virtuosity." (Barba, 2006)

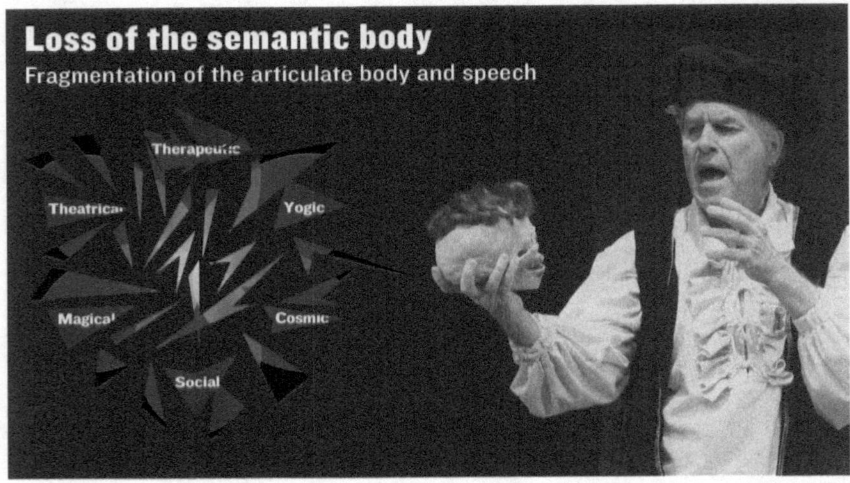

While the dancer may have tremendous athletic power and formal range, their capacity to deliver meaning risks being even inferior to the corporeally impaired actor, who at least has speech to fall back on to provide intelligibility to an audience. The world of dance often compensates through histrionics and athleticism; the latter of which brings the art form closer to gymnastics and circus, in the prioritization form over content.

Barba continues,"To an Asian performer, this distinction seems absurd...We can ask a Noh and Kabuki actor how he would translate the word 'energy' into the language of his work, but he would shake his head in amazement if we asked him to explain the difference between dance and theater." (Barba, 2006)

In the context of Asian theater, a basic but illustrative example of visualization-dependent theatricalized energetics is expressed by Manojo Nomara of the Nōh Kita school; "The actor must imagine that above him is suspended a ring of iron which is pulling him upwards. He must resist this pull in order to keep his feet on the ground." (Barba, 2006 p 10)

As we globally widen our view of theater, we find systems with highly cultivated vocabularies of meaning. For example, from Indian Classical dance, I've collected over 120 examples of narrative hand-gestures in what is likely a far from exhaustive sampling, from Bharatanatyam, Kathak, Odissi, Katkhakali, and many others.

Katkhakali is famous for its dramatic eye movement techniques. It's interesting to note that, from a mimetic perspective, the focus of the actor IS the focus of the audience. What the actor is paying attention to is generally what the audience is paying attention to. And yet, in 'western' systems of theater and dance, are absent the kinds of rigorous gaze training that we find in theater systems with more mature

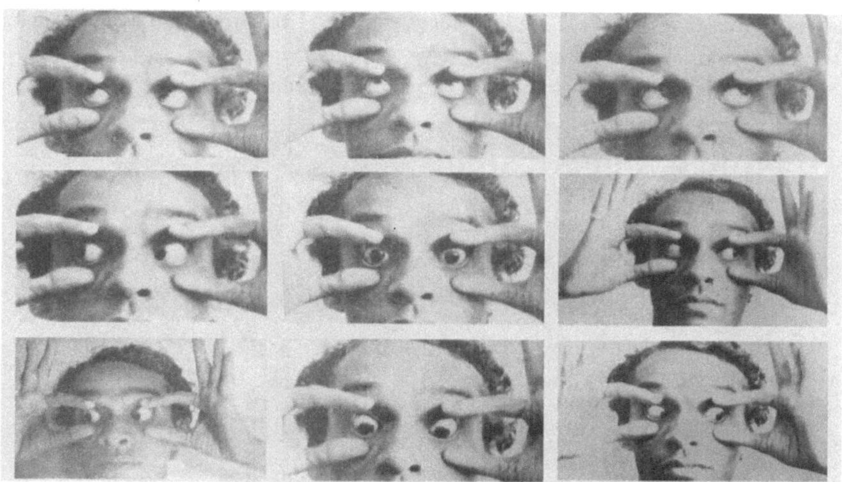

mimetic approaches, such as in Khatakhali, wherein eye movement exercises are a central part of what can be a three-hour training session that begins daily at 3:30am.

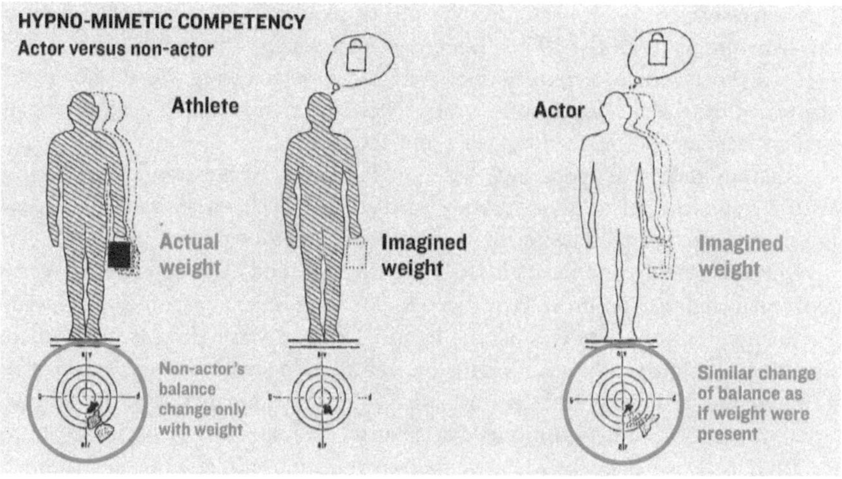

For those who are reassured when reality is measured by machines, the transmission of the imaginal through the semantic body can be shown via kinesimeter— an instrument which measures motion quantitatively. In an experiment, two individuals, an athlete and an actor, stand on a kinesimeter. In the first pass they hold a weight in one hand, and we can see the distribution of force as the body counterbalances the weight. In the second, the participants are just asked to visualize they are holding the same weight. (Barba 2006)

The actor imagining the weight shows a force distribution essentially identically with the carrying a real weight. However, when the athlete imagines the weight, there is essentially no change. The hypno-mimetic competency of the actor is evident here, in the literal translation of an imagined energetic force.

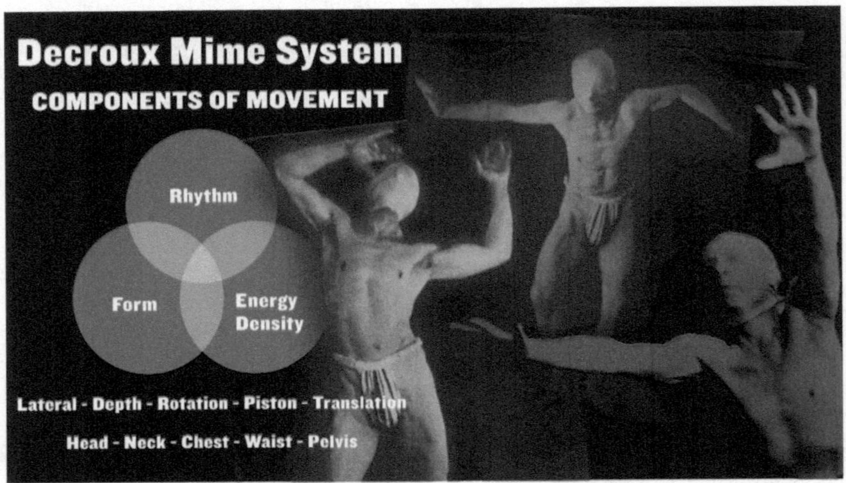

In the modern era, energy systems have played a central role in the renaissance of the semantic body. In the 1930s, Étienne Decroux, the 'father of modern mime', reduced movement to a pure formal system for constructing literal and hyper-abstracted expression. In Decroux's mime system, the three pillars composing all human movements, are rhythm, form, and energy.

Rhythm relates to speed and cadence, fast, slow, acceleration, deceleration. Form involves articulations of the body, such as head, neck, chest, waist, pelvis, and limbs. And also spatial trajectories, such as lateral, depth, rotation.

Whereas rhythm and form are fairly easy to name and describe, 'energy' is a far more challenging concept. In fact, there doesn't seem to be a perfect English term.

Energy, tension, density, and the hybrid 'dension' have all been used in the discourse of mime technique. That the English speaking world struggles to identify a unifying term to designate a performative corporeal energetics is, in this author's opinion, evidence of hypno-mimetic decadence.

And, as always happens when we follow the hypno-mimetic thread that binds us eventually to an energy concept; we begin to question the boundaries between matter and soul, between an individual and the universe.

For Decroux, the corporeal and the spiritual, the ideal, and the communal, were not discontinuous, rather, they completed each other in an expressive and an experiential unity.

Decroux states, "I am overpowered by the spiritual when it has given its form to the material," [Decroux, Leabheart 1978 p. 8] and, "the idea must become material" [Decroux, Leabheart 2012 p. 83] and "when I see the body rise up, it's humanity itself rising up". "When the actor is lying on the ground, it's the whole nation lying down. [Decroux, Leabheart, Franc Chamberlain, *Mime Journal* 1978]

Modernist performance is replete with such transpersonal sentiments. For example, dancer Martha Graham's "Dance is the hidden language of the soul," and "Movement never lies. It is a barometer telling the state of the soul's weather."

And dancer Ruth St. Denis' "I see dance being used as communication between body and soul, to express what it too deep to find for words."

And of course from the artist who made the death of God conditional on his dancing prowess. Friedrich Nietzsche's "I would believe only in a God that knows how to dance."

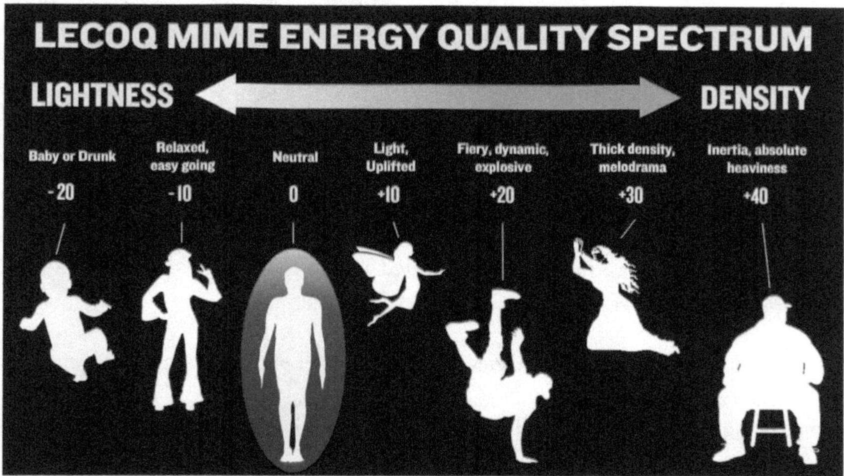

A key focus of hypno-mimetic physicality, is the generation and manipulation of energy qualities in the body. What is seen in the mind's eye, incorporated and translated through the body, becomes what is seen and felt kinesthetically by the audience. As already mentioned, Etienne Decroux, alongside rhythm and form placed energetic density as one of the three pillars of all movement. Other modern mime practitioners continued to develop the energy concept in their work, such as Anne Dennis, Kari Margolis, and Jacques Lecoq.

Lecoq identifies a spectrum of energy qualities that provide a good entry point for conceptualizing the role of energetic density in mimetic systems. We go from the rubbery incoherence of a baby or a drunk; to a relaxed laid-back quality; through to the homeostatic pre-expressiveness of the neutral zero-point; into a fairy-like lightness; then building in intensity to fiery, dynamic qualities; on to increasing heaviness, through melodramatic intensity; until we arrive at the inertia or leaden heaviness of the densest matter.

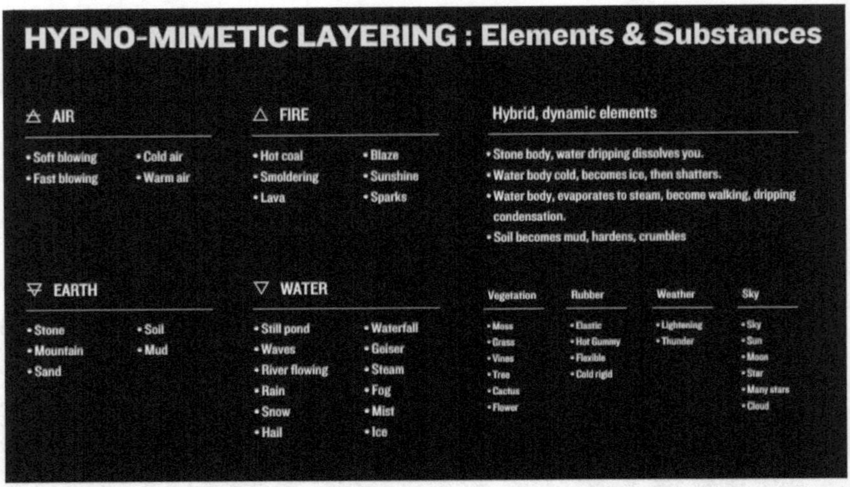

HYPNO-MIMETIC LAYERING : Elements & Substances

△ AIR

- Soft blowing
- Fast blowing
- Cold air
- Warm air

△ FIRE

- Hot coal
- Smoldering
- Lava
- Blaze
- Sunshine
- Sparks

Hybrid, dynamic elements

- Stone body, water dripping dissolves you.
- Water body cold, becomes ice, then shatters.
- Water body, evaporates to steam, become walking, dripping condensation.
- Soil becomes mud, hardens, crumbles

▽ EARTH

- Stone
- Mountain
- Sand
- Soil
- Mud

▽ WATER

- Still pond
- Waves
- River flowing
- Rain
- Snow
- Hail
- Waterfall
- Geiser
- Steam
- Fog
- Mist
- Ice

Vegetation	Rubber	Weather	Sky
Moss	Elastic	Lightening	Sky
Grass	Hot Gummy	Thunder	Sun
Vines	Flexible		Moon
Tree	Cold rigid		Star
Cactus			Many stars
Flower			Cloud

As we reduce the energetics of movements to their elemental and substantial essences, we arrive at a hypno-mimetic alchemy. We work foundationally with visualizations and breathing qualities rooted in the foundational elements of air, fire, earth, and water.

—⁓— Air has the expressive qualities of coldness and warmness, and soft and fast blowing.

—⁓— Fire has the expressive qualities of hot coal, smoldering, lava, blazing, sunshine, and sparks.

—⁓— Earth has the expressive qualities of stone, mountains, sand, soil, and mud.

—⁓— Water has the expressive qualities of a still pond, waves, flowing rivers, tsunamis, snow, hail, waterfalls, geisers, fog, mist, and ice.

—⁓— Vegetation has the expressive qualities of moss, grass, vines, tress, cactus, and flowers.

—⁓— Rubber can be elastic, hot and gummy, flexible, or cold and rigid.

We can mime these qualities simply in isolation. Or, as our hypno-mimetic visualization and breathing capacities improve we move on to more complex enactments. For example, you have a stone body, and dripping water slowly dissolves you. Or your body begins as soft soil. Rain on your soil body transforms you to mud. Then sun dries and hardens you. Then you crumble.

I say we work hypno-mimetically with visualizations and breathing qualities. This is because there are literally endless qualities of breathing. Try breathing at the rhythm of stone when miming stone, and breathing the rhythm of dandelion seeds blowing in the air when miming those. Focus on the rhythm and intensity of your breathing in each case and you will see what I mean. There is a 1:1 relationship between hyper-subtle breathing modulation and tangible energy qualities, rhythms, and distributions.

MIMETIC LAYERING : Entities, Conditions, Actions

Starting in random or specified positions. Transform into animal, real or imaginary so long as it is clear. Let them take their time. Change conditions and actions periodically. Post-exercise, discuss energy qualities.

ENTITIES		INTERNALS	EXTERNALS	ACTIONS		
• Chicken	• Horse	• Hungry	• Cold	• Search	• Retreat	• Shiver
• Frog	• Insect	• Afraid	• Snowing	• Hide	• Part	• Crouch
• Turtle	• Spider	• Angry	• Heat	• Discover	• Welcome	• Cower
• Cow	• Dog	• Sad	• Rain	• Escape	• Threaten	• Fawn
• Eagle	• Cat	• Water-filled	• Rocks falling	• Hurry	• Repulse	• Grovel
• Lion	• Deer	• Air filled (temps)	• Earthquake	• Rush	• Grow	• Flinch
• Snake	• Octopus	• Fire filled		• Hesitate	• Decay	• Attack it
• Elephant	• Fish	• Earth filled		• Delay	• Bloom	• Defend it
• Giraffe	• Butterfly	• Electricity filled		• Linger	• Wither	• Struggle
• Tiger	• Worm			• Meet	• Wilt	• Fight it
				• Greet	• Appear	• Chase it
				• Lurk	• Disappear	• Flee
				• Advance	• Shudder	• Hug it
				• Press Mud	• Cringe	• Tremble

Example: A hungry afraid cow in an earthquake pressing mud

As we move on from the mimetics of elemental qualities, to that of animated entities (such as insects, birds, frogs, snakes, or octopi), which we combine with internal states (such as hunger, impatience, sadness, afraid, water-filled, or fire-filled), and external conditions (such as weather or war), and actions (such as greeting, retreating or decaying).

Combining these categories brings you to quite unexpected expressive territory.

For example; A hungry afraid octopus hesitantly gathering mud, with occasional waves of strong current flowing through and disrupting your effort. Try it.

It often works best when a workshop facilitator calls out cues for the action, and you respond with physical embodiment. But you can do it on your own. Working solo, it can help to record your voice moving through the cues and then work with the recording as your facilitator.

THE HYPNO-MIMETIC CONNECTION TO THE PRIMORDIAL

In opening the body as a territory for esoteric knowledge, the connection with animals, and ultimately to your animal nature, and the animate universe, is crucial. This is not only because animal mimicry helps us transcend normative human conditioning, but as avant-garde theater director Jerzy Grotowski says, "One mustn't forget; the body is an animal. I am not saying we are animals; I say our body is an animal". (Grotowski, Richards, 1995)

Could it even be, that as humans, we merely co-exist with the animal that is our body?

Is there an antagonism between the dual natures of the human?

An ego-operated identity fetishizing rationality and language confronted by a beast which, like a domesticated dog, has lost its feral nature?

What questions can we ask to set free this beast?

What language must we learn so we can understand its answers?

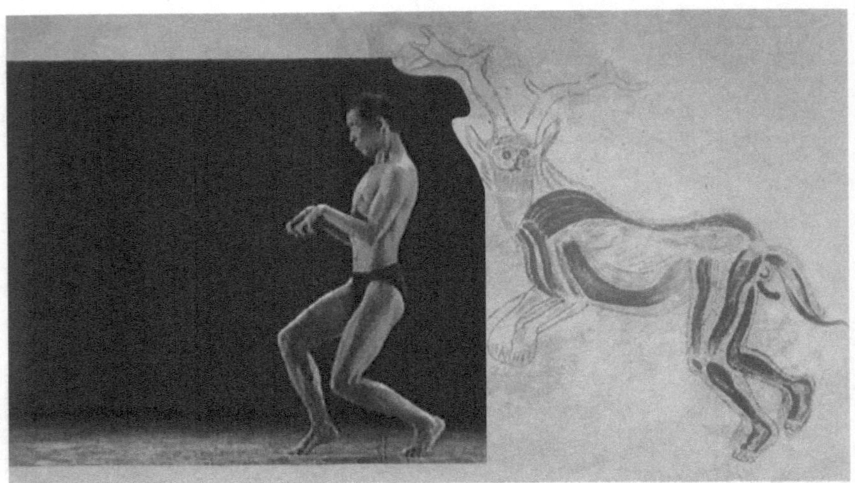

The Butoh Fu of Tatsumi Hijikata contains hypno-mimetic suggestions that invoke archaic hunter cave paintings, as you evoke the fullness of the animal from within your animal. You are able to feel the hide of your own beast enclosing you. Scent of fur and musk. Nostrils filled with dust. The human ego drops.

YOU FEEL THE BULL'S HORNS
YOU FEEL THE BULL'S WEIGHT
YOUR HOOVES, SPLITTING INTO THREE
YOU ARE DANCING THE ALTAMIRA CAVE PAINTING
ANCIENT BULLS
AS YOU DANCE YOU ARE AWARE OF THE BULL'S ELEGANCE
WEIGHT, AND SLIGHTLY WET BODY HAIR
THE HORNS TURN IN PRECISELY SEVEN DIRECTIONS
THE BULL STANDS AT DUSK
IT HAS BECOME CLOUDY
IT IS JUST BEFORE A STORM
THE BULL'S HEAD IS DECORATED WITH DAHLIA FLOWERS
THEY ARE WET WITH RAIN
THE BULL IS AWARE THAT HE MAY BE SACRIFICED
THAT HE MAY SUFFER PAINS
(Paraphrased from Hijikata FU, Waguri 1994)

Physically based psychotherapeutic approaches invite us to mine into things like buried childhood traumas, latent emotions, or significant relational contexts between ourselves and family members, and so on. We may be tempted to refer to experiences as 'going deep'. But what if the body contains or can access knowledge much deeper than what we have experienced within this lifetime? When asking questions of the body, why settle for the catharsis available from exploring childhood trauma, if it is possible to tap into knowledge tens of thousands of years old?

Perhaps, as we descend deeper into the corporeal, we will discover the animal origins of the first humans. And reconnect with the first humans who hunted animals. And the moment those humans became animals again, so as to become better hunters. In other words, the primordial origins of mimesis in the first humans who mimicked their prey to hunt more successfully.

Does hypno-mimesis have an old-school Darwinian survival mandate? Did we evolve bio-physically to become the animal we hunt via our hypno-mimetic faculties?

As poet and ethno-environmentalist Gary Snyder posits, "in ritual and ceremonies that are found throughout the world from ancient times, the key component of the ceremony is animal miming." "... a spontaneous expression of the capacity of becoming physically and psychically one with the animal." (Snyder, 1980)

Between being the hunter and the hunted, what did our agrarian industrial bodies lose? Perhaps that level of stillness that brings us to the "movement-consciousness-mind-presence of animals."

"As the Indians say, 'Hunt for the animal that comes to you,'" Snyder says.

He comments that "Early tradition of life, prior to agriculture, required literally thousands of years of great attention and awareness."

Snyder further remarks, that, as a boy growing up in the American North West, he saw "old Wishram Indians spearing salmon on the Columbia River, standing on a little plank out over a rushing waterfall. They could stand motionless for twenty to thirty minutes with a spear in their hands and suddenly, they'd have a salmon."

This tremendous one-pointedness of concentration led Snyder to speculate that hunting may account for a biologic origin of meditation. "I am speculating simply on what are the biophysical, evolutionary roots of meditation and of spiritual practice", Snyder says.

In my first theater company, Dreaming Crow Puppet and Mask Theater, we explored just this meditative physicality. In our Inuit inspired play *Sedna*, a village is near starvation. They are eating their dogs. People die. A Shaman is enlisted to appeal to Sedna, the Mother of Sea Beasts to send a seal to the village. Perhaps humans have been up to no good again. Hunting just for sport. Wasting skins or other animal parts. Who knows? But she must not be happy. The Shaman goes into trance. Beseeches Sedna her for forgiveness, appealing to her generosity. In the end she sends a seal and the village is saved.

In preparation for our roles, some of the more cognitively intrepid of us would eat hallucinogenic mushrooms with our costumes on to become more fully possessed by the animals. Hunters, seal, polar bear. The hunter and the hunted. We would stand in the snow for long periods. We contemplated what it would be like to stand for 12 hours over an air hole waiting for a seal to emerge. Standing in deep meditation until our legs would shake.

Popular spiritual leader Eckhart Tolle evokes a related hypno-mimetic approach as a means of helping the meditator achieve presence.

> Close your eyes and say to yourself: 'I wonder what my next thought is going to be.' Then become very alert and wait for the next thought. Be like a cat watching a mouse hole. What thought is going to come out of the mouse hole. Try it now." (Tolle)

HYPNO-MIMESIS AND BUTOH

In 20th century dance, the use of a hypno-mimetics approach to dissolve the normative boundaries between the body and objects, between senses and matter, reached a peak in the development of the Butoh Fu of Hijikata Tatsumi. Hijikata is a founder of Ankoku Butoh (Dance of Darkness), a dance genre developed in Japan between the late 1950's-1970's.

Hijikata developed an extensive hypno-mimetic vocabulary, called Butoh Fu, which are composed of over 1,200 hypno-mimetic inputs drawn from painting, sculpture, and many other sources. The Butoh Fu were principally compiled and extended by long-time company member Yukio Waguri. Additional publishing and evolution of Butoh Fu or similar material can be found also in the works of Rhizome Lee, and on the excellent manual.shadowbody.com online resource.

Whereas many post-Hijikata Butoh practitioners tend to defend a subjectivist approach to defining, or rather not defining Butoh, it is clear that as Hijikata's work matured, he developed a very rigorous dance vocabulary and methodology that bears many of the features of a fully transmissible system. It is my point of view that Hijikata/Waguri's Ankoku Butoh Fu are as close as Butoh comes to being a dance tradition on the order of Ballet, Kathakali, Bharatanatyam. Therefore, I generally distinguish much post-Hijikata Butoh as more-or-less a style genre that is missing core components that would cohere it as a tradition. For performative traditions to become mature transmissible systems, rather than just individualist creations with surface stylistic affinities using a common genre moniker, a matured underlying technique must be present, often accompanied by a recognizable formal vocabulary, and often a repertoire. Minus repertoire, in the case of Butoh, the centerpieces of just such technique and formal vocabulary are the hypno-mimetic Ankoku Butoh Fu of Hijikata.

Hijikata's Butoh Fu are verbal and imagistic cues meant to be ingested into the body to shape movement in a space where energetics and form overlap.

Hijikata's hypno-mimetic cues drew from art such as painting and sculptures from source such as Altamira cave paintings, Bacon, Bellmer, Bosch, Bosse, Dali, Dubuffet, Giacometti, Goya, Itō Jakuchū, Kiyochika, Michaux, Rodin, Redon, Turner, and Wols; spirits, legends, and figures such as hungry human ghosts, ghosts of roosters, gaki demons, Jesus, witches, popes; extreme situations such as having burns all over your body walking through war-torn villages, being penetrated by insects, lumps of flesh falling away, schizoid disintegration, soul being torn apart, disembowelment, nerves disintegrating into air, and internal tornadoes; natural objects, qualities, and materials such as dust, caramelized sugar, shadows, straw, flowers, porcelain dolls, smells, walls, flatness, smoke, tangled nerves, eyes becoming bird's nests, a child's crayon drawing, being coated in pus, transparent rubber sheets, hands becoming dead shrubs, being made of darkness or bubbles, falling particles, goats, mannequins, pegasus, torso becoming a horse-neck, exhaling strings, and a wet cat stretched turning into a dinosaur.

An example wherein a painting provides the cue for both a formal facial shape and a visualization for contorting the face into this shape, is the Butoh Fu Francis Bacon's Face.

DISTORTED BY FRANCIS BACON'S PAINTBRUSH
WHICH TWISTS AND CONTORTS THE FACE
DRAGGING FLESH FROM THE OUTSIDE
(Waguri 1998)

From the 1998 DVD of Butoh Fu compiled by Yukio Waguri, we see the actors face contort in visualized response to the visualization of Bacon's paint brush dragging and twisting the musculature in something of a figure 8 pattern.

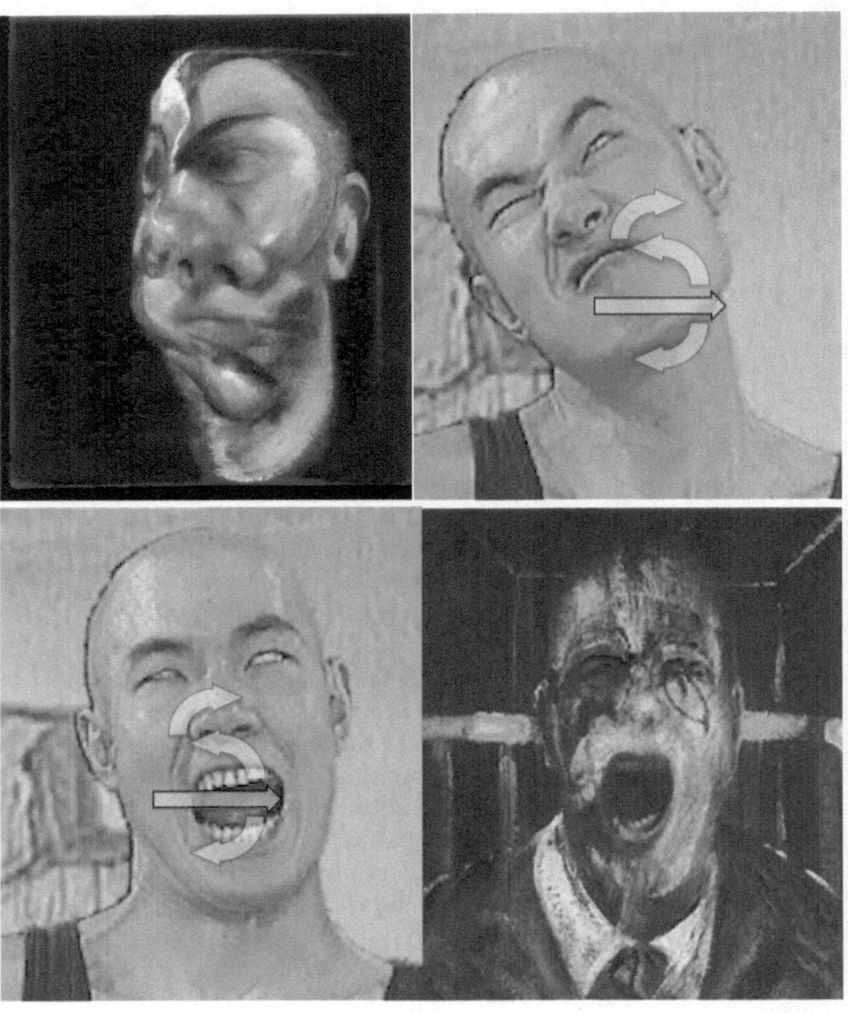

As Yukio Waguri demonstrates Michaux's ink painting, the actor mimes a bottle crashing into his head, and we see semi-involuntary twitches cascade down his head and face in response to visualized lines of ink.

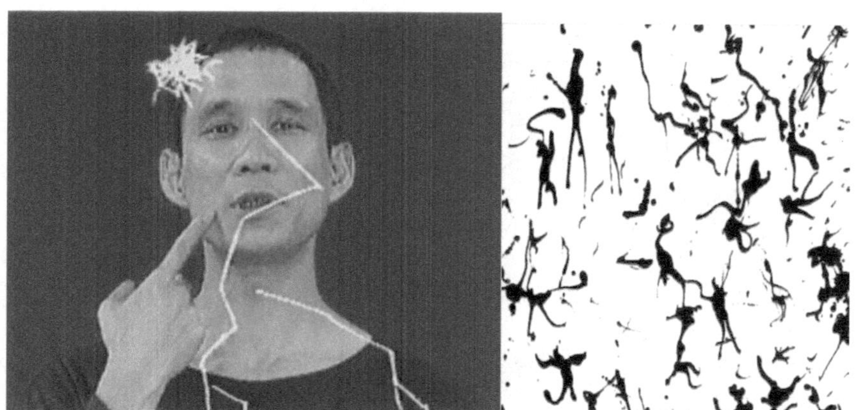

MICHAUX'S INK BOTTLE CRASHES INTO YOUR RIGHT FOREHEAD
THE BOTTLE CRACKS AND SPILLS INTO THE INSIDE PARTS OF YOUR BODY
YOUR NERVES TRACE THE SPILLED INK INSIDE YOUR BODY
FROM THE RIGHT TEMPLE THROUGH THE RIGHT CHEEK AND TO THE TWITCHING SIDE OF THE MOUTH AND TO THE NECK
THE INK IS NOW THROUGH YOUR NECK AND OUT YOUR BACK
THEN IT RE-ENTERS YOUR BACK AND COMES OUT OF YOUR CHEST
THEN IT GOES BACK UP YOUR NECK
THE NERVE TRACING THE INK COMING UP YOUR NECK IS SUDDENLY SVERED
THE NERVES THN BECOME LIKE ROOTS PULLED OUT OF DIRT

(Waguri 1998)

Such cues and movements become both a technique and formal choreographic building blocks. In the following example, we see multiple such building blocks combine in one overall physicalized sequence, one transforming to another.

FOLLOW THE PASSAGE OF DALI AROUND KING SOLOMON'S
PALACE
LION IN THE GROTTO
FACES IN THE FOREST
SLUGS
FRANCIS BACONS FACES
FISTS, SCABS, THREE FACES
THE POPE WEARING CLOTHES MADE OF STEAMING PUS
THE EXECUTIONER DISAPPEARS INTO PUS
SLOW DOWN
THE IDOT WITHIN GOYA'S CHARACTER
STREAMING PUS
PUS ON ODILON REDON'S ONE-EYED GOBLIN
A DOLL IN PUS
PUS ON MANNEQUINS
BECOME THE POPE IN A ROBE MADE OF PUS
THE POPE WITHDRAWS BACKWARDS
(Waguri 1998)

PUPPETEERS OF THE DEAD

The early Butoh milieu directly explored the physicalization of ancestors, pre-birth experiences, and disembodied entities.

Hijikata, directly incorporated the soul of his deceased sister.

I keep an older sister alive in my body.
When I am absorbed in creating a butoh piece," "she plucks the darkness from my body

100

and eats more of it than is necessary.
When she stands up in my body
I sit down impulsively.
For me to fall is for her to fall.
But there is even more to our relationship than that.

Butoh co-originator Kazuo Ohno danced in relationship with his mother, an act both of tribute and reconciliation. Ohno says, "The first encounter with beauty in this life is the encounter with your mother."

His son, Yoshito Ohno, said of him, "he frequently speaks of how she shortened her life by giving of her flesh and blood so as to nourish him in the womb." "Dance, as I see it, is my father's way of telling his mother that he has come to realize the full extent of her sorrow."

In Butoh Ritual Mexicano workshops, Diego Piñon offers an exercise by which our bodies ask of the cosmos regarding the essence of our mothers and fathers. The following actions are performed literally.

Planting your fingers into your perineum between your anus and your genitals
your right hand reaches out into the cosmos
you scrape the essence of your mother from from it
you suck this essence from your fingers
then you plant this essence into your perineum.
Reaching out to the left, you repeat the same for your father.

(Piñon, 2001, from Abler's workshop notes)

Additionally, Kazuo Ohno speaks of direct reconnection with the fetal body:

An embryo's dream.
Mother scrapes her own life to let her child eat it.
The child grows up in a dream..."
"The essence of these dreams is to trace back the origins of life and to dance there."
"My face was covered with a veil. It is like mother's amnion."

FROM THE DANCE AVANT-GARDE
TO THE THERAPEUTIC AVANT-GARDE

The notion of connecting to pre-natal memories through movement is not limited to the Butoh avant-garde. Some Dance and Movement Therapists posit that non-verbal expression may access memory from pre-verbal phases of development. Diane Duggan (1981) citing Kestenberg's research on the role of movement patterns in early development, notes that fetuses are able to respond to stimulation as early as the seventh week after conception, therefore "it is not surprising that individual differences in movement have been identified in infants".

The notion of pre-verbal subjective development raises questions about therapies with overly language focused approaches. Duggan (1981) writes "During this preverbal period, all experience is linked to body sensation and movement. Dance therapists believe that the body is a repository of memories of this period and seek to tap them directly through the body." Dance Therapy favors, as Irma Alperson (1977) says, an "approach to self-awareness", that "does not demand definition prior to expression and therefore potentially limit the experience, as verbalization might."

However powerful direct corporeal access to pre-verbal knowledge might be,

Duggan notes that Dance Therapy has no unified protocols for diagnosis or session structure, and not all therapists are psychoanalytically trained.

In my view, this analytic and diagnostic gap in Dance Movement Therapy is analogous to the dancing and acting schism of Western Theater; that is, the lack of a system capable of interpreting a semantic body. Although whereas in the case of the dancing/acting schism, the gap is of mimetic intelligibility, in therapeutic, the semantic readability is in terms of effects of trauma or conditioning, and the emphasis for mimesis in therapy may lean more toward intervention methods such as dramatic enactments.

Wilhelm Reich's character analytic acumen served well to address this overall gap, with a corporeal semantics that was diagnostic and foundational to somatic therapeutic interventions.

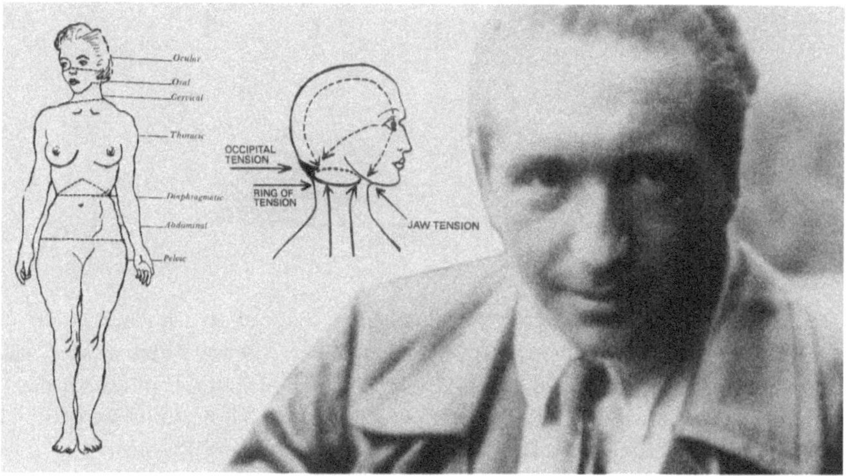

Initially, Reich would mimic the physicality of his patient's defensive manipulative attitudes so as to undermine them. For example, a false acquiescence disguising an unexpressed contempt; as a false positive transference masking the latent negative transference. (Reich, *Character Analysis*, 1949)

Reich ultimately developed a methodical approach to the analysis of rigidified character structures, correlated to expressive and sensational blockages in bodily segments. These segments were Ocular, Oral, Cervical, Thoracic, Diaphragmatic, Abdominal, and Pelvic. These segments suffered from chronic rigidifications, for example resulting from habitual repression, such as shameful avoidance of genital self-pleasure, or repression of fight or flight responses to abusive family members, or traumatically forced bowel movements, and many more.

Trapped in conditioning from our childhood past, the adult neurotic body becomes stuck in a habitual response to historical stimuli that are no longer present. In a sense, the neurotic body is condemned to unconscious perpetual self or situational mimicry, even if the environment no longer places the same dysfunctional demands on the individual.

Building on Reich's work, Bioenergetics Therapy includes an array of mimetic exercises aimed at liberating the bodies' rigidities, such as: Expressing exaggerated emotions in a mirror; Two partners scream yes and no at one another repeatedly; Beating a wadded-up blanket with a tennis racquet while shouting in anger at a target of unexpressed rage.

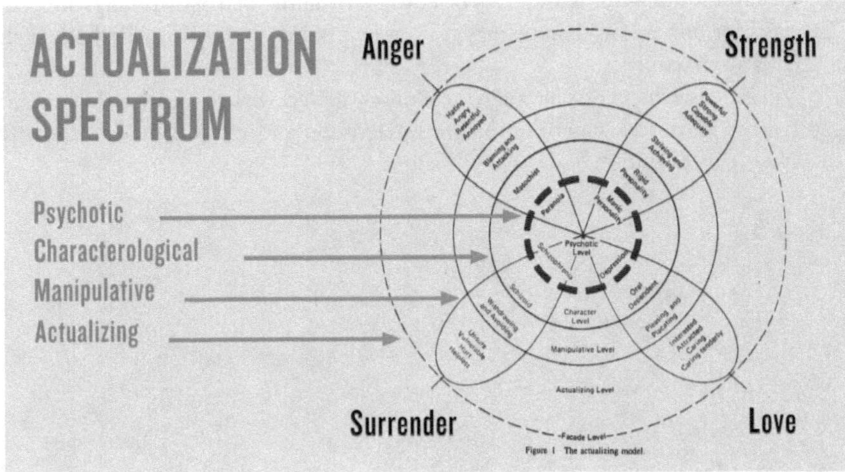

Actualization Therapy uses mimetic role-playing, mapped to a holistic model of healthful capacity to fluidly express what life requires. The actualization spectrum plays out along two axes A) of anger and Love, and B) of strength and surrender.

Anger, love, strength, and surrender are seen has having healthful expressions, but also manipulative, character rigidifying, and psychotic expressions.

For example, the healthful capacity to temporarily experience and suppress anger when the situation requires, anger transposes to chronic blaming, masochism, and paranoia as disease conditions predominate and degenerate.

Mimesis is used for example to help clients access and familiarize themselves with healthier expressions of anger via role-playing or replaying historical scenarios or dynamics that help mobilize the body to familiarize itself consciously with emotions that may have been buried, thereby instigating catharsis. Examples of hypno-mimetic enactments applied to the Actualization model include;

—∞— Re-enactment family argument scenarios.

—∞— Giving 'yes' to those from which you would forever otherwise withhold it. Or accepting a 'yes' from those who never said it.

—∞— Your eyes are closed, a trusted person touches your face tenderly while saying the loving things your parents never said to you, but perhaps wish they could have.

—∞— You slam your fists into the couch and scream into the core of the universe that you will never give up.

—⁓— You releasing the chronic mistrustful holding into the surrender into trustful falling.

—⁓— As the schizoid, you face a therapist playing your rejecting parents, in order activate your rage so you can fully reject your rejection, and ultimately come back to the experience of their acceptance.

—⁓— As the oral dependent you scream your need to a therapist playing a dismissive parent, in order to own the violent rejection of your own need, and then open yourself to embrace its final fulfillment.

—⁓— A therapist mimics your own manipulations, just as Wilhelm Reich did, in order to undermine your false positive transference and evoke the contempt you so artfully mask behind your false acquiescence.

—⁓— You imaginally project your denied manipulations onto the emptiness of a chair, and then switch into it, in order to re-absorb the projection mimetically into the mask of the opposing identity, and then oscillate your identification back and forth between your polarized selves until you harmonize into a more flexible integration.

DO WE EVEN NEED IDENTITIES TO TRANSFORM?

An exercise from the Sub-body Butoh school achieves a somatic integration of a shadow without interpretive mediation.

The space is divided into four stages.

In the first stage, the practitioner moves forward in a neutral walk called an 'ash walk'.

In the second stage, a shadow is allowed to arise and speak in the expression of the body.

In the third stage, the shadow is thanked with a deep prostration, as it returns to the earth.

In the fourth stage, the dancer emerges, blooming as a flower from the shadow's seed.

Do we need to name our pain? Are words truly necessary?

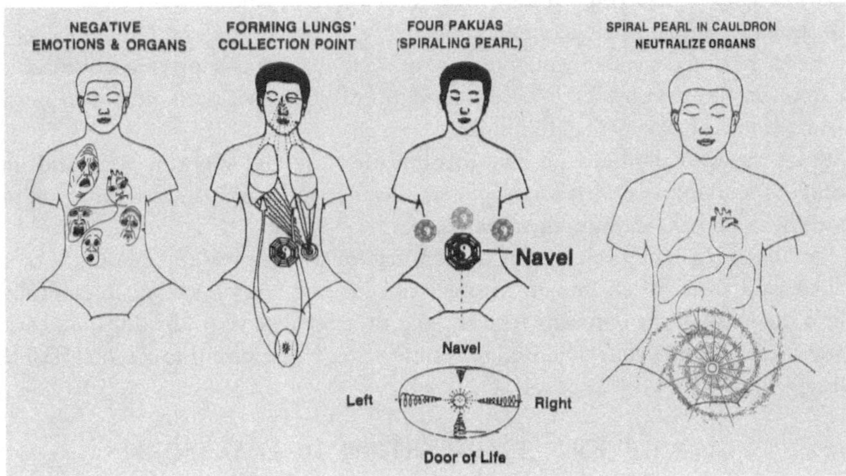

Perhaps the most radical therapeutic rejection of language that addresses psycho-emotional blockages and residues can be found in Taoist yogic alchemies. Taoist yogic practices use extensive visualizations, breathing, and postural approaches to achieve the goal of returning the body to a neutral state of liberated generative potential. Unlike some perspectives of emotional health, that view states such as happiness and joy as the goal, the Taoist model is rather neutrality. An empty vessel state that is relaxed, open, and responsive but neutrally de-stimulated.

In the Chinese medicine model, the various organs in the body are believed to govern our emotions. For example, the kidneys govern both gentleness and fear, the lungs courage and depression. The emotional residues are visualized as draining

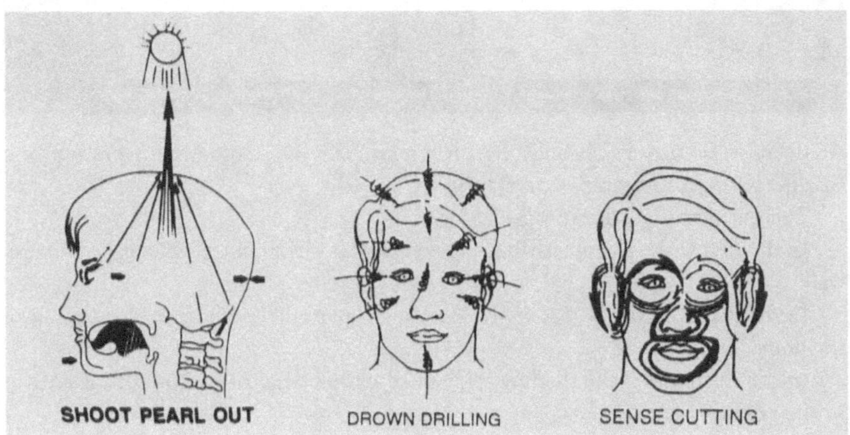

from the organs into collection points, then funneled to and shredded to bits by abdominally located processing units called pakuas. From here the broken down residues are drained to a naval cauldron in your abdomen.

The cauldron processes the emotional residues into a pearl that you shoot up out of the whale-spout at the top of your skull. The pearl then breaks into 50 pearls that penetrates your face, ripping up sediment of facial muscles, ripping up the residue of your brain, and cutting through the congestion of your ocular, oral, nasal, and auditory senses.

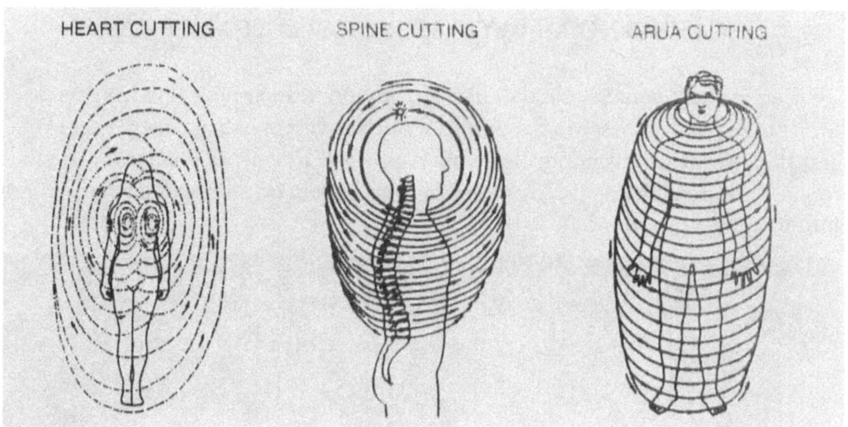

Then you feel the pearls of energy spiraling through the impurities in your heart, shredding tensions from your spine, and slicing the debris from your aura. These activities are repeated visualizing your energetic and spiritual bodies, in addition to the physical. Taking hypno-mimesis from focus on the dense physical body to our subtle bodies.

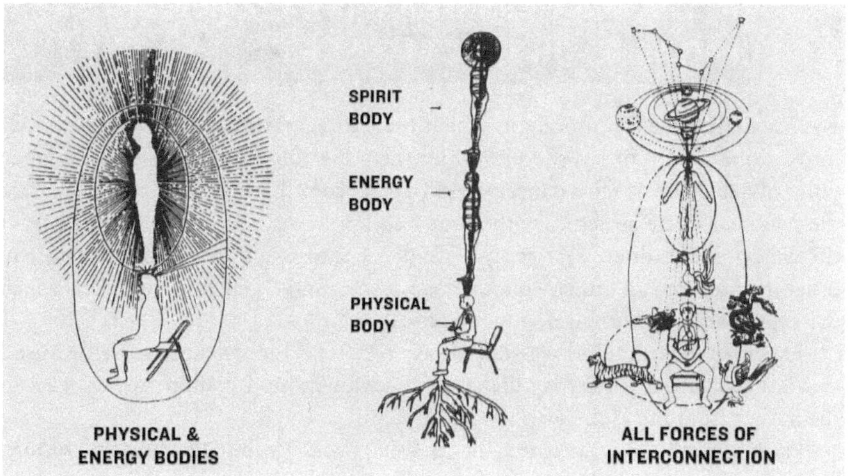

Note here, that time is not spent indulging ego narratives about our interpersonal life dramas, interpreting unconscious elements, or nurturing new identity patterns. We simply annihilate the energy residues and scarifications of our life experience from the energy field of the body directly and move on.

Note that research regarding the efficacy of non-verbal interventions for psycho-emotional conditions will always be limited in cultures that have no theory for energy bodies, notwithstanding their presence in medicinal systems that may have existed for thousands of years.

THE HYPNO-MIMETIC THRESHOLD OF MADNESS

Thus far we have contemplated de-personalization as an approach to transcend the limits of our ordinary selves for purposes of creativity, spiritual experience, magic, and therapeutic intervention. But what happens if this depersonalization is taken too far? Is it possible to push dissociation from a space of volitional involuntariness into total disintegration?

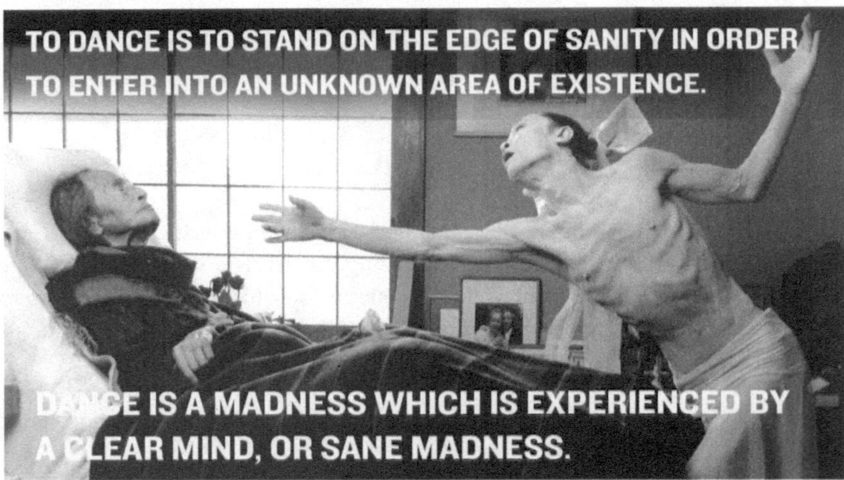

For Kasai, "Dance is a process in which the dancer transforms his/her own body into a work. That is to say, the author him/herself is the work." "This is the original point of departure which a dancer should always come back to. But if a dancer faces the Mobius's-circle structure without any compromise, there is no alternative for the dancer but madness", Kasai says. "To dance is to stand on the edge of sanity in order to enter into an unknown area of existence" And, "Dance is a madness which has experienced a clear mind, or a sane madness."

However, Kasai's mind was not always so clear. "I stopped dancing because I couldn't separate my everyday life as a dancer anymore. I couldn't separate me as the author from me as the work."

Pausing from the intensity of Butoh, Kasai grounded himself through

Eurhythmy, a spiritual form of movement developed by the Anthroposophists, under the auspices of Rudolf Steiner.

Kasai had used the anarchistically oriented Butoh, to dismantle centralized governance in his body; but to a disintegrating extreme. However, through the mystical-collectivist oriented Eurythmy, he hypno-mimetically harmonized his body with the sounds of language of humanity.

Kasai said, "I learned Eurythmy not only related to performance, but also to social art, in which facing the body means facing society." A statement quite close to the earlier corporeally collectivist statements of Decroux aligning the individual body, to society, and humankind. Furthermore, the species harmonization philosophy of Eurythmy's approach, is reminiscent of the collective trust belief earlier mentioned in the context of the Balinese, and a more integrative depersonalization of Vodoun trance.

Kasai said, "I heal myself through Eurythmy so I can get bogged deeper in the mud."

One of the must historically famous cases of dance and madness, cited by Kasai, is Vaslav Nijinsky, whose embodiment of the character become so total that he would remain in character at all times, subjugating his identity to the puppet Petrushka. Kasai says; "The dancer should be able to present his/her own existence as an ultimate action." And consequently, "After Nijinksy it became impossible for a dancer to regard his/her body simply as a means of expression. Today, every dancer faces the question; What is the body, what are the constituents of the body itself?"

The self-disintegration of madness was reflected in Nijinsky's diary from 1919, which "expressed his great fear of hospitalization and confinement. He filled it with drawings of eyes, as he felt himself under scrutiny, by his wife, a young doctor Frenkel, and others." A subjective state well expressed in Hijikata's Butoh.

HE IS AWARE THAT HE IS SLOWY DISINTEGRATED BECAUSE
HE IS BING WATCHED FROM ALL ANGLES.
AT FIRST HE IS AWARE OF SOMETHING
THAT IS STARING AT HIM FROM THE BACK
THEN HE IS AWARE OF SOMETHING
THAT STARES AT HIM FROM THE RIGHT AND FRONT
THEN HE IS AWARE OF SOMETHING
THAT STARES AT HIM FROM THE LEFT AND FRONT
THEN SOMETHING STARES AT HIM FROM HIS FEET
THEN FROM ABOVE
THIS PROCESS IS REPEATED AGAIN AND AGAIN UNTIL
THE BODY IS DISINTEGRATED
FINALLY THERE ARE ONLY PARTICLES
THE PARTICLES ARE AWARE
THAT THE WORLD AROUND THEM HAS ENTIRELY

CHANGED
THE PARTICLES CAN BECOME GHOSTS IF THEY ACQUIRE
SOME DAMPNESS

(Hijikata FU, Waguri 1994)

CONCLUSION

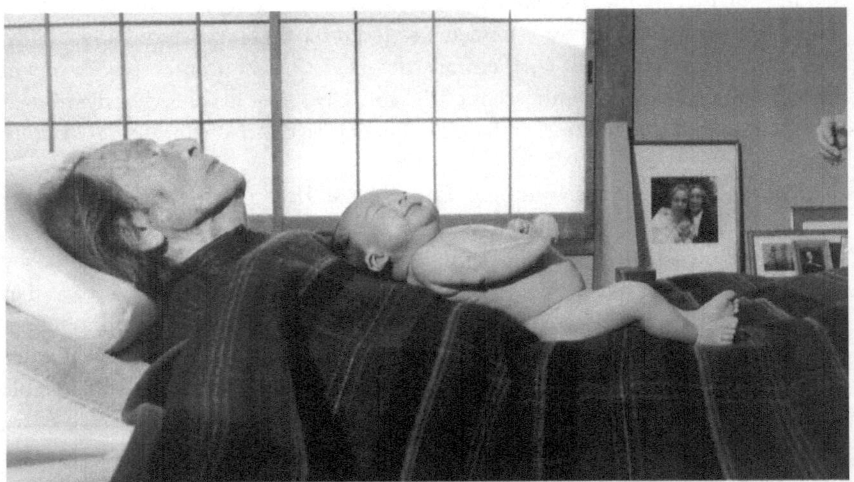

In our time together, we have contemplated the concept of hypno-mimesis in a broad array of contexts; the theatrical, therapeutic, yogic, cosmic, social, and magical. We have explored hypno-mimesis not only within these contexts, but as a challenge to the boundaries of these contexts.

I hope to have exposed you to ideas that will help you enter into deeper dialog with your body.

I would like to conclude this talk as I began it, with that of the child meditating on the corpse of his ancestor.

These questions we ask our bodies, in so many ways invite our ancestors into us. And just as we fall backwards into their nurturing vastness, so do they fall forward into our bodies' blossomings.

I look forward to being in contemplation with you all; asking questions that only the body can answer, as a vehicle of language for the universe itself, beyond our rational minds and egos.

Mantic Staining
– The Magical Paintings of Ithell Colquhoun

Stephanie Moran & Anna Sebastian

How might psychoanalysis and occultism be a means to experience a pre-conscious or mythical state of reality? Is painting a method through which this is most effectively realised? What are the connections between a divinatory painting practice and Carl Jung's thought and practice, specifically around colour theory, psychomorphology and theosophical 'Akashic records'? What is the relationship between psychoanalysis and occultism?

The artistic and occult practices of painter Ithell Colquhoun connect these questions. Colquhoun was a British artist, writer and occultist (1906-1988) who was associated with the British Surrealist movement until her excommunication. She was an initiate of a number of esoteric orders, including the O.T.O. Nu Isis Lodge and Countess Tamara Bourkhoun's Golden Dawn Order of the Phoenix, and was a deaconess of the druidic Ancient Celtic Church. Colquhoun's painting practice combines analytic and magical techniques for scrying. This paper will perform close readings of some of her works and the concepts she worked with, including Hermeticism, Theosophy, Qabalah and Psychism, as well as her use of surrealist techniques.

Introduction

> 1st woman: Where can we find the philosopher's stone, the end of the rainbow, the hole in the hedge or the mark on the sheet?
> A Man: In the holes the trees left when they were uprooted by the wind.[1]

In 1923 Carl Gustav Jung held a series of seminars in Polzeath Cornwall, at the Analytical Psychology club. The seminars covered topics of analytic transference in psychoanalysis, the power of the symbol and magic. In the same year, at the age of 17, Ithell Colquhoun's lifelong interest in occultism was stimulated on reading a newspaper account of Aleister Crowley's Abbey of Thelema.[2]

Synchronicity underpins divination. Interpreted quite simply by Jung as 'meaningful coincidences'.[3] Synchronicity connects to processes of the unconscious in which time moves differently, and events or moments correspond symbolically,

---

1 Colquhoun, Alloway and Southey, 'Question-and-Answer Threesome'
2 https://wrldrels.org/2017/08/11/margaret-ithell-colquhoun/
3 Jung, *Synchronicity, An Acausal Connecting Principle*, ix.

"a correspondence between the physical and spiritual worlds".[4] Jung's arrival in Cornwall, Colquhoun's relationship to Cornwall, and the relationship they both had to the unconscious and automatic processes, creates a correspondence through time. Colquhoun identified nature as an interconnected system. She used Qabalistic and alchemical principles, and the structure of initiations proposed by the Golden Dawn as well as those of the other esoteric organisations of which she was a member.

While still a student Colquhoun wrote 'The Prose of Alchemy' for the *Quest* magazine. In 1928 she also joined the affiliated organisation, G.R.S. Mead's Quest society, an offshoot of the Theosophical Society, where her cousin was secretary. Colquhoun applied to be a member of the Golden Dawn and although her membership was rejected, the Golden Dawn continued to be enormously significant for her. She shared the group's vision of founding a unified magical system, drawing on both eastern and western traditions. She shared their use of an Indian symbolic system called Tattvas and applied the Golden Dawn's colour system in her paintings and Taro cards. Her monograph about the Golden Dawn and its founder, McGregor Mathers, was published in 1975.[5] Evidently, Colquhoun was a powerful and magical thinker from early on, and she continued to follow that path throughout her life.

Ithell Colquhoun attended the opening of the 1936 Surrealist exhibition in London, an event that introduced her art's imaginative power to extend reality, isolating and empowering significant and invisible potentials. She was particularly struck by the artist Salvador Dali's performance as he emerged, with two wolfhounds on a leash, suffocating in diving gear from which he needed to be rescued by his wife, Gala. There was a potency to the atmosphere as though he had evoked 'phantasmic presences'.[6] That summer in France, surrealist painters including Roberto Matta, Estaben Frances and Gordon Onslow Ford, would introduce her to psychomorphology, a practice of automatic processes which would later define her own practice, providing a method through which her artworks became magical objects.

Colquhoun joined the surrealists at a moment of a fundamental shift in the perception of women in society and their role within esotericism. Colquhoun wrote about and powerfully portrayed the landscape as sexually ambiguous, hermaphroditic and powerfully female. Such visions appeared subversive to the male-led surrealists, whose works and writings idealised the erotic power of the feminine.

Despite her membership of various organisations Colquhoun was fiercely independent (which is why she was later expelled from the British surrealists). She was committed to the exploration of magic, the landscape, and the inner self. Connections she perceived between the self and the cosmos drew her attention

---

4 Ibid.

5 Colquhoun, *The Sword of Wisdom: MacGregor Mathers and the Golden Dawn.*

6 Colquhoun, *Surrealism.*

to the Qabalah and the four worlds that comprised the Qabalistic tree of life. Her paintings and poetry, in the spirit of surrealism, extended vision from the sensorial world of the everyday, to parallel and possibly higher realms of existence. She recorded her dreams and used a variety of automatic processes to see into these worlds. She is distinguished from other surrealists by her commitment to mobilising the mediumistic possibilities of these processes. For Colquhoun the occult delivered of the modernist project what the surrealist group only vacantly promised: embrace of female power and emancipation; a collective vision and a living spiritual practice.

SURREALISM

The Surrealist revolution, its exploration of inner worlds and creation of new mythologies, seemed to invite connections between the unconscious and the hermetic to expand reality.[7] Surrealists' overt influences ranged from Sigmund Freud to writers of the French occult revival such as Eliphas Lévi. For Freud, psychoanalysis might be a scientific practice or a therapy, an attempt at understanding the inner mechanisms of the self, accessed via a variety of procedures towards unifying the disintegrated self within wider society. Its relationship to occultism is complicated. Discourses of the mind, symbolic investigation of memory and dream, the presence of spirits and revisiting repressed memory all have histories within older traditions of shamanism and the esoteric. Occultist Israel Regardie correlates psychoanalysis with magical techniques. He describes the mechanisms used to climb the Qabalistic tree of life and rejoin the Ain Soph; these include symbolism, astrology, numerology, geomancy and the tarot.[8] Israel Regardie joined the Golden Dawn in 1938 and Colquhoun was familiar with his work. He was the first scholar to publish the previously secret rituals and thoughts of the Golden Dawn. Surrealism mobilised psychoanalytic techniques, arguably returning the sacred to the desacralised contemporary world.

Surrealism was influenced by developments in psychoanalysis. Surrealist leader André Breton visited Freud in Vienna in 1921 to discuss his work, 'On the Interpretation of Dreams'. Within the dream the surrealists saw the marriage of two states, a "conciliation of opposites".[9] For the surrealists, dreams allowed one to access a variety of states that were complementary to the waking state.[10] Dream states appeared to offer something beyond symbolic reference to repressed memories and an individual's unconscious desire. Surrealists saw in them a connection to myth, fantasy, prophecy and the libido; a space where time moves differently, connecting to something eternal, with no past future and present. They viewed them as an extension that was imaginatively free and difficult to experience in our waking lives. The exploration of the dream world as a legitimate reality asks, what is reality and

7 Balakian, *Surrealism: the Road to the Absolute*, 13.
8 Regardie, *The Middle Pillar.*
9 Ibid, 132
10 Ibid, 127

what is consciousness? To Freud, this experiment in perception would mean the disintegration of the personality; unless the surrealists could unify the personality through their processes, the experiment was perplexing.[11]

The Freudian unconscious was populated by the repressed memories of an individual. By contrast, Jung's unconscious could be an otherwise shared space, populated by archetypes with a commonality found in myth. Jung referred to this space as the collective unconscious; he also defined it against the waking world; the 'spirit of the depths' versus the 'spirit of time' (concerned with 'use' and 'value').[12] Colquhoun approached the collective unconscious as another world, populated by entities and energies which could be encountered through focused thought and realised through her images and poetry. She underwent Jungian psychotherapy and dream interpretation under Alice Buck for an extended period of time around the 1950s.[13] Carl Jung, like Colquhoun, wrote and painted images with strong pagan symbology, as though to invoke these forgotten faiths (explicit in his *Red Book*). Colquhoun's work further expresses this parallel by exploring Jungian psychical dialectical opposites of alchemical hermaphroditism.

Surrealism provided Colquhoun with the tools with which she could make paintings as magical objects. She travelled into the unconscious as a medium and channelled the experience through painting. Her images become not only depictions of a random occurrence, or of images seen in the dream space, but entities themselves. Their stylistic alienness is a manifestation of their inter dimensional status.

Symbolism

> I cannot now think symbols less than the greatest of all powers whether they are used consciously by the masters of magic, or half unconsciously by their successors, the poet, the musician and the artist.[14]

In one of his 1923 Cornwall seminars, Jung proposed that images were equivalent to magical objects. An image or symbol provides psychic energy with form, which is the reason magicians make images, "for such things are energy, magical energy".[15] The image as a symbol predates written language and connects the image maker to the deeper meaning of the landscape, its inhabitants and the energetic forces within it, implementing the subject with a sacred significance. An accomplished magician, like the artist, is capable of utilising symbols with precision to achieve a desired intention, communicate it, and to mediate between planes of existence. A symbol that resonates is capable of instilling an attractive force upon its audience, haunting them after their encounter. For an image to haunt, it relies on its components, such

---

11 Ibid, 132
12 Jung and Shamdasani. *The Red Book, Liber Novus*, 229.
13 Colquhoun, *I Saw Water: an Occult Novel and Other Selected Writings*, 20.
14 Yeats, *Ideas of Good and Evil.* 64
15 Jung, "The Nature of the Value of Objects."

as the colours and composition, to be in the right place. On the surface this appears simple, but the subjectivity of 'the right place', requires subtlety and understanding on the part of the maker.

Colquhoun conducted research into numerous esoteric systems and occult orders. Like many Modernist artists and occultists, she synthesised and incorporated symbols from a variety of different systems, finding correspondences between some and treating others separately, using them as appropriate for what she wanted to achieve. She created alternative diagrams of the tree of life, suggesting its transferability across man, woman, plants, animals and even atomic structures. There is a sense of a mathematical process which may come from much of Colquhoun's source material. She drew heavily on Hindu mystical concepts and Tantric thought, which themselves have been revealed to connect to mathematics. In *The Vedic Mathematics of Sankaracarya*, Bharati Krsna Tirtha applies the Vedic Sutras to mathematical problems, and the Sutras reveal truths about the mathematical structures of the universe, grasped through magical and mystical methods. The Sanskrit religious text *The Science of Breath & the Philosophy of the Tattvas* is also highly scientific.

As an artist, Colquhoun was particularly interested in colour systems. Her 1934 essay 'Explanation of a Design for a Painting on Silk'[16] describes distinctive colour scales attributed by the Golden Dawn to the four worlds of the Qabalistic tree of life. Golden Dawn founder McGregor Mathers devised four colour charts for the four worlds and four trees of life. The four worlds are: Atziluth (the archetypal world), Briah (the creative world), Ietzirah (the formative world) and Assiah (the material world). The corresponding colour charts are King, Queen, Prince, and Princess. The King scale is intended to represent the highest or most abstract of the four Qabalistic Worlds, the world of Atziluth which proceeds directly from the Ain Soph.[17] Colquhoun assigns symbolic power to colour, working between the spaces of intuition and instruction. Symbols and colour become meditative portal guns, allowing the subject to access the invisible worlds of the Qabalistic tree. Her paintings are maps for navigating the space of these unseen, magical forces. She uses colour and line to describe the nature and connection of the subjects she depicts, giving form to the landscape of the 'Anima Mundi', or 'Great record' conceived of by Yeats: a record of all that had happened to mankind, which could be evoked by symbols.[18] In 'Design On Silk', Colquhoun analyses the symbolic and aesthetic choices of a design she had created. She wrote about the colour charts and their relation to her images, demonstrating a practical application of Qabalistic knowledge.

DIVINATION

Although she was never granted initiation into the Golden Dawn, Colquhoun was

16 Unpublished manuscript, Tate Gallery Archive (TGA 929/2/1/23)
17 Colquhoun and Nichols (ed.), *The Magical Writings of Ithell Colquhoun*, 47.
18 Havredaki, "In search of a common myth: Influences of mysticism and occultism in W. B. Yeats's "A Vision"".

extremely interested in their methods and researched them thoroughly. Colquhoun was familiar with their use of the Tattvas and the Akashic record, and referred to both in her research and divinatory practice.[19] The writings of Rama Prasad are the source for the Golden Dawn Tattva teaching and also Colquhoun's likely source. Prasad's series of articles "Nature's Finer Forces", describing ideas from Hindu texts, were published in *The Theosophist* (1887-89). These were combined alongside his translation of the Sanskrit texts in his book *The Science of Breath & the Philosophy of the Tattvas*.

There are five Tattvas (or Tattwas), or elements of the Hindu Pranas, which Prasad describes as "the five modifications of the Great Breath". These are known as: Akasha, Vayu, Apas, Prithivi and Tejas. Tattvas are the things that give birth to the vibration that constitutes the phenomena of sound, touch, taste, smell, light. We do not perceive these ethereal vibrations directly, only as they are mediated through things, materials. These phenomena are constituted from vibrations of the element or Tattva, and each one has a different vibratory motion and function. Prasad suggests 'soniferous ether' for Akasha, 'tangiferous ether' for Vayu, 'gustiferous ether' for Apas, 'odiferous ether' for Prithivi, and 'luminiferous ether' for Tejas. Each Tattva is ascribed a symbol with a specific colour, which were often used as divinatory aids.

The term Akashic comes from *Akasa*, the Tattva that contains a sonic element, or soniferous ether. The Akashic records, originating in theosophical thought, are considered a kind of database of every word, thought or action that has ever happened, stored as sorts of energetic prints and encoded in a non-physical plane of existence, also called the etheric plane. They are thought of as a kind of computational substrate, and more recently related to Quantum Physics, as an enduring memory of the universe stored rather as in a computer memory.[20] The Akashic records can be accessed through deep meditative states. The Akashic records contain information about every Soul that has lived, everything that has happened or been thought, and connects each of us to one another. They are sometimes compared to Jung's collective unconscious, but we believe this is inaccurate. The Akashic records have nothing to do with archetypes or representations, they are a complete historical record contained in energetic matter.

Colquhoun specifically used the Tattvas for scrying, probably not just as symbols to meditate on, but also in considering the Tattvic tides – the times of day associated with each Tattva – when working with elemental forces. We also believe she would have included all nonhuman thoughts and events within her conceptualisation of the Akashic record, from geological substrates and stones to single-celled organisms, to birds, plants and bodies of water.

---

19 Colquhoun and Nicholls (ed.), *The Magical Writings of Ithell Colquhoun.*
20 Laszlo, *Science and the Akashic Field: An Integral Theory of Everything*

Mantic Staining

COLQUHOUN'S PAINTINGS

Root of the powers of earth
Root of the powers of air
Root of the powers of water
Root of the powers of fire[21]

The works of Ithell Colquhoun combine surrealist techniques with esoteric knowledge in order to access and communicate with other realms and a collective, ahistorical, unconscious often referred to as the Akashic record. Colquhoun's use of surrealist automatic process, elaborated in her essay 'Children of the Mantic Stain', aimed to detach her images from personal unconscious or ego, to reawaken and reveal the knowledge of ancient communities. Heavily influenced by the automatic writing, hermeticism and Celtic mythology of W. B. Yeats, she fused myth and landscape in her paintings, drawing intensely from the Cornwall landscape, to excavate a timeless, transpersonal psyche. She drew on historical references to ancient Druid practices and pagan relationships to the land, as embodied in the standing stones that populate Cornwall. The reference to Indian practices such as the Tattvas offered a link to her family history. Generations of her family lived in India but she left as a child, too early to have a direct experience and link with the land and its culture.[22] There was perhaps some nostalgia for what she had missed that propelled her to a deeper understanding of Celtic history in order to construct a bond with the new land she was inhabiting.

Colquhoun systematised her painting divination process, an automatic technique developed from Surrealist psychomorphology. For Colquhoun, the automatism is only the first step and the most interesting images generally come through the work of interpretation, after the liberation of the automatism. Colquhoun outlines thirteen methods for automatic image production. She compares the process to both a kind of inverse (or developed) Rorschach method – the artist or patient evolves their own stains and interprets them – and to reading the tea leaves, or scrying. This is why she names it the mantic stain – mantic, from the Greek word *mantikos*, derived from *mantis*, meaning "prophet".

Colquhoun explains the paintings' divinatory power from her observations that all of these automatic processes, while each leading to their own specific morphologies, reflect the unconscious mood of the 'operator':

> If a number of experiments in a single process are undertaken in one day a great similarity of forms will be noticeable throughout. The same operator experimenting with the same process on another day will produce a quite different series of images, though these latter will be linked to one another

21 Colquhoun, *Decad Of Intelligence*. From Decad 1, Keter, admirable or hidden intelligence.
22 Hale, *Ithell Colquhoun: Genius of the Fern Loved Gully*, 19.

by a certain 'family likeness.'[23]

She connects this mantic psycho-temporal variation of forms to alchemic projection, and Jung's description of the alchemist releasing their own phantasy world into the alembic as they watch its contents intently.[24] She further suggests a correspondence between media of the automatic process and elemental energies: for example, fumage, made by flames, relates to fire; 'shut-eye' drawing to darkness. Ecremage (skimming) and parsemage relate to water: processes that involve floating oil paint, powdered chalk or charcoal on the surface of water and gently skimming the resulting random pattern from it by placing paper or canvas onto it.

The Merry Maidens Circle and The Dance of the Nine Opals, 1942

The Merry Maidens stone circle is a late stone age/early bronze age stone circle near Lamorna, where Colquhoun spent many years. It marked a burial mound but was comprised of nineteen stones of diminishing sizes suggesting an alternative use as a lunar calendar (the lunar cycle being nineteen years). Two standing stones are behind, marking a ceremonial causeway. The name Merry Maidens is an interpretation of its Cornish designation 'Dans Meyn' (the Dancing stones). A story evolved that the stones were petrified women, turned into stone for dancing on the sabbath.

In Colquhoun's painting 'Dance of the Nine Opals', the nineteen stones are reduced to nine and significant colours of red, yellow, blue and purple imbue them with spiritual power. She threads brilliant white lines between and around the stones, creating a protective sphere around them. A tree grows from deep in the earth as though the stones and their musical souls have conjoined their energy, and that of the cosmos,[25] to project a complete tree of life at its centre. The green path through the middle is a line of directive force to a gateway in mountains which she imagines. This could be a pathway for the initiate to enter a next world or level of reality. Or perhaps it is that final gate that one passes through in death, signifying a break from the material kingdom of Malkuth.

Colquhoun clearly used the King colour chart for Dance of the Nine Opals, which is significant. She identifies Atziluth, the archetypal world, as a parallel and utterly real plane of existence. Her painting visualizes the bonds, energetic fields and corresponding natures of the stones to the landscape. The realm of Malkuth forms the ground for the stones, circular like the Sephirot, it is defined by yellow. The sky (much like the cosmic Sky of the Akashic records) is defined by a pale blue representing Chokmah, the principle of wisdom: the second sephiroth, conceived of as formless and creative potential. The crimson of Binah defines the ground

---

23 Colquhoun, "Mantic Stain", 33.

24 Jung, *Psychology and Alchemy.*

25 The Merry maiden stone circle, 'Dans Maen', is thought to have originally been composed of eighteen stones, although today it contains nineteen. The stones could have been used as both a sacred site of a pagan / druidic ritual and a lunar calendar acknowledging the nineteen-year cycle of the moon.

below and around the stones, and Binah is a principle of understanding and an implanting of intelligence and wisdom, identified as a female principle and is a principle of restriction, giving the creative potential of Chokmah form. One could interpret this as an ocean of water, being siphoned into rivers. The mountains, in white, corresponds to the brilliance of Kether, the Crown, positioned at the top of the tree. It is a synthesis of white brilliance which exists when the coloured rays from the other sephiroth are in balance. The mountains as imaginary or rather archetypal, in line with the immaterial nature of Atziluth.

The stones are painted with dancing flecks of all the colours of the scale, as though they are as alive as we are; a testament to her quest to "achieve a union of natural and spiritual forces as well as a union of the disciplines of art and the occult."[26] In all, the image poses a distinction between the Kingdom of Malkuth, the world of matter, and the supernal triangle, that of Binah (understanding), Chokmah (wisdom) and Kether (Crown).

Mên-an-Tol

Colquhoun's engagement and identification with all aspects of the landscape as sacred and mystical is a key to her work. Her three books *Crying of the Wind, The Goose of Hermogenes* and *The Living Stones* can all be read as time-travelling occult travelogues. These are travelogues that map the astral planes of trees, rivers and rocks as well as the landscape's more transient organisms, including humans. Colquhoun identifies herself as an animist in *The Living Stones*. This can be seen in her paintings too. She attempts to uncover eternal and transtemporal fact and truths in communication with the rest of nature, and through manipulation of paint. Paint is a perfect medium – a fluid method for channelling energies and generating imagery for interpretation by those with the knowledge and feeling for it. Many painters feel the sense of being possessed by the process, or channelling forms, ideas, emotions, in a trance-like or meditative state. Colquhoun combined this with research into the mythology connected to the spirit of the land, particularly Celtic myth, through her research and practice as a Deaconess of the druidic Ancient Celtic Church. She was especially interested in the stone: as the geological substrate of the land, which she believed determined its character, and as used in ancient stone circles and rituals. As she says, "the structure of the rocks gives rise to the psychic life of the land", each strata and kind of rock "being co-existent with a special phase of the earth-spirit manifestation".[27]

Colquhoun painted and sketched a rock formation in Cornwall called Mên an Tol. A passage from *The Living Stones* describes an attempt to use the Mên-an-Tol to cure herself of rheumatism. Her attempt was unsuccessful, which she attributes to a prerequisite of nudity in crawling through the stone 'from East to West'. Mên-

---

26 Shillitoe, Richard. "The Major Themes." The major themes. Accessed February 14, 2019. http://www.ithellcolquhoun.co.uk/ordering_the_cosmos.htm
27 Colquhoun, *The Living Stones*, 57.

Activating Mên-an-Tol by Anna Sebastian

an-Tol has unknown origins. It may have been a natural formation, as a tor, turned on its side by ancient inhabitants. It was very likely used for fertility rites. In one of her studies of Mên-an-Tol, Colquhoun dynamically depicts a woman stretched out between the rocks, her chakras aligned with them, and her feet and hands grasping the standing stones on either side. An uncovering of a kind of Celtic earth mother that she identifies with.[28] She painted the formation in 1942, tracing coloured lines between and under it like an energy force field, as though the stones are activated by the ground; these could be seen as manifestations of the Akashic records, or signifiers of natural power centres much like leyline theory, which Colquhoun may have been only vaguely aware of as it had not yet entered into common esoteric usage.

As a practicing artist, Anna Sebastian explores Colquhoun's areas of research through her own art production. Colquhoun's various drawings, paintings and descriptions of sacred sites, such as Mên-an-Tol and the Merry Maidens, highlight their historical importance. Many of the standing stones and stone circles are made of granite, so extraordinarily heavy to move. The myths attached to them, presumably as a Christian deterrent, only add to their mystique. Anna says:

---

28 In *The Goose of Hermogenes* she writes of the appearance of a similar feminine spirit as the soul of Britain and the earth, connecting everything that is alive: "She is the type of hero-woman, both mother and warrior, debased long since as Britannia but stemming from the ancient line of foundered Atlantis... I cannot but search for her everywhere and I find her in the land's own long memory" (p72)

In the past I had spoken to a Haitian Houngan, a vodou priest, who insisted that there were a certain number of gates to another world. These gates had physical locations, and a portal could be constructed by the synthesis of man and nature. In the construction of these sites, did the ancient druids feel closest to the sacred, based on intuitive principles through a relationship cultivated with nature? Did they manifest energetic and sacred significance through the building of these monuments and create portals to alternative locations, and if so could I travel through them? My image hypothesises instructions on how to activate a portal in line with Colquhoun's own writings, by crawling through the central ring from East to West. In passing through the portal that is Mên-an-Tol, one is reborn by stone.

ALCOVE

Alcove, 1948, uses the technique of decalcomania which Colquhoun aligns with Earth. Decalcomania is the process of randomly applying blobs of paint to a primed surface, then pressing a sheet of paper or canvas onto it; when removed, forms found in the blots can be worked into. It can be seen as an interior space, even a bodily interior, perhaps a womb-like space – the walls are fleshy and bloody, visceral. The blue and yellow central motif could be a figure lying on a couch, perhaps a psychoanalyst's couch, or a figure sleeping. The image is a metaphor for creation. In the Qabalistic text, the *Zohar*, King Solomon raises a nut in the air and sees its hard shell and the fruit it contains analogous to the upper and lower world, and to the relation of the body to the nature of the soul.

Colquhoun's image is an abstract formulation of a creation myth. Like the creation of the supernal Adam, the first man, through the twisting forms held in the centre of the frame, resonating with the fundamental twist of the male and female paths of the Qabalah. The image was instigated by an automatic process but by returning to it, Colquhoun demonstrates her desire to recognise the significance of its form. The result is a manifestation of the process used to create it: formless creative potential given form through understanding. It could be described as an act of divination.

TRITON

The entwined form, like that of the hermaphrodite, suggests the conjunction of opposing forces to produce a new entity, grown in the womb. The colours around the object change as though the figure born has altered the womb like vessel it inhabits. The act of pulling apart the paper to reveal this form relates to the notion of the hermaphrodite:

Thou wilt observe that the colours of the Paths and the Sephiroth form a mutual balance and harmony of the Tree. Colours are forces, the signatures of the forces; and the child of the children of the forces art thou.[29]

There is a similar double image in stillomantic process but it is on the same piece of paper, as Colquhoun's painting *Triton* demonstrates.

The figure of the hermaphrodite represents the harmonious masculine and feminine aspects significant for many Modernist occult orders, as well as for the surrealists, which emphasised the need for both male and female divinities, masculine and feminine energies. Eliphas Lévi, who was influential for early 20th century occult orders and for the surrealists, argues for the importance of women's sexuality and connection to nature.[30] They were all interested in male-female duality. Israel Regardie speaks of the importance of balance, and as he says, "It will readily be conceded that every person is psychologically bisexual." He relates the Eastern yin and yang via Jung and his animus and anima, to the Qabalah's Chiah and Neshamah.[31]

Jung, heavily influenced by alchemy, conceived of the hermaphrodite as an archetypal symbol of the philosopher's stone and nature of an individual as a composite of masculine and feminine principles. Jung's concept is contained in the image of the 'Gnostic anthropos, the divine original man'.[32] Encased in the image of the hermaphrodite is the conjunction of opposing forces, both physical and psychic: sulphur and mercury, sol and lunar, fire and water, male and female. Jung regards the physical art of manufacturing the stone akin to a psychological process. Instructions for the manufacture of the stone were often cryptic, demanding the alchemist to use their imagination in the process of making the stone. The instructions may be read as a scaffold for the psychic transformation. Indeed, Jung suggests the work of the alchemist is reliant on their capacity to perceive signs and equivalencies within lived reality:

> To cause things in the shadow to appear, and to take away the shadow from them, this is permitted to the intelligent philosopher by God through nature… All these things happen, and the eyes of the common men do not see them, but the eyes of the understanding {intellectus] and of the imagination perceive them [percipiunt] with true and truest vision [visu].[33]

29 Regardie, *The Golden Dawn: an Account of the Teachings, Rites and Ceremonies of the Order of the Golden Dawn*, 570.

30 Shillitoe, *Magician Born of Nature*.

31 Regardie, *The Middle Pillar*, 31

32 Jung, *Psychology and Alchemy*, 232. "Matter is thus transformed through illusion, which is necessarily that of the alchemist. This illusion might well be the vera imaginatio possessed of 'informing power'" (ibid, 252) "The fact that visions aligned themselves to the alchemical work may also explain why dreams or dream visions are often mentioned as important intermezzi or as sources of revelation" (ibid, 252) "It is repeatedly stated that the much sought after aqua permanens would be revealed in a dream. Generally speaking the Prima Materia, indeed the stone itself – or the secret of its production – is revealed to the operator by God" (ibid, 252-253).

33 Sendivogus. *Novum Lumen. Mus herm.* 574. Jung, *Psychology and Alchemy*, 250

In the act of making the image, Colquhoun acknowledges the synthesis of the primal matter of the unconscious image to its conscious refinement. Her work uncovers the hidden life force within herself, the seed of being itself. It is moving and luminescent, using the colours of Qabalistic forces and shapes which echo the double helix. Tapping into symbols of the basic life force within all living things, arching back to the story of the creation of the cosmos, the conjunction of the moon and the sun, and the supernal Adam.

CONCLUSION

Sphere of Venus
Pillar of fire
Victory a beautiful naked woman
– Ithell Colquhoun[34]

Ithell Colquhoun's later masterworks emerged from automatic processes and use of surrealist psychomorphology. She first selected her colour palette and process, deciding on appropriate systems for what she wanted to achieve or connect to, as in any ritual. The making of all art is to reveal unseen potentials in the internal or external world. It is to explore the invisible, underlying structure of the universe, and of being itself, as an endless quest for the magician, the psychoanalyst and the artist.

Colquhoun's use of colour as a divinatory tool draws on the established colour principles of esoteric organisations in their endeavour to climb the tree of life. But her images break with the conventions of established symbols, falling between figuration and abstraction, as a result of her efforts to strip away the aesthetic form of the representation as an archetype, to find its essence though colour and shape.

Colquhoun developed sophisticated systems of nondeterministic generation through her research and her practice, to produce a divinatory framework for focusing intent that would be open to natural and spiritual forces. Like most modernist occultists, she synthesised and adapted this framework from existing traditions, myth and occult colour systems, including Hindu religious and mystical texts, the Qabalah, Celtic Druidry, theosophy and surrealist techniques.

Colquhoun had a deep fascination for the landscape, performing transtemporal explorations through engaging with land and stone rituals and mythologies, attempting to connect to the earth-spirit, to its transpersonal psyche, and Akashic records. Indeed, in seeking gnosis in the natural and external world, Colquhoun presents an ultimate philosophical dispute with the surrealists who, in basing their movement on psychoanalytic progressions, perceived an external reality as repressive, in contrast to the liberation and transcendence that could be found within an inner psychic world.[35] Ithell Colquhoun fearlessly pursued her connection to the

---

34 Colquhoun, *Decad Of Intelligence,* from Decad 7: Hod
35 Ades, "Notes on Two Women Surrealist Painters: Eileen Agar and Ithell Colquhoun".

landscape through a revival of pagan and druidic thought. Embodying within her art and her life the magical processes she diligently studied, utterly negating the role of 'object woman'[36] that surrealism encouraged.

REFERENCES

—⁓— Ades, D. "Notes on Two Women Surrealist Painters: Eileen Agar and Ithell Colquhoun." *Oxford Art Journal* 3, no. 1 (1980): 36–43. https://doi.org/10.1093/oxartj/3.1.36.

—⁓— Balakian, Anna. *Surrealism: the Road to the Absolute.* 2. 1st ed. Vol. 2. Chicago, IL: University of Chicago Press, 1970.

—⁓— Colquhoun , Ithell. "Children of the Mantic Stain." *Athene* 5, 1951, 2 edition.

—⁓— Colquhoun, Ithell, Peter Owen, and R. W. Shillitoe. *Goose of Hermogenes.* London: Peter Owen Publishers, 2018.

—⁓— Colquhoun, Ithell, Richard W. Shillitoe, and Mark S. Morrisson. *I Saw Water: an Occult Novel and Other Selected Writings.* University Park, PA: The Pennsylvania State University Press, 2014.

—⁓— Colquhoun, Ithell. Edited by Rupert White, Rosie Thomson-Glover, Cat Bagg, and Nigel Ayers. *Surrealism Ithell Colquhoun.* artcornwall.org, January 1976. http://www.artcornwall.org/features/Surrealism_Ithell_Colquhoun.htm.

—⁓— Colquhoun, Ithell. *Sword of Wisdom: MacGregor Mathers and the Golden Dawn.* New York: Putnam, 1975.

—⁓— Colquhoun, Ithell. *Decad of Intelligence.* Somerset: Fulgur Press, 2016.

—⁓— Colquhoun, Ithell. 'Explanation of a Design for a Painting on Silk'. 1934. Unpublished manuscript, Tate Gallery Archive (TGA 929/2/1/23)

—⁓— Colquhoun, Ithell. *The Magical Writings of Ithell Colquhoun.* Edited by Steve Nichols. Morrisville, NC: Lulu Enterprises UK Ltd, 2007.

—⁓— Colquhoun, Ithell. "The Mantic Stain". *Enquiry*, 1949, 2 (4): 15–21.

—⁓— Colquhoun, Ithell, Lawrence Alloway and Paul Southey, Typescript titled 'Question-and-Answer Threesome'. Date unknown, Tate Archives TGA 929/2/2/3/7

—⁓— Ferentinou, Victoria. "Margaret Ithell Colquhoun." *WRSP*, August 11, 2017. https://wrldrels.org/2017/08/11/margaret-ithell-colquhoun/

—⁓— Hale, Amy. *Ithell Colquhoun: Genius of the Fern Loved Gully.* London, UK: Strange Attractor Press, 2020.

—⁓— Hale, A. (2012). 'The Magical Life of Ithell Colquhoun'. In Drury, N. (ed.), *Pathways in Modern Western Magic.* Richmond CA: Concrescent.

—⁓— Havredaki, Irene Georgiou. *In search of a common myth: Influences of mysticism and occultism in W. B. Yeats's "A Vision".* University of Connecticut, ProQuest Dissertations Publishing, 1991.

---

36 Ibid.

—∾— Jung, C. G. Unauthorised notes by M. Esther Harding. "The Nature of the Value of Objects." Human Relationships in Relation to the Process of Individuation. Lecture presented at the Cornwall Seminars, July 1923. Accessed from Yale University Library Beinecke Rare Book and Manuscript Library

—∾— Jung, C. G. *Psychology and Alchemy*. Translated by R. F. C. Hull. 12. 3rd ed. Vol. 12. London: Routledge & Kegan, 1980.

—∾— Jung, C. G., and Sonu Shamdasani. *The Red Book, Liber Novus*. Translated by Mark Kyburz and John Peck. New York, New York: W.W. Norton, 2009.

—∾— Jung, Carl Gustav. *Synchronicity, An Acausal Connecting Principle* . 8. 5th ed. Vol. 8. Princeton, New Jersey: Princeton University Press, 2011.

—∾— Laszlo, Ervin, *Science and the Akashic Field: An Integral Theory of Everything,* Rochester, Vermont: Inner Traditions, 2007.

—∾— Prasad, Rama. *The Science of Breath and the Philosophy of the Tattwas*. London: The Theosophical Publishing Society, 1907.

—∾— Regardie, Israel. *The Golden Dawn: an Account of the Teachings, Rites and Ceremonies of the Order of the Golden Dawn*. St. Paul, MN: Llewellyn Publications, 1982.

—∾— Regardie, Israel. *The Middle Pillar: The Balance Between Mind and Magic*. St Paul MN: Llewellyn Publications, 2004.

—∾— Shillitoe, Richard. *Ithell Colquhoun: Magician Born of Nature,* Morrisville, NC: Lulu Enterprises UK Ltd, 2011.

—∾— Shillitoe, Richard. "The Major Themes." The major themes. Accessed February 14, 2019. http://www.ithellcolquhoun.co.uk/the_major_themes.htm.

—∾— Yeats, W. B. *Magic. Ideas of Good and Evil.* London. A. H. Bullen, 1903

Poetry as Magic

Katy Bohinc

In time, with the European colonization so too came their grimoires, their spirits and their theology, and as Obeah itself moved within this whirlwind of beliefs that was – and still is – the Caribbean, its practitioners inevitably encountered the material, absorbing and adapting its spirits to the technologies they knew.

– From occultist Julio Cesar Ody's *Magister Officiorum*

In 2016 I participated in the Psychoanalysis, Art and The Occult conference in London. The conference was fascinating. It was organized by Vanessa Sinclair (co-founder of Das Unbehagen—a key group of Lacanians in NYC & world-wide) and Carl Abrahamsson (who is a well-known occultist author and artist in Scandanavia and throughout Europe). True to title, the conference focused on the intersection of psychoanalysis, art, and the occult—and the main thrust of the discussion was that Western psychoanalysis needed to open up to occult paradigms if they were going to treat an international audience. So for example, how to treat a Haitian patient who believes that psychotic breaks can sometimes be interpreted as a spiritual message from another realm.

There were discussions of various systems of occult thought from around the world, alongside discussions by experts in psychoanalysis and Freudian history. There was discourse around initial investigations of the occult by founding fathers, Freud and Jung (spoiler alert: Freud was more into the occult than most people acknowledge, and there were strategic reasons for him barring occult discussion in public. Freud wanted psychoanalysis accepted as a "science"). Then there was a focus on how Western art is one portal in the West for understanding occult practices. Needless to say, the conference was fascinating.

There I met the leading occult publishers in Europe, Scarlet Imprint, and publishers/artists/occultists Alkistis Dimesh and Peter Grey (their latest work on the history of their magical collaboration is amazing). About a year later, I had a poetry manuscript I had tried with some US publishers, but the content of the poem seemed like it was too "spiritual" for American avant-garde poetry presses to match with. I sent the poem to Alkistis and Peter, and despite like a three-year waitlist, *Trinity Star Trinity* would be published like, next month. Too cool.

I was completely naïve to the portal I was about to step into. I thought of Scarlet Imprint in a conceptual way. My poem, dedicated to Hera, was all my dreams and visions I had visiting the birthplace of Hera on the island of Samos, Greece. Intuitively, I felt the poem should be performed as an invocation with candles and incense. Alkistis and Peter agreed. I felt I had found a publisher who understood my art – yay! And a framework to help this Oulipian poem jump out of itself to its audience. But I was thinking about this from the perspective of poetry.

Little did I understand this same group of occultists was thinking of me as a "witch." And not only a witch, but an exemplary witch! WHOA OMG. Wait, hold up. What is the definition of a witch? Are all poets witches?! And we just don't know it?

I began a two-year-long digestion of occult materials to try to understand this question. What I have learned has blown my mind. I cannot say I have answered this question; the materials which comprise the occult world would take a lifetime in themselves to master. But at the May 2019 follow-up conference to Psychoanalysis, Art and The Occult – aptly titled 100 Years of Modernism and the Occult – we spoke at length and I got feedback on my thoughts of what defines an artist as a witch.

Please consider a humble offering of my learnings below:

First, I want to lay a foundation by sharing the thing which most blew my mind in getting closer to the occult community. As a thinker, I had been of the position that all gods and religious beliefs seemed interesting to me, so why not believe in Hera? (To me, Hera represents the last of the "female goddesses" before we went to a male hierarchy of gods.) Ok great. I believe Hera exists; I believe I can feel her, and I believe I can write a poem which to the best of my ability represents or captures what it felt like to "speak" to Hera. Ok cool. So it turns out, that would be invocation.

Well, when you get into the occult community and the literature, it's not just about "talking" to or "communing" or "feeling" spirits. It's also at the other extreme, evocation. Evocation is the practice of calling a spirit into a room, getting its signature on a piece of paper, interpreting its messages as divination, and then sending the spirit into the world to do your bidding.

There is a distinction here. Invocation can be partially attributed to imagination or a dreamscape or even wishful thinking. Evocation cannot. It's very material and based on proof and outcomes. While it is easy for me to grasp that people believe such things, it is another to really let it sink in that this kind of magic exists and works (and literally all over the world). And, it is another to dig into the history of how and why this works – what Gloria Steinem called "a politics of the skies." It's an incredible history – this tome of documents around the world regarding magic! I urge you to visit the work of Scarlet Imprint to begin an investigation here, if you are so inquisitive.

So back to my question: are all poets witches and what is a witch…?

Well, what is a witch? To my mind, it would be the following things: do you light candles or incense as a form of catharsis or ritual? Do you combine herbs in specific recipes with the intention of having a concrete result in the world (aka herbalism)?

Have you read and practiced and been initiated into a study of witchcraft? Do you sell your practice? And have you ever been part of a group (coven) which practices these things together?

Personally, I would give the "witch" title a lot of criteria. Turns out I'm wrong, and the working definition, historically, is broader. She (or he) is a witch simply because they sense the spirit realm and create ways to communicate with it.

If you ascribe to this definition, I am a witch. I created a way to communicate with Hera in my book, *Trinity Star Trinity*. The way of creation is obviously not limited to poetry: it can be visual art (Kandinsky comes to mind), it can be film, it can be a candle ceremony, it can be herbalistic, it can really be anything. My favorite artist I have met who does this is Charlotte Rodgers. I look at her sculptures (made largely of roadkill) and – it's uncanny. I see a spirit, a personality, a resonance. It's not about the "what" one is using – it's about a belief in spirit and a belief in communing with it.

Now, we get into a sort of political hole, like the kind I reference in the Steinem quote: "what kind of spirit?" Here it gets tricky. What about those of organized religion who believe they channeled "God"—like St. John the Evangelist who wrote *The Book of Revelation*, or Russell Nelson who channels the word of God for the Mormon church? This would actually fit under the definition of "witch" above – except that in the West, historically, a "witch" is literally outside of organized religion. What about that wrinkle?

OK. So. *I think* the answer is as follows: Historically in the West the term "witch" applied to those who were outside of Western organized religion. (And btw, in my research on this topic, the shocker for me was the sheer volume of women (and some men) who were killed. The volume is so much bigger than I ever realized! And the rape! And the torture! OH MY GOD AND GODDESSES! For background here read Colin Wilson's terrific 1970s collection, *The Occult*.

While these murders have obviously left a terrible, bloody mark of baggage on the term "witch," I would argue that if you are speaking from a contemporary occultist POV, the definition of "witch" should be considered more than the term's usage in Western history.

Here's why – let's go back to Haiti, or West Africa, or Northern Brazil. These communities grew up with a mix of spiritualisms. Christianity, that is, communing with Jesus, went along right next to communing with the local gods. And so, I think it helpful to define "witch" as anyone who communes with any gods.

But ok, if those are the definitions: are all poets "witches"? Well, here's my humble schema: There are two axes: the axis of process versus content/outcome, and the axis of spiritual versus secular. On the process versus content/outcome axis we have spiritual techniques (of process) and spiritual forms (of content). On the secular side we have secular process and secular content.

One question unanswered: Is spiritual content necessary for being a witch? For example, Dodie Bellamy's Cunt-Ups or John Cage's I Ching paintings. Bellamy uses a witchy technique to create her work, which William Burroughs and many witches

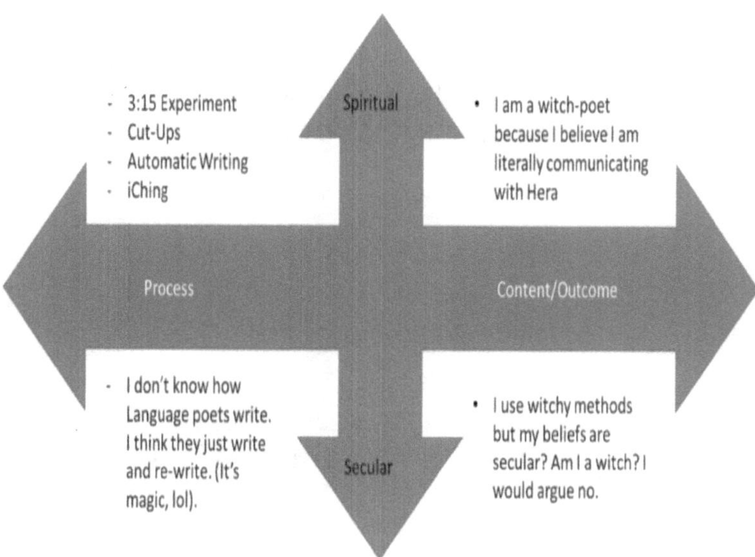

use to divine art or spells: cut-ups. But is Dodie's work witchcraft? Is John Cage's? Not that it matters to the valuation of the art, but the delineation proposed here around the witch category is whether Dodie or John believes they are channeling something from a god or spirit. So in short, are you a poet-witch? To me it's a question of the artists' belief in spirit.

Do you believe in the spirit world? And are you channeling this in your art? If so, I conclude grandly and humbly, you are a witch.

Investigating Initiation – Inside the Temple ov Psychick Youth Camp-outs

Tom Banger & Koshka

*Dedicated to Genesis, who dared us to touch ourselves,
and to the other Fallen. TheY are still HerE.*

In all systems of religion is to be found a system of Initiation... Though none can communicate either the knowledge or the power to achieve this, which we may call the Great Work, it is yet possible for Initiates to guide others. Every man must overcome his own obstacles, expose his own illusions. Yet others may assist him to do both, and they may enable him altogether to avoid many of the false paths, leading no whither, which tempt the weary feet of the uninitiated pilgrim. They can further insure that he is duly tried and tested, for there are many who think themselves to be Masters who have not even begun to tread the Way of Service that leads thereto. Now the Great Work is one, and the Initiation is one, and the Reward is one, however diverse are the symbols wherein the Unutterable is clothed...[1]

      – Aleister Crowley

Magic is dangerous or it is nothing.[2]

      – William S. Burroughs

It's Summer 1988. Thirteen strangers are camping deep in the Colorado mountains for eight days. They are members of an underground magickal organization, and have travelled from all over the US, the UK, and Canada. They think of themselves as part of a Tribe and want to deepen their commitment and take the Next Step in their spiritual journey. Although not all of them knew it yet, or put it in those words, they were looking for an Initiation. For lack of a better term, each of these Individuals was a "member" of Thee Temple ov Psychick Youth.

Thee Temple ov Psychick Youth, or TOPY, was formed in the early 1980s by Genesis P-Orridge and other members and allies of the band Psychic TV. Thee Temple assimilated a number of disparate elements of occultism and culture in an original and nondogmatic way: the methodicalness and skepticism of Aleister Crowley, the freeform sorcery of Austin Spare, the cut-ups and subversion of

---

1 Aleister Crowley, *Liber LXI vel Causae*
2 William S. Burroughs, *Between Spaces: Selected Rituals & Essays from the Archives of Templum Nigri Solis*

William Burroughs and Brion Gysin, the magico-cultural syncretism of JG Ballard, with a very open sexuality, and just a twist of mischievousness. Disguised in a pop music package, Psychic TV's pop packed a wallop – many of their tracks were ritual soundtracks, and the liner notes were filled with occultural musings.

An Ordo Templi Orientis elder once described Thee Temple as "nursery school for occultists", and, albeit intended flippantly, this may be one of the best thumbnail descriptions of TOPY. We aimed to re-evaluate traditional occult systems and to attempt to strip these processes down to their most effective, primal and non-dogmatic forms, and thus revitalize what Genesis derided as "the Museum of Magick" into a living, practical way of being for the late 20th Century and beyond. Templars were exhorted to experiment, and not accept any inherited assumptions or dogma.

Individuals came to Thee Temple from varied spiritual paths. For some, it was their first exposure to occult ways of doing. Others were attracted to or had backgrounds in Thelema, or Chaos Magick, or Buddhism, or shamanism or Gardnerian Witchcraft, even Butoh and Mormonism. TOPY unabashedly appropriated doctrine and iconography from all of them, while remaining agnostic, if not downright atheistic when it came to putting a name on the forces behind the results of our experiments. Although much less open than today, many Templars were exploring non-binary gender identities, and sexual preferences: TOPY encouraged this as part of the systematic questioning of all societal "norms".

At its inception, Thee Temple had only one ritual: The Sigil ov Thee Three Liquids. On the 23rd day of each month at 23:00 hours, all current and prospective templars would masturbate while focusing on a desire. The desire could be for something as concrete and mundane as hooking up with a specific person, or getting a better job, or something as subjective and nebulous as wishing for inspiration or a certain state of mind. Most templars chose to represent this desire in a textual or pictographic form, but others opted to embody their wish in sculpture, music, photography, or even multimedia. Once they had achieved their focused orgasm, they would anoint the object with the three liquids: blood, spit, and "ov" (TOPY's word for sexual fluids), as well as a snip of head hair and pubic hair, let it dry, and mail the result to Thee Temple.

Thus, the only way to become a "full" member of Thee Temple was to commit: to perform the ritual, and put your precious bodily fluids and deepest desires into the postal system, and send it to strangers. It placed every member in a very vulnerable position because it required a suspension of the inherited belief that these fluids had any inherent power per se, as well as a trust that the people on the other end were honorable. Incredibly, hundreds, if not thousands, of Individuals opted in. Once the Temple received their sigil, it was locked up. To protect her anonymity, each Sigilizer received a Temple name, followed by a number – Kali xxx for those who identified as females, Eden xxx for males. In order to honor the spirits of North America, we opted to call male Sigilizers Coyote rather than Eden. We were never able to alight upon a name for females that projected the same empowering feminine image as Kali, so we stuck with Kali.

We founded the US TOPY Station in Denver, Colorado on September 12, 1986. Individuals across North America began contacting us, and we began receiving first inquiries, and then sigils. Since there was no internet, and long distance phone calls were prohibitively expensive, nearly all of our communications were by post. Our engagement model was a sort of pre-digital hodgepodge of pen pals, ebay, Wikipedia, with perhaps just a dash of Tinder thrown in. We exchanged long letters, at first discussing magical and cultural theories and observations, then sharing results, and eventually intimate details of our personal lives. Many of these correspondences blossomed into lifelong friendships. By 1988, some of the Sigilizers had been active within TOPY for a year or more, and most of them had never met the people to whom they were entrusting their vital fluids. Many desired to take their involvement to the next level, and to press flesh with other members, so to speak. We needed to organize a Gathering.

Due to logistical and financial constraints, both of the Station and the Templars, the Gathering had to be a campout. It would also give us space and privacy for rituals, and a natural environment that would provide both a retreat and a sanctuary, and give everyone room for solitude, if they desired it. We decided to hold the first Gathering in Colorado for three reasons: it was in the center of North America, it had remote camping areas we could use for free, and since the US Station was located in Denver, it would be easier for us to organize logistically. We believed that a Gathering should last at least a week for the following reasons:

—⁓— To justify the expense, both in money and travel time
—⁓— To provide everyone an opportunity to become comfortable as a group
—⁓— To allow enough time for serious rituals

It now befell upon the Denver Station "staff" to develop a rough agenda for our guests. We originally planned to have quite a bit of structure, loosely based around the notion of Outward Bound, where there would be a couple days' period of enforced solitude, followed by some kind of group ritual or Initiatory experience. When everyone got together, however, we decided instead to spend the first couple days acclimating both to the mountains around us, and one another. Our campsite was at approximately 10,000 feet (3000 m), so simply breathing took effort for many of us. We suggested having an Initiation, and a couple of us had discussed a basic framework.

TOPY took a special interest in Initiation – this type of ceremony, in whatever form, seemed to be a common denominator of all religion, regardless how primitive or sophisticated. In fact, it could even be said that so-called rites of passage are of central importance to the human being, and perhaps the religious practices were developed to fill this basic need. In many ways, these ceremonies empower us to close the door on past behavior patterns, and give us the sanction of the Tribe to move forward towards a new chapter in our lives.

In many ways, our Tribe was on its own: the campfire burned out long ago, the storyteller got into radio. The temples were empty; their priests convicted on statuatory rape and tax-evasion charges. The tribe was scattered, the extended family bickers on the phone. Now, more than ever, rather than stagnate in the tribe we were born into, we wanted to create the tribe we wanted to be in. We chose to create this tribe on the basis of shared philosophies, values and goals. It was crucial for this new tribe to have its own ceremonies, or lapse into the very vacuity it sought to escape. To quote the TOPY *Black Book*:

> Our concern is with thee Individual in thee modern world. Accordingly our methods are designed to meet thee circumstances that prevail today. They are not occult in thee way that word is usually understood, they rely only on thee intuitive use ov that which we already know, directed with purpose. It is a maximization ov thee powers ov thee brain, a joining together ov conscious and unconscious will so that through thee use of Sigils thee Individual can move towards a desired goal free from thee constraint ov confused ideals and personal contradictions. Unlike much that is called occult, we do not rely on dogma, mystification, references to orthodoxy or thee mimicking ov previously effective butter now redundant rituals, rules and experiences.[3]

Because we live in a secular society, rites of passage, when performed at all, generally ring hollow and fall short of their purpose. They become rote because the words and formuli have lost their power, or perhaps the other way around. Regardless, we felt that in order to regain our spiritual power as Individuals, we had to rethink and repotentiate Initiations. Our goal was to reclaim Ceremony and make it *our own* again.

We were told that initiation had to be ancient, handed down across the generations from teacher to disciple. That the wisdom of the ages had to be inherited from the Elders. But the very essence of Thee Temple rejected that inherited wisdom. We were told that you can't just make up an initiation out of thin air. Where is the tradition? Where is the disciplic succession? If you don't have those crucial elements, it won't achieve anything. We said, as we did with most things magickal, "let's try it and see what happens". So we did, and here's what happened.

The ceremony had to be timeless – in order to be legitimate, the Initiation had to draw on traditions, but also have a unique and contemporary feel and incorporate elements unique to TOPY. For maximum effect, the experience had to be visceral to create a meaningful imprint: it had to take the Candidate out of her head, out of her body, into a timeless state. It also had to be non-denominational in order to respect and embrace the beliefs and non-beliefs of all the participants. While Initiates were welcome to incorporate whatever liturgy they wished, there would be no prayers, no invocations – the Psychick Cross would be our only symbol.

---

3 TOPY, *Thee Black Book*, quoted in *Thee Psychick Bible*

In order to do so, we had to work our way backwards: first we had to ask, *what are Initiations for?*

> Initiation fuses Spirit and Matter in a transcendent unity that partakes not at all of the qualities of either.
>
> … The aim of purging consciousness of the dual polarities of Spirit and Matter is to arrive at a state of "mindlessness" that prepares consciousness to retain its equilibrium in the flood of illumination characteristic of samadhi.[4]

One common feature of ritual seems to be to create a shared experience among a group, to forge a bond beyond kinship or friendship. It establishes a normal. As Seth Godin says, "People like us do things like this".[5] In other words, Initiation not only bonds the Individual to the Tribe, it also bonds the Tribe to the Individual. It also serves to establish a norm for the group. However, it also separates the Initiate from the non-initiate, and distinguishes her as a member of the Tribe, as opposed to the herd. It further distinguishes them as an exceptional member of the Tribe, part of a real or imagined Inner Circle.

But this dichotomy begged the question whether Initiation is for the community or the Individual, or both? From its beginnings, Temple literature was adamant that Temple members owed no fealty to the Temple. The agreement was that nobody on either side of the relationship was *obligated*: Individuals were encouraged to wander in and out of the Temple, according to *their* needs, not the Temple's. Therefore, our ritual would be focussed on bonding the Individual to herself. Any benefit to the TOPY Tribe must be ancillary.

For inspiration, we looked across all kinds of groups, both secular and religious.

- Masons
- Occult Orders
- Indigenous and tribal rites of passage
- College Fraternities
- Sports Teams
- Military
- Outlaw Bikers

We identified three factors that seem to contribute towards a successful Initiation. By successful, we mean one which creates a new frame of mind for a Candidate, triggers altered states of consciousness and gives the Candidate a feeling of a new physical or emotional threshold delineated – and successfully crossed. Individual Initiations in a given tribe must be similar enough to one another to form a shared experience between those who have undergone them. Then, and only then, can the

---

4 Kenneth Grant, *Cults of the Shadow*
5 Seth Godin, *This is Marketing*

Initiation function as a form of tribal bonding.

—∿— Initiation by scarring or marking the body
—∿— Initiation by various mind-altering substances or trance-inducing activities
—∿— Initiation by physical rigors/ordeal. As Joseph Campbell puts it. "The agony of breaking through personal limitations is the agony of spiritual growth."[6]

We recognized that Thee Sigil ov Thee Three Liquids provided a common foundation on which we could construct a meaningful, transformative Initiatory experience. The basic ritual was already familiar to each of us, so we could expand and build upon it while not veering too far into the unknown. The orgasm could provide the mind altering state. The scarring was already part of the ritual. All we needed was a physical ordeal.

In the case of the more secular groups (bikers, fraternities, military), so-called initiations tended to take the form of hazings, or ordeals, while overlooking the physical and trance aspects, unless one includes alcohol as a mind-altering substance. We felt that the physical ordeal was an important piece of the puzzle, as it could help the Initiate get out of their head and into their body. By combining this with pleasure, we could then help the Initiate achieve an altered state and effectively get them out of the body into a transcendental samadhic state.

We knew that in order to create a shared experience, the ritual had to have consistent elements, but we also wanted to keep the structure loose enough to be able to adjust for the needs and wishes of each Individual. We also wanted to ensure that the ceremony could be conducted anywhere with a minimum of props or accoutrements.

We settled on the following components:

THE SECRET – If the Candidate knows what is going to happen to her, it's going to be that much harder to cross a threshold without risking physical or emotional injury. It also builds the mystery and suspense for non-initiates. To maximize this effect, we led each Candidate out of the common area bound and blindfolded.

THE INEVITABILITY – It must be made clear to the Candidate that, once she has made the decision to undergo the Initiation, there is no turning back – if the ceremony is not completed successfully this time, it will not be offered again. As Norman Mudd (Frater O.P.V.) wrote,

> All Initiation must begin with an Act of Truth… It is therefore an absolute rule in this work that every aspirant is compelled, right at the start, to make an important decision, Yes or No, on the instant, without adequate information, and without security. The slavish clinging to safety must be simply broken.

---

6 Joseph Campbell, *The Hero with a Thousand Faces*

… it must be understood clearly that unless such a test is passed on the spot, the gate is shut, once and for all.[7]

THE ATMOSPHERE – You have to make every effort to create a novel setting for the experience. You need to keep the Initiate - and the Initiators - slightly off balance in order to maximize the effect. Placing the Candidate in an unfamiliar space reflects that they will be entering a new psycho-magickal space when the ritual is complete.

The nature of the experience depends almost entirely on set and setting. Set denotes the preparation of the Individual, including his personality structure and his mood at the time. Setting is physical – the weather, the room's atmosphere; social – feelings of persons present towards one another; and cultural – prevailing views as to what is real.[8]

THE BINDING – It needs to be clear to the Candidate that she will have no personal control over what happens to her during the Ceremony. This *must* be made clear *before* she agrees to it. The concept of "Perfect LovE, Perfect TRusT" is implicit here. It also dramatizes how little control the Candidate has in her "daily" life.

Photo: Koshka

---

7 Frater OPV (Norman Mudd), quoted by Kenneth Grant, *Cults of the Shadow*
8 Timothy Leary, *The Psychedelic Experience: A Manual Based on the Tibetan Book of the Dead*

Photo: Koshka

THE PAIN – Very few thresholds have ever been crossed in situations of extreme comfort! In the same way, the Candidate needs to be made physically uncomfortable, so that she can transcend pure physical consciousness and rise above. The Initiatrix *must* have the empathy to distinguish between *pain* and *injury*. A Candidate must never be injured by the tribe.

THE BLISS – the pain/pleasure dichotomy should be played with as much as possible in order to narrow the distinction between the two. This also turbocharges the consciousness out of the body and into a more spiritual state.

> I go deeper into mysticism through erotic delirium; perversely polymorphic, I translate each new awareness into gluttony. Eroticism is a royal road of the soul of God. It flows in the molecular structures. To me, it is the foundation of heterosexual urges. In exploring my desire, I explore my life.[9]

THE SURRENDER – At some point, the Candidate must surrender all emotions in regard to the rite – must give in to the sensations – and rise above them, into the Neither-Neither State where one feels as though all this is happening to some other

---

9 Salvador Dali, *Unspeakable Confessions of Salvador Dali*

self – not the "I". Similar to the samadhic state to which Grant refers.

The Mark – A permanent mark must be made on the body to match the mark made on the mind. This can take the form of a tattoo, a scar, or a piercing. It is crucial that this experience be documented, commemorated in such a way that it can never be forgotten or denied – *indelible and non-repudiable*. The mark also provides Initiates a means of identifying other Initiates.

The Welcome – the Candidate is then welcomed back into the Tribe as a Sister, who has proven her commitment and strength to all.

Though most Initiations include an Oath to the organization or Tribe, the TOPY ceremony did not, because any kind of forced credo seemed to contradict Thee Temple's foundational value of Individualism. It was implicit that each Individual was signing a silent oath to her Self, vowing to always be true to that Self and to never waiver from her Intention.

The Initiatory rite from the 1988 campout formed a solid template for subsequent campouts. Sadly, there aren't many details and artifacts from this first campout. It was held in a remote area of the San Isabel National Forest near Grant, Colorado, and thirteen Individuals attended. After settling in to the campsite, we did an exercise where we formed a Native American medicine wheel[10] and placed ourselves in the elemental direction we thought best represented our current state, and then spoke about where we wanted to be. As well as a good way to get to know each other more deeply, it was also an opportunity to get input about our goals. Later in the week, each of us spent a day and night in complete solitude, spread out far enough away from one another as to not have visual contact, but close enough to signal vocally if there was an emergency. This isolation gave each camper an opportunity to reflect on her life and goals, and also to face the fear of being alone.

Following the solo time, each of the participants painted a symbol on the naked body of every other Camper and briefly explained the meaning of the symbol. This was a way of simultaneously gifting each of our companions with feedback, a blessing, and a path for future reflection and work. We drummed and chanted, roamed around naked and generally had no concern for being "discovered". Although we were miles from the nearest paved road, we were camping and frolicking on public land. As we were to discover later in the week, our privacy was not guaranteed...

The Initiations took place toward the end of the trip and followed the formula outlined above until we reached the final Initiation of the campout. It began as the others had. The Initiate herself was clearly apprehensive about the ritual but proceeded, as time was running out. A few minutes into her ordeal, unforeseen circumstances came into play when the "lookout" informed the group that we were not alone. A group of people on horseback had definitely spotted us and began

---

10 See Hyemeyohsts Storm, *Seven Arrows*

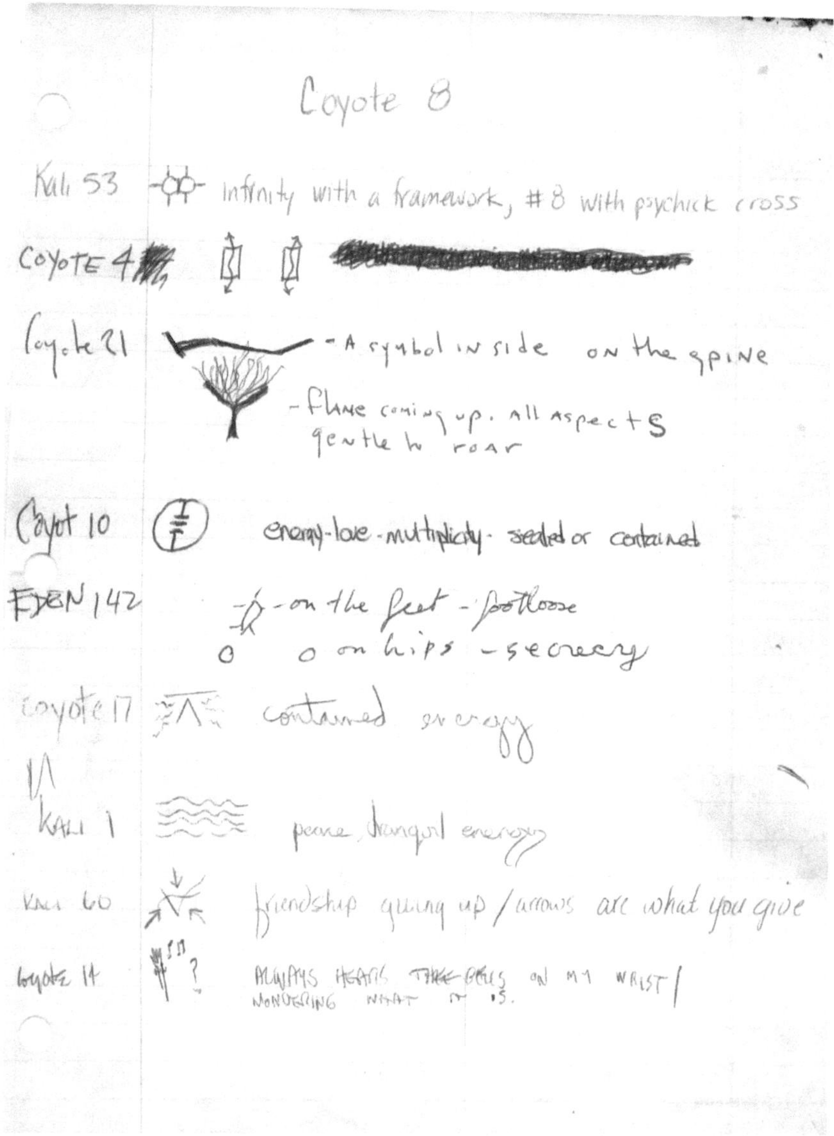

Coyote 8's markings explained (Authors' collection)

crossing themselves. The Initiate, blindfolded and naked, bound to an upright wooden structure (the psychick cross) was quickly and frantically unbound, clothed and led back to the base camp. At first the Initiate thought this was part of the ceremony, meant to test and frighten and push personal limits, but it quickly became clear to her that this was not part of the plan. It was the first and only time that an Initiation had to stop, mid-ceremony. She was successfully initiated on the

Happy campers, 1988 (Photo Koshka)

second campout. We never found out if the interlopers alerted the "authorities" after they stumbled upon our ceremony.

A fair bit of documentation exists for the second campout. In March of 1989, we sent out the following announcement (misspellings intact) from the Denver Station:

CAMP-OUT TIME IS ROLLING BACK AGAIN!!! We need to start planning for it, so if you could fill in thee bottom ov this page and send it back or (if you're a packrat like me, xerox it and send it). IN A SEPARATE ENVELOPE. Thee Trip will probably be in S.W. Colorado this time and will probably last about 9 days (2 weekends). That is leaving early on a Sat a.m., and returning on thee following Sun pm. I know that many ov you have jobs or school, so we're going to try and find a time that will enable thee maximum number ov us to attend. We will be taking thee bus, so the total cost ov thee trip, incl. food for thee trip and gas, will probably cost 50 dollars, which isn't bad for a weeklong ov fun and magick!!

1. WILL YOU WANT to go ON THEE CAMPOUT AT ALL? (if NO, then skip thee rest....)
2. WHEN IS THEE BEST TIME FOR YOU (between July1 and Labor Day)
3. HOW WOULD YOU BE GETTING TO DENVER?
4. IF DRIVING, WOULD YOU BE WILLING TO HELP GET PEOPLE OR GEAR TO THEE CAMPSIT?
a. if YES, how big is your vehicle?
b. WOULD YOU BE WILLING TO PICK SOMEONE UP ON YOUR WAY HERE?
5. IF YOU DON'T HAVE A WAY HERE, WOULD YOU BE WILLING TO GET TO A MEETING PLACE TO CATCH A RIDE?

6.   IS 8 OR 9 DAYS TOO LONG FOR YOU TO GET TIME OFF?
7.   ON A SEPARATE PAPER, PLEASE WRITE DOWN WHAT YOU WOULD LIKE A PERFECT CAMPOUT TO LOOK LIKE: WHAT WOULD YOU DO, WHAT WOULD YOU HOPE TO GET OUT OV IT.

Thank you for your trouble., remember, send this SEPARATELY, marked ATTN: CAMP clearly on the envelope.

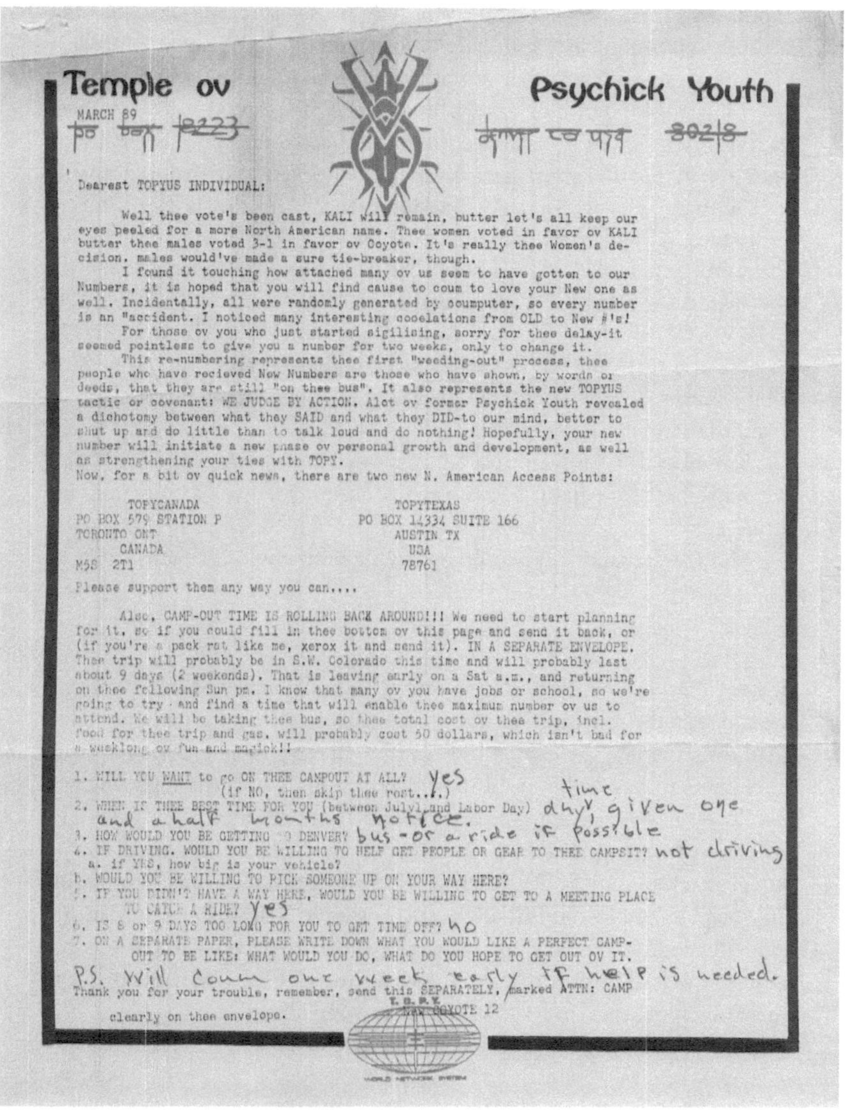

Temple ov **Psychick Youth**

MARCH 89

Dearest TOPYUS INDIVIDUAL:

Well thee vote's been cast, KALI will remain, butter let's all keep our eyes peeled for a more North American name. Thee women voted in favor ov KALI butter thee males voted 3-1 in favor ov Ocyote. It's really thee Women's decision. males would've made a sure tie-breaker, though.

I found it touching how attached many ov us seem to have gotten to our Numbers, it is hoped that you will find cause to coum to love your New one as well. Incidentally, all were randomly generated by ocumputer, so every number is an "accident. I noticed many interesting cooelations from OLD to New #'s!

For those ov you who just started sigilising, sorry for thee delay-it seemed pointless to give you a number for two weeks, only to change it.

This re-numbering represents thee first "weeding-out" process, thee people who have recieved New Numbers are those who have shown, by words or deeds, that they are still "on thee bus". It also represents the new TOPYUS tactic or covenant: WE JUDGE BY ACTION. Alot ov former Psychick Youth revealed a dichotomy between what they SAID and what they DID-to our mind, better to shut up and do little than to talk loud and do nothing! Hopefully, your new number will initiate a new phase ov personal growth and development, as well as strengthening your ties with TOPY.

Now, for a bit ov quick news, there are two new N. American Access Points:

```
     TOPYCANADA                    TOPYTEXAS
PO BOX 579 STATION P          PO BOX 14334 SUITE 166
TORONTO ONT                        AUSTIN TX
     CANADA                          USA
M5S  2T1                            78761
```

Please support them any way you can....

Also, CAMP-OUT TIME IS ROLLING BACK AROUND!!! We need to start planning for it. so if you could fill in thee bottom ov this page and send it back, or (if you're a pack rat like me, xerox it and send it). IN A SEPARATE ENVELOPE. Thee trip will probably be in S.W. Colorado this time and will probably last about 9 days (2 weekends). That is leaving early on a Sat a.m., and returning on thee following Sun pm. I know that many ov you have jobs or school, so we're going to try and find a time that will enable thee maximum number ov us to attend. We will be taking thee bus, so thee total cost ov thee trip, incl. food for thee trip and gas. will probably cost 50 dollars, which isn't bad for a weeklong ov fun and magick!!

1. WILL YOU <u>WANT</u> to go ON THEE CAMPOUT AT ALL?   *yes*
              (if NO, then skip thee rest....)
2. WHEN IS THEE BEST TIME FOR YOU (between July1 and Labor Day) *dhy, given one* *time* *and a half months notice.*
3. HOW WOULD YOU BE GETTING TO DENVER? *bus - or a ride if possible*
4. IF DRIVING. WOULD YOU BE WILLING TO HELP GET PEOPLE OR GEAR TO THEE CAMPSIT? *not driving*
   a. if YES, how big is your vehicle?
b. WOULD YOU BE WILLING TO PICK SOMEONE UP ON YOUR WAY HERE?
5. IF YOU DIDN'T HAVE A WAY HERE, WOULD YOU BE WILLING TO GET TO A MEETING PLACE
      TO CATCH A RIDE? *yes*
6. IS 8 or 9 DAYS TOO LONG FOR YOU TO GET TIME OFF? *no*
7. ON A SEPARATE PAPER, PLEASE WRITE DOWN WHAT YOU WOULD LIKE A PERFECT CAMP-
      OUT TO BE LIKE: WHAT WOULD YOU DO, WHAT DO YOU HOPE TO GET OUT OV IT.
P.S. Will coum one week early if help is needed.
Thank you for your trouble, remember, send this SEPARATELY, marked ATTN: CAMP
      clearly on thee envelope.

T.O.P.Y.
NEW COYOTE 12

Original announcement for 1989 campout. (Authors' Collection)

Responses to the question about what the campout should look like ranged from the banal: "drink beer & roast marshmallows and chocolate" to the profound:

YES I too would like to see the campout not be so much ov a Living Room. Having a home base perhaps but not necessarily where we spend all our time. Especially after spending a winter sitting around in a living room. Why bring such a boring yenching[11] thing into the wilderness, old habits. Habits from having your real space be an apartment or living room. And then there's the aspect of why we sit. And talk. And not live together, communicate, and share on other levels.

Part of the lameness that was at last years camp out was subtle fear of touching. Or kind of like writer's block.

For myself these things were there, but I see them more when I look back on it. For the most part I was just knocked and tripping and in love with the fact we were ACTually together. And this is by no means something to reject but something to be careful ov if we want to feel the camp out with life. Do not fall back on old patterns. Realize the specialness ov WHERE we're at as well as WHO we're with. E X P L O R E. WANDER. PRY. So wow – we're together. Let's celebrate it. I'd like to hike and be in the wilderness myself cuz that's where I like to turn on all my senses. Strengthen my self by losing my personality. Being physical. Unfolding other aspects of me.

As well as this – more direct talking, too. Sharing where we are. Where we may go. The medicine wheel was a good thing. Also X's body painting ritual.

More direct talking if people are having problems with each other too.

—m—

If everyone who's actually coming brings (or finds) power objects or totems we can start the process of charging and adorning them for perhaps chain-mail totems when the campout is over.

I'd like to have solos again too. At least a full day and a night. Maybe two days. It was really good to write and think about where we are and where we're going and how our lives fit in T.O.P.Y./how we'd like to integrate more into TOPY. WHAT TOPY means to us. And formulating an image to use in the Initiation. There should definitely be Initiations. And depending on how many people show up having Initiations fall around the middle of the week. To permit the EFFECT they may have to open any blockages, to let that life expand and spread.

I like to play hide and go seek. Stalking games.

---

11 *yench*. slang To be deceived, swindled, or defrauded. The con artist managed to *yench* the wealthy widow out of her entire fortune.(thefreedictionary.com)

The campout is a time for the tribe. A place where dreams meet. Where we meet. Thee TEMPLE ov PSYCHICK Youth. Our Space WILL be a Temple. To the horizon. No holds barred. As it should be everywhere. Doing a group ritual about that would be a good thing.

So as well as talking and hiking I'd like to do more Official Magic be it frenzy or directed. Altered states. Seeing how many levels we can communicate with in those hills. How much we can see. Invoke ACTion. I'll be thinking more about more Actual tasks and Activities. This letter is a good idea. People should KNOW – they MUST be prepared for the elements so we aren't held back by fussiness on that level.[12]

Many had high expectations:

Camping as with any activity outside work eye would want to be as stimulating as possible, eye want things incongruous and varied. Eye want my existance altered. A perfect trip is one eye couldn't describe because that would calculate and establish boundaries. Eye want grow. I love living. All eye would like to get out of the trip is all eye want to get out of anything growth. Eye am not too good at social situations always had trouble interacting in any way so eye am not sure what eye would do but relish the thought of trying.
Your forever in my dreams[13]

Others were more circumspect:

First of all, I have never personally met a sigilizer (Temple devotee ha!) and that would be great. I picture it as a time to really cum to understand what the Temple really means to me thru the perceptions and actions of others. I am intimidated, actually, tho I know I shouldn't be just the idea of being out in the woods w/ people I trust already (naive?) is almost frightening. I have friends, tho none that are really interested in the things I consider thee most worthwhile, and sharing w/ others of a similar bent is going to be great, an adventure. It will be a great time to explore thee pagan aspect of myself Group rituals would be incredible, I have never done anything like that and it wold be power full. Commune ity I guess. Closer to action communi-ication w/ more than words. Specifics, if your

---

12 Coyote 21, letter to TOPY NA, 1989 Collection of the authors
13 Coyote 7, letter to TOPY NA, 1989 Collection of the authors

Photo: Koshka

looking for them, I'm at a loss because in so many ways I don't know what to expect but thats why I'm so excited about it, for a week trying to define myself in a different way, not with my usual tethers to "reality" but a less temporal, more instantaneous perception. Vague, hm? I don't know.[14]

Twenty three Templars took the challenge in 1989. The campout was held on tribal lands in the Four Corners area of Colorado. We were surrounded by Anasazi cliff dwellings and ancient petroglyphs, which put everyone into a very atavistic state of mind. Although they didn't know the whole story, the tribe members we interacted with were very welcoming and supportive. They gave us a tour of their lands, some oral history and a hind quarter of a freshly killed deer to eat.

The activities on the second campout followed the pattern of the first campout, but we made an effort to organize more activities so there would be less "living room time". We were able to roam naked around the campsite, and dammed up the muddy creek so we could swim in it. Some of our activities bordered on the absurd: we competed in wheelbarrow races and danced the "Hokey Pokey" together with only a touch of innuendo. This time, there were a total of 23 campers, which also meant that a lot more time would be consumed with the Initiations themselves.

Some of us were already friends and/ or lovers and had done ritual work together

---

14 Coyote 6, letter to TOPY NA, 1989 Collection of the authors

Modern Primitives. Photo: Koshka

previously. This enabled us to fine tune the ritual with regard to the thresholds of an Individual. Keep in mind that the ages ranged from 19 to mid 50's. Some Individuals came alone, others in small groups familiar to one and other. Some had prior experience with other systems of magick or practices which included an Initiation, others none. Some were "straight-edge" while others were well versed psychonauts. All sexual preferences and identities were represented. The range of the Candidates' vulnerability was fairly extreme — some were very timid and introverted while others verged on the sycophantic.

For this reason, the Initiators had to adjust their behavior, and sometimes the "rules", to help each Individual get the most out of her experience. One Candidate became notably disturbed to the point of panic. While there was no verbal communication during most of the Initiations, we decided that this person needed some reassurance, which allayed his fear and allowed the ritual to continue successfully. It was a poignant reminder that each of us was having their own experience and that not everyone had the same threshold for discomfort, be it physical, psychic or mental. The dynamic nature of the ritual allowed for this flexibility so that we could meet the needs of each Individual without compromising the effect or relative intensity of their personal experience.

To ensure surprise for the next round of Initiates, each Individual who participated in the rituals – Initiatrix and Initiate alike – promised not to reveal any

Photo: Koshka

details of the ceremony. In so doing, we intentionally built an aura of danger and mystery around the ceremony that would encourage speculation and exaggeration. This would frighten outsiders and dilettantes away and also ensure that future Initiates would have a healthy amount of discomfort around consenting to their Initiation. As far as we are aware, this promise has been kept by all participants to this day.

Initiation has a zombie effect: one Initiate infects another until all eligible members of the community have crossed the threshold. As William S. Burroughs put it,

> Remember the life cycle of a virus ... penetration of a cell or activation within the cell, replication within the cell, escape from the cell to invade other cells, escape from host to infect a new host. This infection can take place in many ways and those who find themselves heavy with the load of a new virus generally use a shotgun technique to cover a wide range of infection routes...[15]

However, zombies are known to run amok, so the experience also has to be carefully controlled. It needs to be performed in an empathetic manner to ensure that each Candidate has been pushed slightly beyond her physical/emotional/psychic limits, but no farther. To push too far is to create trauma – to not push far enough denies them the transcendent experience that is the intended effect.

As more Initiates became Initiators, a sense of frenzy threatened to turn the experience into something more akin to the Stanford Prison Experiment than the Kama Sutra. Mass psychology started to kick in, creating behavioral feedback loops reminiscent of Lord of the Flies. This is widely reported in secular hazing/initiations:

> The fraternity initiation tests a person's dedication to be a part of the fraternity, not to mention teach them values like humility and brotherhood. Unfortunately, some fraternities become violent, and will often cross the line in their initiation rituals.[16]

Things were beginning to get out of hand and some of us began suffering from a sort of "Initiation burnout". To ensure that everyone had a positive experience, we agreed to limit the number of Initiators to four per Candidate. Once this limit was in place, things became less hectic and more focused on the Initiates' wellbeing. This optimized communication and cooperation: each Initiator knew her role and each role acted with unity of purpose and l-ov-e to create an optimal experience for each Candidate.

From an Initiatory standpoint, the experience of being an Initiator may have been at least as transformative as the experience of being Initiated. It taught each of us the compassionate use of pain and fear, to be able to sense other people's thresholds and to push just to that point, and not beyond. It broke our sexual inhibitions and taboos and made us more gentle, more vulnerable, more able to express ourselves nonverbally through touch and silence. But we became stronger, too – able to wield power more confidently, yet more compassionately. And although many of us haven't seen each other for more than thirty years, most of us are still in touch with one another, and there is a special bond between us that will

---

15 William S. Burroughs, *Between Spaces: Selected Rituals & Essays from the Archives of Templum Nigri Solis*

16 Student Assembly – Fraternity Initiation: What It Is, Why It's Important, And Why People Have a Problem With It https://www.studentassembly.org/fraternity-initiation-what-it-is-why-its-important-and-why-people-have-a-problem-with-it/

1989: "Now you are a group." Photo: Koshka

be there forever and cannot be effaced.

However, the second campout was not completely over yet. Koshka had taken two rolls of black and white, as well as color, photos of the campout. There were group photos, landscape photos, photos of us dancing "skyclad" as well as photos of some of the rituals. Knowing that the nature of these photos would most likely rouse suspicion, we were lucky to have an ally who worked in a photo lab. This person agreed to personally handle the processing of the film. When Tom and Koshka picked up the developed prints and negatives they were short on cash, so Koshka paid with a check. Unbeknownst to them at the time, their ally at the lab had called in sick the day the film was processed, and the technician had been disturbed by the photos and alerted the police.

A few days later, there was a knock at Koshka's door. Two plainclothes Denver police detectives were standing on her porch and demanded her ID. Koshka presented hers and asked what this was regarding. In response, the cops presented 8x10 prints of her photos, mostly close-ups of faces. She was asked the identities of a choice few. Feeling very intimidated, she gave a couple of fake names which turned out to be fruitless as they already knew Tom's full name and address. Obviously they had gotten Koshka's name and address off of the personal check used to pay the photo lab. Listening from upstairs, Koshka's roommate, Coyote X, who was featured prominently in the photos, came downstairs to join the conversation.

The police identified themselves as members of the Gang Unit and basically said that the photos suggested occult or satanic rituals that suggested torture, pornography and possible involvement of minors. This was during the "Satanic

Panic," which was at its height across the US at the time. Coyote X stepped up and asked if these were arrestable offenses and once the police assured him declared that they indeed were not and no charges were being pressed, the cops left their business cards and asked to arrange a meeting with Tom. Koshka and Coyote X contacted Tom immediately, who scheduled a meeting with the detectives.

Tom met with the detectives and recorded the conversation. Unfortunately, the cassette perished in a subsequent fire or flood. Ironically, the end result was the cops asking Tom for his expertise when dealing with issues of this nature in the future. It was clear to the investigators that we were consenting adults camping and engaging in "strange" but not illegal behavior. These were not kids sacrificing animals and spraypainting pentagrams as was being sensationalized in the tabloids at the time. We were relieved that we avoided public exposure – we feel that it was in large part due to our transparency about what we were doing, and our policy to require all Sigilizers to be legal adults.

What happened to us after the Initiation? Nothing and Everything. Life went on. Both of us eventually just drifted out of Thee Temple, and in 1991, Genesis attempted to dissolve it. Repeatedly. But It had grown bigger than any of us – there was more to Thee Temple ov Psychick Youth than any of us knew or understood, and no person could stop it any more than Canute could (apocryphally) stop the tide. It kept going, almost of its own accord. Various Individuals kept the post office box open, and kept assigning Temple Names to new Sigilizers. And for all we know, they still are today. Because the system works.

So what remains? These experiences can never be forgotten, nor taken away. Many of us have stayed in touch, and some of us have remained close friends for over thirty years. Thee Temple ov Psychick Youth was a temporary autonomous zone that allowed intellectual freedom of expression and exchange of information. The campout created a second temporary autonomous zone, interior to that of Thee Temple at large, which allowed its participants as close to total freedom to express themselves on the physical, psychic, and emotional levels. We were all present as perhaps we had never been before, and have seldom been since.

In a very short period of time we were an organic, human, analog version of the Internet which would be in part the downfall of TOPY at large. Within that minimal time frame we became the Tribe we all wanted to be a part of, in and of the flesh. We built it and we came! In the 30+ years that have passed, many of us have left the physical realm. Some have adamantly wanted nothing to do with attempts at documented recollections. The implicit trust and respect have betrayed no one in their actions. We were free agents of chaos whose paths crossed in a most unusual way, beholden to no one but ourselves. It existed because we believed in it.

Are we enlightened? Perhaps. Are we Initiates because of it? Illusion? Perhaps. Pull back the camera....

The Fin-de-Siècle Magical Aesthetic of Austin Osman Spare
– Siderealism, Atavism, Automatism, Occultism

Simon Magus

Fig. 1: *The Eye of Ecstasy* from *The Book of Pleasure* (1913)

Introduction

The art and occult psycho-philosophical writings of the late Victorian/Edwardian artist and occultist Austin Osman Spare (1886-1956) can be described as entertaining a creative and magical dialectic. There is as yet little scholarly work on Spare, though his oeuvre has been an area of rapidly expanding interest in recent years.[1] Analytical trajectories have tended to adopt the critical methodologies of either the art historian or the historian of esoteric ideas. More recently, Stephen Pochin has gone so far as to deny any dialectic between two separate aspects,

---

1 One of a number of reasons for the limited academic investigation of Spare – aside from the obvious obscurity of his language – is that much of his work and its commentaries still only appear in the original, expensive antiquarian originals or 'collectable' collections of essays. For this reason – and in this paper – I have elected to use more readily available reprints and compilations of Spare's work where possible, which hopefully will prove more readily accessible to the reader intending to develop an interest in his oeuvre. In addition, I have focussed almost exclusively on Spare's thought rather than the man himself. For the biographical context, see Phil Baker, *Austin Osman Spare: The Life and Legend of London's Lost Artist* (London: Strange Attractor Press, 2011).

preferring to describe what he sees as a unity which is only apparently divided – as in the birefingent refraction of Iceland spar.[2] In this essay I consider the two aspects of Spare's work as coterminous, and demonstrate how his art is both a product of his magical praxis *sensu lato*, and illustrative of the principle elements of his occult philosophy. In keeping with the theme of esoteric practices, rather than focus primarily on the lineaments of artistic influence, I shall focus on the *phronesis* of Spare's occultist imagination, considering some of the esoteric influences on Spare and contextualising him within the compass of the nineteenth-century occult milieu. In the first part and introduction, I shall present an overview of the main ideas in Spare's psycho-philosophy and provide a sparse précis of their interconnections. In the second part, I shall analyse these ideas in detail under the four rubrics of 'Siderealism,' 'Atavism,' 'Automatism,' and 'Occultism.'

By way of a prolegomenon to the study of Spare's work, I should mention a number of caveats. Firstly, there is the problematic of Kenneth Grant's mediation of Spare, and secondly the misappropriation of his ideas by subsequent modern esoteric groups. To elucidate the former, Robert Ansell has introduced the term 'Grantisms'[3] the significance of which will become more evident as we proceed. Spare is frequently incorrectly described as the founder of a 'Zos-Kia Cultus.' In reality, this is a product of Kenneth Grant's mediation:

> His iconoclasm, distaste for the props and symbolism of ceremonial magic and his aversion to moralism as well as his innovative use of sigilization served to distinguish his personal style of magic which his friend and associate Kenneth Grant called Zos Kia Cultus.[4]

It appears that Grant's mediation of Spare's thought has become widely influential amongst the scant academic studies of Spare, serving to blur the boundaries of what is Grant and what is Spare. For example, in a passage in *Imagining Language,* Spare is introduced as 'an English magus of the Zos-Kia cult.'[5] In addition, Christopher Miles has noted that "Grant dubs this complex of techniques with the phrase that has come to be associated with Spare's magic … "atavistic resurgence." Spare does not use this phrase anywhere in his published works."[6] However, one should not be too quick to be critical of Kenneth Grant, as it is quite clear at times that Spare very much intended their work to be a collaboration. In a letter to Kenneth and Steffi Grant dated Tuesday 10th October 1950, Spare writes:

---

2 Steven Pochin, "A Curious Double-Refraction" in Steven Pochin ed., *Austin Osman Spare, Fallen Visionary: Refractions* (London: Jerusalem Press, 2012), 12.

3 Robert Ansell, personal communication, September 2008

4 Wolftrappe, "Austin Osman Spare," last modified December 12, 2006, accessed September 19, 2015, wolftrappe.blogspot.com/2006/12/austin-osman-spare-austin-osman-spare.html.

5 Jed Rasula and Steve McCaffery (Eds.) *Imagining Language: An Anthology,* (London: MIT Press, 1996), 368.

6 Christopher J. Miles, "Journey into the Neither-Neither: Austin Osman Spare and the Construction of Shamanic Identity," *The Pomegranate*, 8.1 (2006): 74.

I'm mapping out a really good thing on magic in general which we can both work on. You, an intro. to Magic generally and I, a specific formula. I'll give you my portion first but you will be quite safe working without [me] as yours will corner the field in a general way.[7]

In fact, they did collaborate on *The Witches' Sabbath*. Grant reports that Spare "gave me rough notes for an article on Witches Sabbath which is to be published under my name."[8] It was, published in 1992, forty years later – under Spare's name.[9] Grant freely admitted at the time "I can't always disentangle my own phantasies from what you are actually saying, i.e. I tend to read into your books too much of my own experience, thus (probably) missing the vital point of the whole thing."[10] Seemingly suspecting at times that Spare was deliberately obscuring some esoteric truth, he asks in their correspondence: 'If you have time would you *please* jot down a few *private* notes for my benefit.' Robert Ansell comments on Grant's mediation:

> I have publicly said in the past that Grant's Spare is like a sidereal portrait [see below]: you can recognise the subject, but liberties have been taken with his likeness. In some respects it speaks deeply of the connection between the two men, but while it is good sorcery, it is bad sourcery.[11]

The second caveat involves misconception and misappropriation of Spare's ideas. This continued apace through the twentieth century, and continues to the present day. Spare has been co-opted by modern witchcraft groups, Neo-shamanistic practitioners and so-called 'Chaos' magicians.[12] In addition he has been linked with Amerindian Spirituality, as outlined by Miles.[13] This inevitably detracts from Spare's insistent individualism and efforts at de-traditionalization, which are considered further below. A more accurate title for Spare's thought would be Kiaism, especially in view of his following statement and his description of the 'Kiaist':

> The wise pleasure seeker, having realised they [i.e. Heaven or Hell, Purgatory or Indifference] are "different degrees of desire" and never desirable, gives up both Virtue and Vice and becomes a Kiaist. Riding the Shark of his desire he crosses the ocean of dual principle and engages himself in self-love.[14]

---

7 Kenneth and Steffi Grant, *Zos Speaks!: Encounters with Austin Osman Spare* (High Wycombe: Fulgur Ltd., 1998), 62.

8 Ibid., 281.

9 Ibid., 68.

10 Ibid., 68.

11 Robert Ansell, personal communication, September 2008

12 A series of essays by Spare appear under the subtitle *Austin Osman Spare and the Zos Kia Cultus* in the 'Chaos Magic' section of the Internet Sacred Text Archive, accessed September 20, 2015, http://www.sacred-texts.com/eso/chaos/

13 Christopher J. Miles, "Journey into the Neither-Neither": 54.

14 Austin Osman Spare, "The Book of Pleasure" in *Ethos*, 35-36.

Bearing in mind some of the above mentioned caveats, we are now in a position to consider the principal psycho-philosophical ideas of Spare's oeuvre in some depth, in order to facilitate an understanding of how these nuanced conceptualisations are deployed in his aesthetic and magical praxis.

PRINCIPAL IDEAS

Some of Spare's key ideas can be very difficult to pin down precisely: on occasion, it does feel a little like trying to knock rivets into quicksilver. In his earliest published work, *Earth: Inferno* (1904) he quotes freely from Omar Khayyam, Dante and the *New Testament*. William Wallace is critical, commenting that "the quotation [from Dante's *Inferno*] is lax in its translation, being very literal, translating word for word from the Italian in a heavy-handed amateurish fashion."[15] Nevertheless in this volume, Spare presents "potent images of death, sensuality and the grotesque [which] exude an aura of elusive mystery and revelation; cryptic juxtapositions of word and image amply convey his burgeoning philosophy.'[16] It is here that Spare first presents his concepts of Kia and Zos, and had thus "divined his pathway, and determined its twin polarities"[17] (Though as we shall see, one should be careful with the use of the term 'polarity', in the light of the concept of the 'Neither-Neither' which is considered further below). Spare does little at this stage to adumbrate the meaning of Zos and Kia. This would wait until the publication of *The Book of Pleasure (Self-Love): the Psychology of Ecstasy* in 1913 where Austin Spare provides a series of definitions by way of introduction to his psycho-philosophy:

DEFINITIONS

The words God, religions, faith, morals, woman, etc. (they being forms of belief), are used as expressing different "means" as controlling and expressing desire: an idea of unity by fear in some form or another which must spell bondage – the imagined limits; extended by science which adds a dearly paid inch to our height: no more.

Kia: The absolute freedom which being free is mighty enough to be "reality" and free at any time: therefore is not potential or manifest (except as its instant possibility) by ideas of freedom or "means," but by the Ego being free to receive it, by being free of ideas about it and by not believing. The less said of it (Kia) the less obscure is it. Remember evolution teaches by terrible punishments – that conception is ultimate reality but not ultimate freedom from evolution.

---

15 William Wallace, *Austin Osman Spare: The Artist's Books 1905-1927* (Thame: Mandrake Press, 2005), 4.

16 Gavin W. Semple, *Zos-Kia: An Introductory Essay on the Art and Sorcery of Austin Osman Spare* (London: Fulgur Ltd., 1995), 8-9.

17 Ibid., 9.

Virtue: Pure Art

Self-Love: A mental state, mood or condition caused by the emotion of laughter becoming the principle that allows the Ego appreciation or universal association in permitting inclusion before conception.

Exhaustion: That state of vacuity brought by exhausting a desire by some means of dissipation when the mood corresponds to the nature of the desire, i.e., when the mind is worried because of the non-fulfilment of such desire and seeks relief. By seizing this mood and living, the resultant vacuity is sensitive to the subtle suggestion of the sigil.[18]

Zos

Spare does not mention 'Zos' in the *Definitions*. Zos generally acts as his 'alter-ego' in his writings; more accurately, his embodied self. Semple notes:

> Spare states, *"The body considered as a whole I call ZOS"*; Zos therefore designates all that which is embodied or manifest – the apperceptive or conative Ego that 'receives' Kia, and is indeed the bodying forth of the Absolute into being. *"What is unmanifest is Absoluteness; what is manifest is reality as all differentiations of that." (The Logomachy of Zos).*[19]

Shah suggests a number of possible sources:

> Zos, in the terminology of Spare, seems to be an amalgamation of Nietzsche's Zarathustra and Blake's Los of *Jerusalem*. For Spare, Zos was very much a self-representation of a self-willed and self-disciplined artist seeking to redeem society, who also acted as metaphor for the efforts of Imagination to reawaken mystical vision in Mankind.[20]

Semple argues that Spare is adopting a fundamental element of gnostic philosophy – that of dualism and that "this dualism of Being and Non-Being, I and All-Otherness is a fundamental doctrine of gnostic philosophy, and Spare had seized upon it before he was out of his teens."[21]

KIA: ATTEMPTS AT APPREHENSION

The title of this section is quite deliberate. As has been seen above, 'the less said of it

---

18 Austin Osman Spare, 'The Book of Pleasure' in *Ethos*, 32.

19 Gavin W. Semple, *Zos-Kia*, 11.

20 Sunny Shah, *Austin Osman Spare: An Introduction to his Life & Writings* (Edmonds, WA: Holmes Publishing Group, 1998), 20.

21 Gavin W. Semple, *Zos-Kia*, 11.

(Kia), the less obscure it is.' This did not deter William Wallace in his provision of a Kabbalistical attribution, relating it to the 'Tree of Life' glyph: "These permutations [of letters of the 'Sacred Alphabet' as representing the Kia] are the means by which the Kiā progressively reveals itself along the Middle Pillar."[22] A better approximation to the Kia may be Rudolf Otto's concept of the 'numinous.' In his *Das Heilige – The Idea of the Holy* (1923) Otto formulated his concept of the *Numinosum*. As the 'ominous' pertains to the omen, so the 'numinous' pertains to the 'numen' – the 'spiritual' Other – the 'uncanny.' This is distinct from the Kantian noumenon – the *Ding an sich* of which the 'phenomenon' was the human perceptual experience. For Otto,

> The magical is nothing but a suppressed and dimmed form of the numinous, a crude form of it which great art purifies and ennobles. In great art the point is reached at which we may no longer speak of the 'magical', but rather are confronted with the numinous itself, with all its impelling motive power, transcending reason, expressed in sweeping lines and rhythm.[23]

He relates this to the experience of religious painting of China in the classical period of the T'ang and Sung dynasties:

> These works are to be classed with the profoundest and sublimest of the creations of human art. The spectator who, as it were, immerses himself in them feels behind these waters and mountains the mysterious breath of the primeval Tao.[24]

In Spare's art, theriomorphic efflorescence and vegetal anthropomorphism combine. For example, in *The Book of Ugly Ecstasy*, penis becomes anther or stamen, breasts are multiplied and confused with plant ova. Though one might not be comfortable with calling the weird swarms of Spare's art 'sublime,' one cannot deny the presence of his 'sweeping lines and rhythm,' or doubt the 'frisson of the uncanny.' Otto's term *Numinosum* was appropriated by Carl Gustav Jung who altered its meaning: for Otto the numinous pertains to the external 'spiritual' object, whereas Jung gave it a psychological interpretation whereby the feeling of the numinous, the 'uncanny' relates to the subject, and indicates the activation of Archetypes. Richard Noll in his anti-Jungian polemic *The Jung Cult: Origins of a Charismatic Movement* (1996) makes this comment:

> After the appearance of Rudolph Otto's *Das Heilige (The idea of the Holy)* in 1917, Jung referred to the mystery initiations forged by his psychological

---

22 William Wallace, *Austin Osman Spare: The Artist's Books 1905-1927*, 272.
23 Rudolf Otto, *The Idea of the Holy* (Oxford: OUP, 1923), 67.
24 Ibid., 67.

method as an experience of the *numinosum*. "Everyone who has achieved this breakthrough always describes it as overwhelming," the hierophant Jung says in 1931 about those who sacrifice themselves in the Jungian mysteries of analytical psychology.[25]

We can only conclude with the observation that Spare's concept of the Kia transcends subject-object dualism. Otto also makes the following comment with regard to the 'magical' in art which is pertinent to a study of Spare's work: "The actual impression of 'magic' is quite independent of [the] historical bond of connexion with magical practices."[26]

The Neither-Neither

Throughout his work, Spare rejects both orthodox religion and magical traditionalism. His wide reading had provided him with a broad knowledge of religions, cults and assorted arcana. However, unlike Aleister Crowley (see below) and his syncretic approach in occultism,

> Spare's master stroke was to separate the process of believing and *how* to believe from the content of *what* is believed. *The Book of Pleasure* opens with the words, *"What is there to believe, but Self?"* and continues with a meticulous iconoclasm of beliefs both orthodox and unorthodox.[27]

In this way, Spare makes way for his essential concept, the Kia, which we attempted to elucidate above, and which he called "The Consumer of Religion." Spare says of the Kia:

> Of name it has no need, to designate, I call it Kia – I dare not claim it as myself. The Kia which can be expressed by conceivable ideas, is not the eternal Kia, which burns up all belief – but is the archetype of 'self, the slavery of mortality.[28]

Spare's concept is predicated on the following argument: fundamental to all religions is the human desire, in the knowledge of personal ephemerality, to reach out towards a divine or transcendent Other. In so doing, however, a dualism of self and other is created which in itself cannot be transcended – so that all doctrines fail at their commencement: "Self gazes upon self through the mirror of its own making. This is the Law of Duality – the nature of belief, and the very substance of

---

25 Richard Noll, *The Jung Cult: Origins of a Charismatic Movement* (London: Harper Collins, 1996), 282.
26 Rudolf Otto, *The Idea of the Holy*, 66-67.
27 Gavin W. Semple, *Zos-Kia*, 19.
28 Ibid., 19-20.

Ego."[29] Spare's solution to this problem is "to disengage the mutual tension between the 'believer' and 'believed in' by simply removing that which at once unites and separates them – the *believing*."[30] He escapes the clutches of duality by means of the 'Neither-Neither.' With any idea which implies its opposite, the usual way to escape the polarity is to say that your solution is 'neither this – nor that' and thereby transcend both. However, as Semple points out:

> By the negative process of believing 'neither this nor that', the consciousness is located ever between subject and object. This attitude is common to several mystical schools; however, Spare takes it a step further. The 'neither' position still infers the two polarities between which it lies, yet can itself be transcended, *by* itself; this Spare calls the 'Neither-Neither' principle.[31]

That is, neither is it 'neither.' As Spare says in *The Logomachy of Zos*, "THE ABSOLUTE appears to become other than itself, for it is sufficient; it is and is not, neither is it beyond, nor in, nor of me or any thing: it is 'Neither-Neither.'"[32] One may attempt to align the concept of the 'Neither-Neither' with apophatic gnosis, but should beware reducing it to or equating it with this. One also thinks of the *via negativa* of Pseudo-Dionysius the Areopagite, and negative theology where God is described in terms of what he is not.[33] Other suggestions include a comparison with the *Tao* in the *Tao Deh Ching*:

> Spare's magicks make use of a state of mental vacuity he called Neither-Neither and Peter Carroll calls gnosis. This is a state in which dualities are annihilated and consciousness enters an undifferentiated state which is not conceptual, nor verbal nor cognitive. It may be understood – in Taoist terms, for Spare was obviously influenced by Taoism – as a mutual negation of yin and yang effecting a return to the ineffable Tao.[34]

The Neither-Neither could also be compared with the *Ungrund* of the German Christian theosopher Jacob Boehme. One of the dominant themes in Boehme's writings is the utter transcendence of God: His existence outside time and space, inaccessible to all human thought, ineffable by any human tongue.

What then is left which we can conceive of? Nothing is left, a nothing

---

29 Ibid., 20.
30 Ibid., 20.
31 Ibid., 20.
32 Austin Osman Spare, Aphorism 290 of "The Logomachy of Zos" in Kenneth and Steffi Grant, *Zos Speaks!*, 180.
33 David Luscombe, "Dionysius Areopagita (Pseudo-)" in Wouter J. Hanegraaff, Ed., *Dictionary of Gnosis and Western Esotericism* (Leiden: Brill), 312-313.
34 The Ultimate Comment, "Austin Osman Spare," accessed 18 September 2015, http://theultimate-comment.com/austin_osman_spare.

which Boehme calls the *Ungrund*, often translated into English by the word Abyss, a depth which has no end, a bottomless empty nothingness.[35]

Put more radically – and simply – the 'Neither-Neither' is an empty hermeneutic. Shah's comments are amongst the most elegant and succinct: "Spare's Neither-Neither principle – the interminable deferral of meaning through an incessant series of negations perhaps has its theoretical forebear in Hegel."[36] A Hegelian dialectic, in which every positive determination is defined by its negative, and via the interplay of opposites, a third term is motivated. However,

> The Neither-Neither is a perpetual transcending of linguistic terms – neither this, neither that, neither the Hegelian synthesis of the two. Signs are defined by their negative valency to another. The search through the chain of signifiers for that final term which transcends even the Neither-Neither is an impossible quest – as Spare says, "it cannot be balanced". The point of the Neither-Neither is that there is no *telos* – there is no finality,
>
> No transcendental signified, no outside-text that can be the final resting place for meaning.
>
> For Spare, there is no stasis. His psychology of ecstasy is governed by movement. An aesthetics of kinetics.[37]

This emphasis on movement is a reflection of the psychodynamic model of the psyche that dominated the period. Shah invites the reader to trace the language of action in Spare's writing. Sigils (see below) are activated by *motivation*, "the Neither-Neither is a continual chase. The Death Posture may seem a moment of quietude, but is a dynamic equilibrium – an on-going struggle between conscious and subconscious."[38] The 'Neither-Neither' can be considered then as the pathway to the gnosis of the Absolute, Kia. Spare relates the intimate relationship of the two in *The Book of Pleasure*: "The Kia which can vaguely be expressed in words is the "Neither-Neither," the unmodified "I" in the sensation of omnipresence."[39]

It is quite apparent from the above account that the 'Neither-Neither' serves a more mystical and gnostic than simply magical purpose in providing access to the ineffable Kia, resulting in the *mysterium coniunctionis* of the Zos and the Kia. As Semple has observed:

---

35 Robin Waterfield, ed., *Jacob Boehme: Western Esoteric Masters Series* (Berkeley: North Atlantic Books, 2001), 26.

36 Sunny Shah, "AOS Theory" in Geraldine Beskin and John Bonner, eds., *Austin Osman Spare: Artist Occultist Sensualist* (Suffolk: Beskin Press, 1999), 24.

37 Ibid., 2-3.
38 Ibid., 2-3.
39 Austin Osman Spare, "The Book of Pleasure" in *Ethos*, 45.

Spare walked the paths of both mysticism and magic. To a mystic seeking reunion with and dissolution in Godhead, magical powers – the *siddhis* – are unwanted side-effects of his practices; for the sorcerer, observation of magical mechanism may lead to speculations of a purely mystical nature. The two paths are refractions of one Path.[40]

The 'Neither-Neither' is attained via the *Death Posture* which is discussed below.

THE DEATH POSTURE

In Spare's phronesis, the attainment of the 'Neither-Neither' is via the stages of the Death Posture. Spare elaborates the stages of this procedure in *The Book of Pleasure*:

THE RITUAL AND DOCTRINE

Lying on your back lazily, the body expressing the emotion of yawning, suspiring while conceiving by smiling, that is the idea of the posture. Forgetting time with those things which were essential reflecting their meaninglessness, the moment is beyond time and its virtue has happened.

Standing on tip-toe, with arms rigid, bound behind by the hands, clasped and straining the utmost, the neck stretched-breathing deeply and spasmodically, till giddy and sensation comes in gusts, gives exhaustion and capacity for the former.

Gazing at your reflection till it is blurred and you know not the gazer, close your eyes (this usually happens involuntarily) and visualize. The light (always an X in curious evolutions) that is seen should be held onto, never letting go, till the effort is forgotten, this gives a feeling of immensity (which sees a small form), whose limit you cannot reach. This should be practised before experiencing the foregoing. The emotion that is felt is the knowledge that tells you why.[41]

Physiologically, this appears to involve hyperventilation almost to the point of loss of consciousness, and an exaggerated version of 'progressive muscular relaxation' where various muscles groups may be sequentially contracted and relaxed to promote deep relaxation. The key point is achieving *exhaustion*, thereby extinguishing conceptual thought and continuous internal dialogue. Interestingly, it has been noted, from a parapsychological perspective that:

Some of those taking part in PK [psychokinesis] studies ... clench

---

40 Gavin W. Semple, *Zos-Kia*, 20.
41 Ibid., 67-68.

their fists and screw up their faces when faced with a micro-PK task on a computer. While this muscular preparation seems to work well in a real physical task, PK curiously seems to occur more frequently in the quiescent period characterised by release of effort.[42]

The importance of this exhaustion may have either or both of two sources, both of which Spare was exposed to: mediumism (see below) and the yogic practices which he would have been familiar with as a probationer with Crowley's Group the *Argenteum Astrum*. Crowley's *Liber HHH* makes reference to *Shavasana*, the 'Pose of a Corpse,' but the Death Posture is similar to this technique in name only:

> 0. Be seated in thine Asana, or recumbent in Shavasana, or in the position of the dying Buddha.
> Think of thy death; imagine the various diseases that may attack thee.[43]

The Death Posture, then, leads into an extended visualisation process. The idea of experiencing the 'emotion of yawning' and smiling is of particular note, as it appears that "mentation is suspended during a yawn or a smile (this can be ascertained by attempting a simple calculation)."[44] Thus, it can be said that:

> With a smile and a mighty sigh that awakens nostalgias of the infinite, the sorcerer shifts between the domain of the living and the otherworld of the dead; dead in life and vital in death, within the perfect equipoise of Neither-Neither.[45]

The Death Posture should not be thought of as a mundane, work-a-day yogic practice. As has been noted:

> This death-feint mimetises in terms appreciable to both body and mind the fundamental principle of magic; *the reduction of all properties to simplicity, making them transmutable to utilise them afresh by redirection, without capitalization, bearing fruit many times.*"[46]

SIGILS AND THE SACRED ALPHABET

The creation of his 'Sacred Alphabet' and the process of creating sigils is important, though not central (see below), to the magical praxis of Austin Osman Spare. Like

---

42 Carl Williams, "Conceptual Metaphor: A Meaning- oriented Approach for Parapsychology," *Journal of the Society for Psychical Research*, 7.2,892 (July 2008):137.
43 Aleister Crowley, "Liber HHH," accessed 18 September, 2015, http://www.sacred-texts.com/oto/lib341.htm.
44 Gavin W. Semple, *Zos-Kia*, 25.
45 Ibid., 18.
46 Ibid., 18.

many students, Spare would have visited the British museum and there have been exposed to the "primal scripts from the ancient kingdoms of Egypt, Assyria, and Sumer"[47] and would have been aware that "although the original meanings were largely forgotten, these glyphs had survived through time, carrying the exotic ambience of the cultures which gave birth to them."[48] The secrets of the meanings were at one stage the preserve of hierocracies and royalty: these only were permitted to know the sacred meanings. It has been observed that:

> The Sacred Alphabet, as Spare describes it, consists of the root forms of … evocative sigils, it is the veritable script of the familiars thronging the magician's Circle, and epitomizes the mother tongue of that oblique dominion. Ultimately abstract and inscrutable, it articulates via aesthesis.[49]

Wallace provides a detailed comparison of Spare's 'Sacred Alphabet' – called by both Grant and Wallace 'The Alphabet of Desire' – with the Enochian letters of Dr John Dee.[50] At times the similarity is striking, but elsewhere it is hard to see anything similar. The actual sigillisation process itself uses the ordinary alphabet, and involves conjoining letters. Grant explains:

> Spare gives as an example the desire for superhuman strength which he formulates as follows: *I desire the strength of a tiger*. In order to sigillize this desire, put down on a piece of paper all the letters of which the sentence is composed, omitting repetitions. The resulting sequence of letters, IDESRTHNGOFMY, is then combined to form a single glyph.[51]

The first sigillic formula appeared in his *Book of Satyrs* (1907). During this period Spare signed himself with a monogram, conjoining his initials, in the style of Albrecht Dürer (1471-1528), an artist who Spare greatly admired.[52] It was commonplace for artists and writers to sign themselves with a monogram during this period. One thinks particularly of the 'butterfly signatures' of James McNeill Whistler:

> Whistler's monogram 'J.W.' was developed into a 'butterfly' signature in c.1869 and gradually evolved over the next thirty years, acquiring antennae, veins and a tail. In the more barbed of his letters, he would sign himself with a stinging tail, like a scorpion.[53]

---

47 Ibid., 7.
48 Ibid., 7.
49 Austin Osman Spare, *Two Tracts on Cartomancy: With an Introductory Essay by Gavin W. Semple* (London: Fulgur, 1997), 22.
50 William Wallace, *Austin Osman Spare*, 268-270.
51 Kenneth Grant, *Images and Oracles of Austin Osman Spare* (London: Fulgur, 2003), 55.
52 Gavin W. Semple, *Zos-Kia*, 8.
53 "The Correspondence of James McNeill Whistler: A Chronology of Whistler's Butterfly Signatures" University of Glasgow, accessed Sept 18, 2015, http://www.whistler.arts.gla.ac.uk/miscellany/butterflies/.

It is from the basic idea of the monogram that Spare derived his idea of using sigils as a magical method. Hence, with the development of this idea during 1910, he ceased to sign his work with a monogram, and instead used AOS which became his trademark. As has been noted, "The distinction was necessary as the Sorcerous application of the sigil became apparent."[54]

In the Spring of 1910, Spare was working on material which would eventually form *The Book of Pleasure*, his 'magical grimoire.' A sketchbook coincident with this period shows

> Exemplars of letter-forms from a variety of ancient alphabets, which would appear alongside Spare's personal calligrams and sigils. Stylised Hebrew, Coptic and Cuneiform letters appear, as well as geomantic figures and letters from the Enochian script of Dr John Dee, an eclectic re-alignment of earlier traditions to Spare's intent.[55]

Note the wording: 'an eclectic re-alignment' rather than a syncretic acquisition. It is also important to distinguish between 'sigillisation' and 'symbolisation.'

> *The Book of Pleasure* is perhaps Spare's principal work and what is interesting is the methodological objection to the role of symbol and symbolisation within magical praxis. It is important to distinguish very clearly Spare's form of sigillisation from any commonplace idea of symbolism. There are a number of models that can be distinguished: a symbol can stand for something; it can point to something; it can contain something or it can communicate something. In each case it is essentially an adjunct of 'something.'… It is in one of the sections on sigils, subtitled 'the psychology of believing', that we find the following: "We are not the object by the perception, but by becoming it".[56]

That is, the symbol implies perception of object by subject, the sigil: subject-object resolution.

THEOSOPHY, ERNST HAECKEL AND SPARE'S ATAVISM

Spare was certainly influenced by the ideas of Helena Petrovna Blavatsky's Theosophical Society. It has been noted that:

An early influence on his youthful mysticism had been Madame Blavatsky's

---

54 Gavin W. Semple, *Zos-Kia*, 8.

55 Ibid., 8.

56 Matt Lee, "'Memories of a sorcerer': notes on Gilles Deleuze-Felix Guattari, Austin Osman Spare and Anomalous Sorceries," accessed September 18, 2015, https://fulgur.co.uk/artists/austin-osman-spare/memories-of-a-sorcerer-notes-on-gilles-deleuze-felix-guattari-austin-osman-spare-and-anomalous-sorceries/.

Theosophy, reflected by the appearance of terms such as 'Ikkah' and 'Sikah' in the *Earth: Inferno* of 1904. [*Iccha* and *Sikkah* are Sanskrit terms for 'Will' and 'Method' respectively].[57]

William Wallace suggests that there is some historical evidence for this:

> There is a prevailing family tradition, emanating from Spare's younger sister, Ellen Victoria and recounted by her son Martin Lapwood that Spare, in his youth, made use of the Theosophical Library.[58]

However, for an indicator as to the origins of Spare's concepts of 'atavism' we have to look beyond Blavatsky to the work of the embryologist, artist, and racial anthropologist, Ernst Heinrich Philipp August Haeckel (1834-1919). Haeckel was imbued with German Romantic thought as represented by *Naturphilosophie*, and the conceptualisation of a 'living nature.' As is a commonplace for the science of the period, he considered it appropriate to interpolate his own Romantic and aesthetic intuitions into empirical material. In his *Die Welträtsel* (1899) Haeckel tellingly entitles two chapters 'The Embryology of the Soul' and 'The Phylogeny of the Soul.'[59] However, simultaneously his perhaps surprising espousal of a monist position attributed life to mechanistic processes. Rudolf Steiner, Blavatsky's contemporary, who later evolved his own ideas in the form of Anthroposophy had this to say about Haeckel:

> Haeckel's phylogenetic idea is the most significant event in German intellectual life in the latter half of the nineteenth century. And there is no better scientific foundation to esotericism than Haeckel's teaching. Haeckel's teaching is exemplary, but Haeckel is the worst commentator on it.[60]

It is evolution in general, and, more specifically, Haeckel's 'Biogenetic Law' and his now largely abandoned concept of *Ontogeny recapitulates* Phylogeny, and Blavatsky's *responsum* to it, which explains her quasi-empirical searches for the spiritual, couched as they are in a specific evolutionary metaphysics, and Spare's subsequent interpretation of these ideas. Haeckel promulgated the idea that vertebrate embryos passed through all of the documented Darwinian stages of vertebrate evolution *in utero*. He gave as evidence the similarity of vertebrate embryos at an early stage of development – which he exaggerated, as was later demonstrated. In addition, in his *Natürliche Schöpfungsgeschichte* (1868), "he included woodcut prints represented

---

57 Austin Osman Spare, *Two Tracts on Cartomancy*, 21.
58 William Wallace, *Austin Osman Spare*, 19.
59 Ernst Haeckel, *The Riddle of the Universe: At the Close of the Nineteenth Century*, trans. by Joseph McCabe (New York: Harper & Brothers Publishers, 1905).
60 "Defending Steiner: Rudolf Steiner and Ernst Haeckel," 4, accessed September 18, 2015, http://www.defendingsteiner.com/articles/rs-haeckel.php.

as embryos of various animals to support the idea that during development, an embryo recapitulated its supposed evolutionary history."[61] In addition, "Haeckel placed woodcut prints of dog and human embryos [and] stated that the actual embryos possessed the same likeness represented in the woodcuts. In fact, they were all fraudulently printed from the *same* woodcut."[62] Blavatsky would use Haeckel's 'law' in her formulation of a cyclical ascendant metempsychosis.[63]

PLACING SPARE PHILOSOPHICALLY

Spare's thought resists easy explication by comparison. His influences are at the best of times difficult to discern, and in any case the desire for original thought (not necessarily an original 'synthesis' with its Hegelian overtones) and to reject dialectic and pursue the 'Neither-Neither,' makes this even more problematic. Robert Ansell remarks

> I have always been uncomfortable with the attempts to project philosophies upon Spare's work, but accept it seems necessary for some. One might as well say of one bird to another, they [are] similar: they both have wings, they both have beaks, they both have clawed feet – they must be related. Yes, but not in any way relevant to the present incarnation.[64]

Sunny Shah concludes an essay with the following comments:

> Isn't this a pointless exercise, all this theorising over the theories of Spare? Isn't it so much navel gazing? Austin Osman Spare himself said that the modernisms of the day, what he called 'atavistic nostalgias' are "the fear of facing and expressing reality." … I regard this intellectual posturing as a form of wilful re-appropriation. To drag him through the critical machine to revitalise his comments. And perhaps to bring the attention of the academic community to one of England's lost theorists.[65]

Admittedly, where Spare is concerned, the empirico-historical technique does seem to propose a 'frogs' legs taste like chicken' approach. Having said this, his thought cannot be said to be entirely autochthonous, and a number of observations on documented sources can be made. Many of the putative influences on Spare and his literature and art have been analysed in depth by William Wallace in his monolithic

---

61 Eric Weisstein's World of Scientific Biography: "Haeckel, Ernst (1834-1919)," 1-2, accessed September 18, 2015, http://scienceworld.wolfram.com/biography/Haekel.html.
62 Ibid., 2.
63 Helena P. Blavatsky, *The Secret Doctrine* (London: The Theosophical Publishing House, 1893)
64 Robert Ansell: personal Communication August 2008.
65 Sunny Shah, "AOS Theory" in Beskin and Bonner eds., *Austin Osman Spare: Artist Occultist Sensualist*, 27-8.

work.[66] A few brief observations will be made with regard to Wallace's work. One should remark at the outset that he is frequently rather speculative. Consider the following:

> Spare may have noted with interest Crowley's use of the Platonic oppositional conditions of phenomena and noumena.[67]

> Spare may have encountered Dee through the tercentennial publication of two biographies: Thomas Smith's *The Life of John Dee* (1908) and Charlotte Fell Smith's *John Dee 1527-1608* (1909).[68]

> Spare's comments on mediumism hint that he may have considered it, perhaps witnessed it and discarded it.[69]

Whilst he remains within the domain of art criticism and the interpretation of Spare's pictures, this is not a problem. However, when he steps outside of this, he frequently goes beyond the boundaries of the documented written word. In addition, he expounds at some considerable length on the form of Spare's writing rather than the content. His literary focus means that he concentrates on the origins of the florilegium that Spare gathers to articulate his ideas, rather than upon the ideas themselves. Of note also is that Wallace presents a table of correspondences between Sparian hypostases, Kabbalah, and ancient Egyptian theology,[70] thus attempting to petrify Spare into the very fossilised magical tradition that he eschewed. As Spare said:

> Their symbolism is chaotic and meaningless. Not knowing the early rendering, they succeed in projecting their own meagreness by this confusion, as explaining the ancient symbols. Children are more wise. This conglomeration of antiquity decayed, collected with the disease of greed – is surely the chance for charity? Forgetting trumpery ideas, learn the best tradition by seeing your own functions and the modern unbiased.[71]

This is reminiscent of the Welsh poet R. S. Thomas, who in the poem *Welsh Landscape*, commenting on the traditionalism of his own countrymen, sums up very well Spare's view on ceremonial magicians of the so-called 'Western Occult Tradition,' where he calls them:

---

66 William Wallace, *Austin Osman Spare*. Passim.
67 Ibid., 264.
68 Ibid., 265.
69 Ibid., 291.
70 Ibid., 66-7.
71 Austin Osman Spare, "The Book of Pleasure" in *Ethos*, 40-41.

> An impotent people
> Sick with inbreeding
> Worrying the carcase of an old song[72]

This is the paradox of Spare: a faltering desire to express new ideas employing archaic idioms.

SPARE AND THE ROMANTIC TRADITION

Whilst there are a number of Romantic ideas in Spare's work, there are two which stand out for brief consideration here. Firstly, the importance of the imaginative faculty, and secondly the prominence he gives to the notion of the 'Fatal Woman.' The Weimar Neo-Classicist view of the imagination saw it as a purely *passive* function of the mind associated only with sense perception. As has been noted:

> This is in direct contrast to the whole conceptual and cosmological basis of Spare's system and his perceptions of the Imagination as *praxis*. That is, the Imagination as the means by which the Divine becomes accessible through Inspiration and the divine (*Kiā*) as the repository for the countless myriad forms of inherent ancestral wisdom.[73]

A central feature of Romantic thought is the importance of the Imagination as a spiritual, noetic organ of 'ungrasped truth.'[74] Spare sees it as a truly creative faculty, not just a means to rearrange sense data and memory. In his writing, it is the faculty which subsumes reason and habitual thought, and facilitates the apprehension of the divine.

Secondly, we consider the idea of the 'Fatal Woman,' which remained prominent in the *Décadent* pantheon of the *Fin de Siècle*. The 'Fatal Woman' is

> Seen to persist in in Spare's books from *Earth: Inferno* onwards, with the Woman in both positive and negative guises, as human or demonic, as witch and virgin and, at times, crossing the gender divide as androgyne and hermaphrodite. ... The hero can be either aided or beset by a variety of female or hybrid types; these range in Spare's books from incarnate women to allegorical types of varying nature and character.[75]

---

72 R.S Thomas, *Selected Poems:1946 – 1968* (London: Hart-Davis, MacGibbon, 1973), 9.

73 William Wallace, *Austin Osman Spare*, 12.

74 Defining what constitutes 'Romanticism' has always been a thorny issue, see Chapter 1. "In Search of a Definition" in Isaiah Berlin, *The Roots of Romanticism*, ed. by Henry Hardy (London: Pimlico, 1999). On the importance of the imagination in this context, see C.M. Bowra, *The Romantic Imagination* (London: Oxford University Press, 1957).

75 Ibid., 13-14.

SPARE AND THE RABELAISIAN GROTESQUE

Spare was particularly fond of illustrating what others might find repulsive in his art work, and frequently employed very elderly female nudes, in what might be described as the pursuit of Rabelaisian grotesque realism: his *faute de mieux* 'hagography.' In *Gargantua* we find sexualised the elderly female: "By means of those laws, widow women, for two months after the deaths of their husbands, can frankly play at bonkbum, pricking on regardless."[76] In *The Witches' Sabbath*, Spare unveils his esoteric reasoning in relation to magical praxis:

> The Sabbath is an inverse-reversion for self-seduction; an undoing for a divertive connation: Sex is used as the medium and technique of a magical act. It is not only erotic satisfaction; the converting sensual-sublimation detached, controlled until later and final sublimation. His whole training is submissive and obedient until he can transmute, control and divert him or her self where desired by transference and cold amoral passion.[77]

He elaborates further that "The Witch so engaged is usually old, usually grotesque, libidinously learned and is as sexually attractive as a corpse; yet she becomes the entire vehicle of consummation. This is necessary for transmutation; the personal aesthetic culture is destroyed."[78]

We are now in a position to consider the practical aspects of the magical and aesthetic work of Austin Osman Spare. For the purpose of this paper I have elected to consider this under broad thematic rubrics rather than as component parts of a diachronic evolution, but will mention developmental aspects where necessary.

SIDEREALISM

Fig. 2 Portrait of Joan Crawford (1933)

---

76 François Rabelais, *Gargantua and Pantagruel* (London: Penguin, 2006), 217.
77 Austin Osman Spare, "The Witches' Sabbath" in *Ethos*, 154.
78 Ibid., 154.

In the 1930s, Spare began to experiment with a method of portraiture which he termed 'Siderealism.' Often known for the gritty realism of his portraits of the everyday street people of South London, here Spare turned his hand to document the images of famous Hollywood stars (see Fig.2), hence the pun on 'sidereal' – pertaining both to images perhaps drawn in starlight and the 'stars' of stage and screen which were his subject.

The portraits were painted using a process of anamorphic translation, a mathematical trigonometric process by which the image is distorted becoming elongated and etiolated. In its extreme form, *anamorphosis* produces an image which may only be seen from a particular position of the observer in front of the painting. The most famous example of this is of course Hans Holbein the Younger's *The Ambassadors* of 1533 which has an extreme anamorphic skull at the base of the painting, only seen for what it is by viewing the painting far out to the left or right. (Fig.3)

Fig. 3 Hans Holbein the Younger, *The Ambassadors* (1553)

We may speculate as to the purpose of such an artistic idiom in Spare's practice, as he does not specify. It has been suggested that the intention of the distortion, which was effectively akin to a trigonometric translation, was to "suggest much more of the sitters' personality and magickal content than is apparent in a more conventional depiction."[79] However, Frank Letchford has denied this, quoting Spare, and saying that the purpose of the distortion:

---

79 Marcus M. Jungkurth, "Tree of Knowledge – Good and Evil" in Geraldine Beskin and John Bonner, eds., *Austin Osman Spare: Artist Occultist Sensualist*, 51.

... was *not* to illume the subjects character but to represent several aspects of an idea or: "The geometric plasticity or rhythm released by an exact application of knowledge as opposed to fortuitous derivation."
... His 'sidereal' technique is better known to tutors and students as 'Anamorphic' art, a technique whereby they can only be viewed from a certain perspective or angle.[80]

Perhaps Siderealism was Spare's answer to Surrealism. In the context of this account, the technique does not at first sight appear to bare any specific relation to magical praxis. One might speculate that the images are simply unsettling to visual perception and quite literally compel the viewer to see things 'from a different angle.' However, a number of the portraits in this series are entitled 'Experiments in Relativity.'[81] Salvador Dalí's famous 'soft watches' in his *The Persistence of Memory* (1931) were at one time considered a meditation on Relativity and the distortions of Space-Time.[82] It is likely that Spare, who called himself the 'English Surrealist,' was carrying out a similar experiment in the distortion of space and time, deriving 'sidereal' from the notion of a relative 'sidereal time' used by astrologers when plotting the natal chart and so on. Certainly, after the incorporation of Vaihinger's philosophy he would talk about the relative nature of 'sidereal truth' (see below). I shall now move on to consider Austin Spare's ideas regarding 'Atavism' – and what Kenneth Grant termed 'Atavistic Resurgence.'

ATAVISM

SIGILLISATION AND ATAVISM: DESIRE, WILL AND BELIEF; IDS AND KARMAS

To understand how the process of sigillisation receives its sorcerous application one has to understand, firstly, the relationship of Desire, Will, and Belief in Spare's writing, and secondly, how these relate to Spare's notions of atavism. In Kiaism, Belief and Desire constitute Spare's great conceptual binary. By obtaining the vacuity of the 'Neither-Neither,' Spare aims to suspend believing, and thus neutralise a plurality of distracting and conflicting desires. The Will and the Desire are then freed up to provide a cathexis for magical purposes. The sigil can embody this focussed 'beam' of desire, which then must be lost in the 'subconsciousness' – a sleight of mind which can be viewed as a *reverse-anamnesis*. Whereas in the psychoanalytic process, the analyst facilitates the recovery of the contents of the subconscious which have been long repressed by the individual, Spare advocates that the conscious desire must be buried and forgotten. Only in this way, by the desire becoming an 'organic' subconscious desire, will the magical procedure be

---

80 Frank Letchford, *Michelangelo in a Teacup: Austin Osman Spare* (Thame: mandrake Press, 2005), 215.
81 Spare entitled a series of the Sidereal portraits as numbered 'Experiments in Relativity.' See "Star Time: Famous Faces" in Stephen Pochin, ed., *Austin Osman Spare, Fallen Visionary: Refractions*, 70-71.
82 Dawn Ades, *Dalí* (London: Thames and Hudson, 1982), 179.

effective. Spare also describes how sigils may become the vehicle for personified desires which he calls, using Freudian terminology, 'Ids.'

These reside in the personal subconscious. These may be ensorcellated by the sigil and induced to materialise in the form of elemental *telesmata*. According to Spare, there are other unconscious desires and drives which he termed 'Karmas':

Spare realized that *any* symbols must be effective provided that they are congruent with the patterns of the operator's innate beliefs and personal aesthetic [i.e 'innate' rather than externally imposed belief systems]. This is certain to be the case if they are drawn from his or her own subconsciousness. He understood 'Karmas' to be those elements of past experience and desire which dwell unrecognised within the deep mind, periodically resurging into waking life in new, sometimes discomfiting guises. They seem autonomous, even demonic, because they elude conscious control.[83]

Fig. 4 Evolution of the Human Race (1929)

The Karmas may arise from pre-human phylogenetic strata of the unconscious mind, which may even include vegetal strata. Kenneth Grant seems to group the

83 Austin Osman Spare, *Two Tracts on Cartomancy*, 22.

Ids and Karmas together. However, my impression is that the Ids relate to more superficial and personal layers of the subconscious/unconscious, and personal memories and history.

When isolated and given the sigil through which to manifest, the "'Ids' become transformative potentials, their knowledge spoken forth in primal languages of desire."[84] This is the process Grant termed 'Atavistic Resurgence.' Spare's sorcery therefore involves a two-way exchange between the conscious and unconscious mind – a process of *amnesis-anamnesis.*

On the Atavistic and Shamanistic

Spare's atavism sees animal 'Karmas' as representing Man's evolutionary and reincarnatory history or perhaps more accurately metahistory: elements of his psyche which remain dormant but can come to the surface at any time. (see Fig.4). As aforementioned Spare has been appropriated by many post-modern and 'New Age' currents, and perhaps because of his use of trance states in his automatic drawing and writing, Spare has been cast in the guise of some kind of Edwardian Shaman:

> One may view Spare as a cartographer of the human psyche, whose shamanistic talents enabled him to traverse both space and time. In addition it has been suggested that: "All of the Janus-headed, multi-faced, theriomorphic swarms which proliferate in Spare's paintings threaten to break out of their world and spill into ours."[85]

And in addition:

> Spare is a sorceror and a shamanic artist – He attempts to represent the occult, the hidden, the unseen, to illustrate the unseeable, to portray sensations and subconscious energies. ...The shaman is a person who deliberately remains in a perpetual spiritual crisis and this can sometimes conflict with his earthly needs.[86]

Christopher Miles points out that past ethnographic and anthropological studies have created a number of problematics in terms of what he calls 'the construction of shamanic identities.' One dominant theme is the construction of a 'universal shamanism' rather than respecting differences between tribes and even across continents. He mentions the work of Michael Harner ('core-shamanism') and Mircea Eliade as examples: "Harner, then, shares Eliade's urge to construct a

---

84 Ibid., 22.

85 Geraldine Beskin and John Bonner, Introduction to Geraldine Beskin and John Bonner, eds., *Austin Osman Spare: Artist Occultist Sensualist*, 1.

86 John Balance, "Tree of Knowledge, Good and Evil" in Geraldine Beskin and John Bonner, eds., *Austin Osman Spare: Artist Occultist Sensualist*, 52.

universal "shamanism," a generalized, for-all-cases description of the essentials that is thus able to link a vast panoply of cultures around the world." He argues that labelling any practice as "shamanism" or any individual as a "shaman" "is a highly problematic act that carries far more information about the person creating the label and their cultural contexts than it can ever do about any possibility of indigenous practice."[87]

How does Sparian atavism compare with the shamanic use of tutelary animal spirits? As aforementioned, Spare considered these entities to be a deep part of his own psyche so that, although employing an occultist spin on evolutionary theory, he couches his notions in the framework of depth psychology:

> All geniuses have active subconsciousness, and the less they are aware of the fact, the greater their accomplishments. ... Know the subconsciousness to be an epitome of all experience and wisdom, past incarnations as men, animals, *birds, vegetable life, etc.,* [emphasis S.M.] everything that exists, has and ever will exist.[88]

From a modern paleontological perspective, of course, birds are an off-shoot of the reptilian phylum and never part of human evolutionary history, but this is a residue of Haeckelian Biogenesis, which persists to the present day in esotericism. Semple summarises Spare's approach:

> Spare's sorcery has been described as becoming 'shamanistic' in emphasis; this comment was probably intended to contrast his pure and uncluttered method with the ceremonialism which he derided. The true link however is his formulation of Atavistic Resurgence [sic.] as the means of eliciting creative *genius*. Bestial transformation is perhaps the most ancient magical art, used, used by shamans to establish rapport with animals – essential for tribal societies dependent upon the hunt – and to ensorcel beast spirits and familiars for spirit journeying and shape shifting. ... However, the assumption of atavistic powers can take other forms, apart from possession and mimesis: the bestial and vegetal forms which writhe and weave through Spare's artwork ... indicate the ways in which he preferred to interact with atavisms.[89]

The shaman is classically a spiritual healer who typically employs totem animal spirits in a spiritist/animistic worldview. As Robert J. Wallis has discussed in a recent paper *Austin Osman Spare: Visionary 'Shaman': Deconstructing the Myth*, since at least as far back as the eighteenth century and the concept of the 'noble savage,' the identities of artist, madman, genius and Shaman as peripheral, marginalised

---

87 Christopher Miles, "Journey into the Neither-Neither", 58.
88 Austin Osman Spare, "The Book of Pleasure" in *Ethos*, 121.
89 Gavin W. Semple, *Zos-Kia*, 26.

and yet paradoxically celebrated individuals have become semantically 'entangled,' with little reverence for their individual historical construction.[90] As a result the term 'shaman' has become diffuse and disparate in its qualification to the point of being meaningless. As Wallis says, a priest delivering the Eucharist might be considered a 'shaman.'

In some parts of the world, the shaman acts as a *psychopompos* who undergoes a *katabasis* to seek the lost soul of the sick tribal member in the underworld and return it to him. This is very different to Spare's magical philosophy and aesthetics – the shaman perhaps becoming possessed by a 'bird spirit', whereas Spare would liberate an avian 'Karma' from the unconscious. (See above regarding Spare's sigillisation and 'obtaining the power of a tiger.') For Spare, the unconscious mind is 'The Storehouse of Memories with an Ever-Open Door.'[91] Spare adopts Haeckelian ideas in his notion of 'Atavism' describing as we have seen elements of the psyche considered as entities from previous existences in non-human form. It is these deep-seated psychological entities which appear to be the source of the 'animal spirits' which he was allegedly able to conjure to physical manifestation. Intriguingly, Spare seems to have anticipated the work of Paul MacLean, who postulated a 'triune brain theory.'[92] MacLean theorises that there are three phylogenetic 'layers' to the brain. The deep structures he calls the 'Reptilian Brain' concerned with the appetites, autonomic nervous system and homeostasis. The next layer is a mammalian 'Paleocortex' concerned with the emotions and social interaction; and finally, the latest phylogenetic human addition, the 'Neocortex' concerned with logic and ratiocination. It is to the suspension of ratiocination that we now move on to in a consideration of the role of Automatic phenomena in Spare's writing and art work.

AUTOMATISM

In her book, *Surrealism and the Occult*, in a chapter entitled 'The Surrealist Manifestoes, Automatism and Austin Osman Spare,' Nadia Choucha notes that:

> The writings of André Breton are essential to gaining any understanding of surrealism. … In the first *Surrealist Manifesto* (1924), Breton called for the recuperation of lost mental powers. 'Under the pretence of civilization and progress, we have managed to banish from the mind everything that may rightly or wrongly be termed superstition or fancy: forbidden is any kind of search for truth which is not in conformance with accepted practices.'… Surrealism is defined not simply as a new style or form of culture, but as a re-evaluation of the past and an attempt to explore

---

90 Robert J. Wallis, "Austin Osman Spare, Visionary 'Shaman': Deconstructing the Myth" in Stephen Pochin Ed., *Austin Osman Spare, Fallen Visionary: Refractions* (London: Jerusalem Press, 2012), 123.
91 Austin Osman Spare, "The Book of Pleasure" in *Ethos*, 121.
92 See Paul D. MacLean, *The Triune Brain in Evolution: Role in Paeleocerebral Functions* (New York: Springer, 1990). The hypothesis though useful has been criticised as simplistic in recent years.

obscure and neglected aspects of human experience.[93]

Breton elaborates further when he says that "We cross what occultists call dangerous territory."[94] The investigations transcend logic and rationalism, and do this mainly by the technique of automatism. Breton defines this as follows:

> Surrealism, noun, masc., pure psychic automatism by which it is intended to express, either verbally, or in writing, the true function of thought. Thought dictated in the absence of all control exerted by reason, and outside all aesthetic and moral preoccupations.[95]

Breton had been influenced by the French psychologist, Pierre Janet (1859-1947). Of particular note is that he had read Janet's book *Psychological Automatism* (1889): "Breton had been a medical student at the Sorbonne, and practiced psychiatry upon shell-shocked soldiers in an army hospital during the war."[96] Whilst Breton was more concerned with automatic writing, André Masson produced automatic drawing. Masson was unconvinced that drawing in this way could be completely 'automatic':

> It was I who became the severest critic of automatism. I still cannot agree with the unconscious approach. I do not believe you can arrive by this means at the intensity essential for a picture. I recognize there are intense expressions to be obtained through the subconscious, but not without selection.[97]

In England, one Austin Osman Spare had been "successfully producing automatic drawings at least ten years before the surrealist movement had begun in France."[98] Spare had experimented with both automatic techniques. In fact, some of *The Focus of Life* was written in a trance state:

> It is interesting to note several references to breathing and breath-holding, states which induce trance and self-hypnosis. Perhaps the automatic writing therein was penned in a state of detachment in order to reach down into the lump of material which the mind had the ability to marvellously organize. Some of the writing in *Focus* was automatically produced while other parts were edited.[99]

---

93 Nadia Choucha, *Surrealism and the Occult* (Oxford: Mandrake Press, 1991), 47.
94 Ibid., 47.
95 Ibid., 47-48.
96 Ibid., 48.
97 Ibid., 49.
98 Ibid., 49.
99 Austin Osman Spare, *The Book of Automatic Drawing* (Thame: I-H-O books, 2005), 4.

Hannen Swaffer describes Spare's technique of automatic drawing:

> On some occasions, in order to do automatic drawings, Mr Spare stares into a mirror and induces self-hypnotism. In a hypnotic state, he sometimes goes on working for hours, awakening to find that he has covered pages and pages full of the most beautiful work. He cannot always control it. There are periods, sometimes for months at a time, he says, when, receiving no promptings from outside, he cannot work at all.[100]

Spare says that he believes that although they are not cognisant of it, many artists are inspired by outside forces, or that they work through their subconscious minds. He recommends the development of these powers:

> All significant art, I believe, comes from that source. It is inspiration, revelation, spiritual truth, which men express in the different ways they have developed.

> I am now trying to perfect a technique of automatic drawing, so that the best can be brought out in me. If we study the subconscious we have much to learn. …

> The prophets and seers were hermits. Because of circumstances I have lived for months a hermit's life. Poverty has made me live alone. It has been partly choice, partly compulsion. The result has been psychic development.[101]

In 1936, the International Surrealist Exhibition opened. Salvador Dalí was to lecture in July of that year and Austin Osman Spare, who had published *The Book of Pleasure*, anticipating the first Surrealist manifesto by eleven years, was ignored. However, "Spare set out to redress the balance; the very term 'Surrealism' which Breton had appropriated from Apollinaire was now assumed – with calculated irony – by Spare as his own."[102] It is of note that at Christmas and on her birthday, Spare's friend Ada Pain "received affectionate cards from *"Your Surrealist – Austin O. Spare."*[103] Although Spare continued to use both automatic drawing and writing techniques in his work, "automatic drawing only flourished amongst the Paris group for a few months of 1920, after which emphasis shifted to automatic writing."[104] The following comment from Oswell Blakeston, a critic and film-maker, which appeared in the catalogue for Spare's exhibition of October 1936 is particularly cogent for this account: "Surrealist in Surrealism", … "How many 'movements' he

---

100 William Wallace, *Michelangelo in a teacup*, 121.
101 Ibid., 5.
102 Austin Osman Spare, *Two Tracts on Cartomancy*, 12.
103 Ibid., 13.
104 Ibid., 13.

has originated the near future will show, even as modern psychology is developing along lines suggested by Spare's outstanding mystical writings."[105] From an early age Spare's father reported that he used to draw and write in a trance state, and although as aforementioned Breton and his group eventually abandoned automatic drawing in favour of automatic writing, Spare continued to use both. *The Book of Ugly Ecstasy* and the *Book of Satyrs* contain examples of Spare's automatic drawing and elements of *The Focus of Life* were written in a trance state; *The Eye of Ecstasy* is an example of automatic drawing from *The Book of Pleasure*. (Fig.1).Using such methods, Spare hoped that through his art he would tap the energies of the deep strata of the psyche. The painting itself could be said to have an amuletic quality, both as a record and document of this process.

Fig. 5 Ascension of the Ego from Ecstasy to Ecstasy (1910)
published in *The Book of Pleasure* (1913)

The picture *Ascension of the Ego from Ecstasy to Ecstasy* of 1910 could be considered as one such amuletic image (Fig.5). It shows therianthropic i.e. human-animal hybrids, representing the 'resurgence' of the so-called Karmas typical of Spare's work. In other works, Spare presents images of the divided self as a conglomerate of Ids, representative of personified desires, some resulting from previous human incarnations. A classic example of this is *Mind and Body* from 1953, where these previous selves are shown either side of the central self- portrait. (Fig 6.)

---

105 Ibid., 13.

Fig.6 Mind and Body (1953) Self-Portrait flanked by 'Ids'
as personifications of Desire

Finally, we move on to consider some of the most prevalent ideas and common misconceptions concerning Spare's Occultism.

OCCULTISM

MAGIA SEXUALIS: TANTRA AND SELF-LOVE

'Desire' and its directionality play an important role in Spare's magical praxis. Here we consider the role of *magia sexualis* in Spare's schemata in relation to his concept of *Self-Love*, and his idea of 'The New Sexuality,' as these ideas are likely to be confused. There are distinct sexual elements to Spare's magical philosophy, as well as the erotic nature of many of his pictures. Although much of the modern Western approach to yoga in general and tantra in particular owes much to the mediation of Helena Petrovna Blavatsky's Theosophical Society[106] and the writings of Aleister Crowley,[107] Spare does appear to demonstrate some elements which make him a more authentically South Asian *Tantrika*. In one passage, he appears to condone the consumption of 'nectar' which seems to be his own semen:

---

106 Helena Blavatsky, *The Secret Doctrine* (London; Theosophical Publishing House, 1918), passim.
107 Aleister Crowley, *Book 4: Liber ABA* (Maine: Weiser, 1994) is a good example.

Now let him imagine an union takes place between himself (the mystic union of the Ego and Absolute). The nectar emitted, let him drink slowly, again and again. [In the foot note he says here: 'If it becomes physical, let him imagine another's body.'] After this astonishing experience his passion is incomparable, there is nothing in the world he will desire: unless he wills. That is why people don't understand me. The ecstasy in its emotion is omnigenous. Know it as the nectar of life, the Syllubub of Sun and Moon.[108]

The consumption and/or retention of sexual fluids are ancient tantric practices:

One of the oldest Tantric schools, the Kaula (from *kula, lineage* or *family*), centered around the oral consumption of sexual fluids. By consuming the combined semen and menstrual fluids, the initiate was literally "incorporated" into the esoteric family and lineage, physically infused with its most powerful essence: "the Tantric Virile Hero generated and partook of his own and his consort's vital fluids in a 'eucharistic' ritual, whose ultimate consumer was the Goddess herself, [Shakti, embodied as Kali, Durga or Chamunda] who pleased, would afford the supernatural enjoyments and powers the practitioners sought."[109]

It has been observed that there is actually a plurality of different sexual rites:

Some would call for a difficult act of seminal retention and sublimation during the rite: others would use an even more complex procedure called the *vajroli mudra*, which involves not only seminal retention but actually the sucking or withdrawal of the female sexual fluids out of the woman's body (what some call the "fountain pen technique").[110]

Spare seems to favour the idea of the sexually transgressive as a means to the abandonment of morality:

For Spare, the most hypocritical sort of morality, and the one that must be absolutely overcome, is the vain Christian asceticism that denies sensual pleasure. Sexuality can never truly be denied, for it will only turn into a repressive cesspool of repression and guilt.[111]

---

108 Austin Osman Spare, "The Book of Pleasure" in *Ethos*, 105.

109 Hugh B. Urban, *Magia Sexualis; Sex, Magic, and Liberation in Modern Western Esotericism* (Berkeley: University of California Press, 2006), 88. See also Chapter 3, "Solve et Coagula: Attitudes toward the Ambrosial Aspects of Human Seed in Certain Yogic Traditions and in the Sexual Magick of Aleister Crowley" in Gordan Djurdjevic, *India and the Occult: The Influence of South Asian Spirituality on Modern Western Occultism* (New York: Palgrave MacMillan, 2014).

110 Ibid., 88.

111 Ibid., 231.

As an introduction to his 'Plotinus Formula (see below),' Spare announces:

> Now unto this period [i.e. before he discovered the formula] I had copulated only the atmosphere or rode whores, lined old hags, witches and bitches of all kinds, there being few virgins.[112]

And he fulminates in *The Anathema of Zos: The Sermon to the Hypocrites*:

> Think ye to curb the semen SENTIMENTALLY? Ye deny sexuality with tinsel ethics, live by slaughter, pray to greater idiots. ... For ye desire saviours useless to pleasure. ... Honest was Sodom! YOUR theology is a slime-pit of gibberish become ethics.[113]

Spare felt that, like the unlocatable, ineffable Kia, the human self was by nature radically free and blissful. In *The Book of Pleasure*, he expounds that the sole imperative of the human is 'Self-Love', the recognition of and pleasure in one's own nature. More specifically he identifies sexual pleasure with the innermost nature of the Self: ""The 'Self,' will pleasure in all things. There is only one sense, the sexual. There is only one desire, procreation... 'I multiply I' is creation: The sexual infinity."[114] There also appears to be evidence of sexual practices being used in a magical context. For example, the so called 'Plotinus Formula.' Kenneth Grant describes this procedure:

> Most interesting item of the evening concerned the 'Plotinus Formula'. He told us the secret of the real meaning of the word Urning. This is the "Earthenware Virgin" mentioned in the ms.{See Part II, Section II.} [*Zos Speaks!*] He drew a phallus as an illustration, and pointed out that an essential feature of the operation consisted in the fact of the tremendous suction generated by the specially constructed vase. He bought a "Japanese" vase for about 3/- and used it.[115]

Spare outlines the procedure in *The Zoëtic Grimoire of Zos*:

> Second Formula: The Formula of Plotinus – as sent me through the Delphic Pythoness via Automatism, called "Giving life to the Autistic By Virgin Earthenware."...

The autotelic wish into heterotelic conception is by consummation using an urn of correct shape and dimension which must correlate nearly to that of the lingam used – so that there is sufficient vacuum. At the moment of orgasm the wish

---

112 Kenneth and Steffi Grant, *Zos Speaks!*, 233.
113 Austin Osman Spare, *The Anathema of Zos* (Thame: I-H-O Books, 2001), 14-
114 Hugh Urban, *Magia Sexualis*, 231.
115 Kenneth and Steffi Grant, *Zos Speaks!*, 37.

must be *imperatively stated*. After ejaculation seal the vessel with your sigil and with the secret formula of your desire. Bury same at midnight, the moon being quartered. When the moon wanes, disinter and pour contents as libation into earth with suitable incantation, and re-bury same. This is the most formidable formula known, never fails and is dangerous – hence what is not written must be guessed. From this formula was derived the legend of the *Genii of the Brazen Vessel* as related by Solomon.[116]

Spare's 'New Sexuality' may be described in terms of his interaction with the Archetypal 'Universal Woman' who he mourned in *Earth: Inferno*: "The desertion of the "universal Woman' lying barren on the parapet of the Subconscious in humanity; and humanity sinking into the pit of conventionality Hail! The convention of the age is nearing its limit, and with it a resurrection of the Primitive Woman."[117] Spare's 'Universal Woman' – "the mediatrix of the unknown acting as psychopompos ... underlines the dark aspect of his anima."[118] His encounters with this entity,

> The luring quintessence of desire, with whom he "strayed into the path direct", led to the formulation of 'The new sexuality of ZOS', a sexuality not being limited to mere sensuality, but defined as pure cosmic consciousness embracing reality, freed from all convention and condition.[119]

Fig. 7: Frontispiece to *The Book of Pleasure* (1913)

---

116 Ibid., 223.
117 Austin O. Spare, *Earth: Inferno* (Thame: I-H-O Books, 2005), 9.
118 Marcus M. Jungkurth, "Neither-Neither: Austin Osman Spare and the Underworld" in Beskin and Bonner Eds., *Austin Osman Spare: Artist Occultist Sensualist*, 56.
119 Ibid, p.56.

Also suggestive of tantric and yogic methods is a breathing technique – aside from the one involved in the Death Posture – which Spare employs. If we look at the frontispiece to *The Book of Pleasure* (Fig.7), we can see that Spare appears to be closing his left nostril. This yogic technique is believed to stimulate the right hemisphere directly: the olfactory systems 'plug' directly into the ipsilateral hemisphere rather than crossing over as nerve fibres do for many systems of the body. Many will be familiar with the now somewhat revised idea of the right hemisphere as being associated with creative expression. One may speculate that there is indeed a neurobiological substrate to the Left Hand and Right Hand paths of magical praxis: the Dionysian right hemisphere controlling the left hand, the Apollonian left hemisphere controlling the right hand.[120]

THE ARENA OF ANON: SPARE, CARTOMANCY AND VAIHINGER

There are three types of cartomancy that Austin Spare employed. Tarot, divination by playing cards, and his 'Surrealist Horse Racing Cards.' Of the first and last types we have little to say here: it is known that Spare created a set of Tarot cards but these were lost many years ago. They have recently been discovered at the museum of the Magic Circle and will be published with a commentary shortly.[121] The general aspect of divination by cards involving Spare's unique ideas is described below. Before proceeding, however, we should first introduce the work of Hans Vaihinger.

There appears to be a clear connection between elements of Spare's philosophy and the work of Hans Vaihinger (1852-1933), the German philosopher and Kantian scholar. Early in their friendship, "Kenneth Grant lent [*The Philosophy of 'As if'*] to Spare, who enthusiastically assimilated its themes."[122] In *Philosophie des Als Ob* (1911), Vaihinger employs a phenomenological approach to argue that human beings can never really know the underlying reality of the world, and as a result:

> It is the purpose of the organic function of thought to change and elaborate the perceptual material into those ideas, associations of ideas and conceptual constructs which, while consistent and coherent among themselves are, as the phrase goes and as we can say provisionally, "clothed in objectivity."[123]

---

120 The early 'New Age' constructions of a 'Left Brain-Right Brain' hypothesis – based as they were around mid-twentieth century neurology and neurosurgical interventions for epilepsy involving the division of the corpus callosum of the brain and the resulting perceptual and cognitive changes – have been significantly overhauled in recent years. The brain remains 'divided,' but in a much more sophisticated and scientifically appreciated manner. See Iain Mc Gilchrist, *The Master and his Emissary: The Divided Brain and the Making of the Western World*: New Haven and London: Yale University Press, 2009).
121 Jonathan Allen and Mark Pilkington, eds., *Lost Envoy: The Tarot Deck of Austin Osman Spare*, (London: Strange Attractor Press, 2016).
122 Austin Osman Spare, *Two Tracts on Cartomancy*, 23.
123 Hans Vaihinger, *The Philosophy of 'As If': A System of the Theoretical, Practical and Religious Fictions of Mankind*, trans. by C.K. Ogden, (New York: Harcourt, Brace & Company Inc., 1925), 8.

Vaihinger uses examples from the physical sciences, such as protons, electrons, and electromagnetic waves. None of these phenomena have been observed directly, but the world behaves 'As if' what he terms such 'Scientific Fictions' science exist, and thus they are functional and useful. This in spite of the fact that "we do not know objective reality but only infer it."[124]

This philosophy extends wider than the compass of natural science: in society, it implies that one behaves 'as if" ethical certainty were possible. Likewise in the sphere of religion and theology one acts 'as if" there were a God. In the text of *Mind to Mind and How by a Sorcerer* (1997), Spare expounds on his ideas on cartomancy:

> He sets out by reiterating several themes from *The Book of Pleasure*, and interweaves them with a Kantian thesis (derived from Vaihinger) addressing the relationship between cause and effect as these are perceived by the individual consciousness. In accord with Vaihinger, Spare contends that our ordinary waking reality is fictive – a purely subjective and apparitional world.[125]

Spare criticises scientific method in this regard (*Mind to Mind and How* is subtitled 'Rendered in an idiom other than for scientists'): "Man is a vehicle of thought, and thought governs the world. Scientists constantly mistake the 'means' for the cause: brain, nerves, body etc., are the media of thought, and when thought is dynamic in them we say it is 'the mind."[126] Spare also alludes to Vaihinger's thought in *The Witches' Sabbath* (1997):

SYNOPSIS OF THE SABBATH

> THEORY OF FORMULA: Differentiation is the stimuli of recreation: hence perversion and contra-practices are used to that end: ceremony and ritual is the matric of form and order. The belief being, that by the "as if" act and wish is fleshed when endowed by continuity, ecstasy on ecstasy.[127]

In his correspondence with Kenneth and Steffi Grant in a list of 'essentials' for the efficacy of the sigillisation process and its accompanying ritual he says that, to paraphrase, the process of active anamnesis of the wish associated with the sigil ritual "may be & must be 'to an extent' "as if.""[128]

At a more metaphysical level, in *The Logomachy of Zos*, he draws on Vaihinger in relation to the 'Absolute,' and the nature of Truth itself. He also aligns this with his own concept of the 'sidereal,' which may provide some hint as to what his enigmatic Siderealism and its portraiture actually meant to him:

---

124 Ibid., 8
125 Austin Osman Spare, "Mind to Mind and How by a Sorceror" in *Two Tracts on Cartomancy*, 22.
126 Ibid., 31.
127 Austin Osman Spare, "The Witches' Sabbath" in *Ethos*, 155.
128 Kenneth and Steffi Grant, *Zos Speaks!*, 106

> Truth is all things past, actual and potential in the conceptive – therefore Truth is relative. What is true for me may not be true for you, and what is true now may not be so later, or at other times and places, hence truth has a chronology in space and 'time-space' truth. There are truths we create from our 'as if' realities – environment, character, temperament, learning etc. … Truth may be induced by the obsessive, by faith, or by something committed: these are 'personal truths', the 'as if truths'. I assert that *all lies are true* when accurately reorientated to time and place, and may be called 'sidereal truths.'[129]

If we return to Spare's 'Sidereal' portraits, this suggests that the anamorphic distorted images of the 'stars' and their contiguous media personalities and stories have their own particular relative 'truth'; this would certainly explain the 'Experiments in Relativity' rubric. Perhaps they are akin to Jean Baudrillard's 'simulacra'[130] – standing alone and apart from the mimesis of any original.

The Philosophy of 'As if' also relates to the concept of 'the Anon' in Spare's ideas of divination, which is vitally important to any overview of his theories. The 'anon' – i.e. the 'future' is more precisely described as the field of a future *in potentia*. In Spare's logic, if personal reality consists of a series of conceptualised Vaihingerian 'fictions,' the very act of cartomancy becomes not merely an act of divining the future, but the possibility of *determining* it. As the cards are mapped out, the querent constellates the 'Ids' – the coalesced personified 'desires' associated with each card. These are the entities which – as unconscious desires, and including the aforementioned *Karmas* – arise from the querent and determine the future. So in Spare's psycho-philosophy, the future is not so much *read* in the cards as predetermined and predestined, but apprehended, manipulated and *changed*. Here, again, the 'Ids' and 'Karmas' appear – now ensorcellated by the cards – here acting in lieu of sigils. This then, in terms of esoteric practice, is more *cartopraxy* than cartomancy. The process of shuffling the cards at the start marks the departure of conscious awareness – again featuring automatism as a process and portal to the *Subconscious(ness)*.

Spare on 'Mediumism'

As we have seen, it appeared that Spare had encountered spiritualist practice or 'mediumism' but didn't rate it: "Spare saw "mediumism" and "séances" as typified by a "passivity" "which opens up the mind to what is called external influences or disembodied energy, usually having no better purpose than to rap tables."[131] The spiritist idea of contacting the 'spirits of the departed' would have not been in keeping with his own occult psychological perspective of the

---

129 Ibid., 178.

130 Jean Baudrillard, *Simulacra and Simulation*, trans. by Sheila Faria Glaser (Michigan: The University of Michigan Press, 1994).

131 Christopher Miles, "Journey into the Neither-Neither": 67.

manifestation of atavisms from his own subconscious:

> Spare is not strongly interested in the existence or otherwise of such "external influences" – as we have seen, the magical practices that he expounds are based upon the magician causing effect upon her/himself through the making organic of a particular wish.[132]

However, it is of note that a contemporaneous account of mediumistic practice, Baron von Schrenck Notzing's *Phenomena of Materialisation: A contribution to the Investigation of Mediumistic Teleplastics* (1920) did mention the importance of exhaustion which Spare emphasises in 'The Death Posture' (see above):

> Assuming that mediumship comprises genuine telekinetic and teleplastic performances, the possibility of such action is no doubt confined within definite limits. Its production corresponds to a certain degree of exhaustion of the medium's organism, and this conversion must be accompanied by a strong bodily reaction of the medium.[133]

This volume contains several purported photographs of 'teleplastic manifestation' i.e. manifestation of material 'out of thin air' which appear overtly and amateurishly fraudulent (poorly drawn 'spirit faces' and muslin as 'ectoplasm'). Spare had clearly seen material like this a few years before, as he tellingly makes this comment in *The Book of Pleasure*:

> All [your] desires, however mighty, you will one day incarnate – yea photograph. These things already exist – very soon you will have spiritual photographs (unfaked) – but not by the camera you use at present. The pioneer is ever the old fool. An afterthought: some spirits are already photographed – the microbes.[134]

CONCLUSION AND SUMMARY

As we have seen, under the influence of Kenneth Grant the process of sigillisation, and the 'Alphabet of Desire' have come to be perceived as dominant components of what has been termed – again by Grant – the 'Zos Kia Cultus.' The interplay between the two elements of the Zos-Kia dyad actually represents the more mystical aspect of Spare's psycho-philosophy. As Michael Staley has pointed out, there was a chronological shift in Spare's conceptualisation of the Zos-Kia:

> In Spare's early work the Zos and the Kia were analogous perhaps to the Tao and the Teh, or the Self and any point which experiences the Self. In later

---

132 Ibid., 67.
133 Baron von Schrenk Notzing, *Perspectives in Psychical Research: Phenomena of Materialisation: A Contribution to the Investigation of Mediumistic Teleplastics* (New York: Arno, 1920), 14.
134 Austin Osman Spare, "The Book of Pleasure" in *Ethos*, 83.

years this philosophy became more dynamic, with the Kia being the rough equivalent of the pleroma, the cosmic entirety, what is sometimes referred to as Cosmic Mind.[135]

Spare actually describes his 'system' – such as it is – as *Kiaism*. Grant places emphasis on an Alphabet of *Desire*, called by Spare the 'Sacred Alphabet,' as this emphasised the Ids as embodying *sexual* energies which the magician focusses in magical procedure; this was in keeping with Grant's own interests in sex magic. As Staley also observes, by the time of the production of the *Book of Zos vel Thanatos*, appearing in the compilation *Zos Speaks!*, "Spare explained that across the years he had largely forgotten the principles behind his systems of sigillisation, but stimulated by Grant's interest he set about reconstructing the methodology.'[136] Thus the 'Alphabet of Desire' was a reconstruction – again under Grant's influence.

I have attempted to provide an overview of the major – though not all of the components of the complex thought of Austin Osman Spare, in order to facilitate an examination of his magical praxis. I can conclude by concurring with Robert Ansell that what we have been looking at for some years is in reality a *Sidereal* portrait of Austin Osman Spare, yet in keeping with Spare's 'sidereal truth,' this is still, in a relativistic sense, valid. We must be aware of the Grantisms, whilst at the same time not decrying the importance of the Grants' preservation and curation of Spare's ideas and imaginarium. Nevertheless, our primary focus of study should rest on *Kiaism*, rather than a 'Zos Kia Cultus;' *Atavism* rather than 'Atavistic Resurgence;' and a *Sacred Alphabet* rather than an 'Alphabet of Desire.' We should understand that Spare could not really be termed a shaman, though there are elements in his practice which chime with indigenous South Asian tantric practice. Finally, we can add that the importance of the sigillisation process is hyperbolised by later groups who retrospectively assigned Spare as their progenitor.

---

135 Michael Staley, "Transmitting the Sacred Fire" in Stephen Pochin, ed., *Austin Osman Spare, Fallen Visionary: Refractions*, 107-10.
136 Ibid., 111.

Automatic Drawings and Oracles

Ugo Dossi

Oracles are messages from a different level of reality, which are supposed to provide an advantage over the usual way of looking at reality.

The term oracle itself probably comes from the Latin word for mouth, because most oracles have been translated into language, and passed on orally, often as a saying or an aphorism.

Traditionally oracles have been consulted before making important decisions about the future, asked about unresolved questions of the past, or queried in order to understand the ever new and confusing present.

In addition, an oracle refers to the geographical location where these messages are made accessible, in Western antiquity, for example, in Delphi or Cumae. It also refers to the person through which the message flows; in Delphi it was the oracle priestess, the Pythia "the one who comes from the earth;" in Cumae the Sybil, the "whisperer."

The process itself with which the connection to the other level of reality is established, is also called oracle.

All advanced civilizations, which had their cohesion in a consensus to a common world view, developed oracle forms. These meant an opening of the world view beyond their conventions.

The means used were different. The Germanic tribes threw beech sticks on the ground and examined the random patterns and configurations with which they came to lie and called them "runes", signs, because they were expected to point to something hidden from their usual vision. The Romans watched the inner organs of sacrificed animals as well as the flights of birds. In Delphi, the Pythia exposed herself to the fumes of the volcanic underworld in order to achieve a trance-state in which habitual thinking had no disturbing influence.

Regardless of which approach was preferred, all these attempts had a common root: a healthy distrust of habitual rational thought and the certainty that, alternatively, other resources must be available, perceptual paths that run in the unconscious but touch a broader spectrum of reality than everyday thinking in words.

Automatic drawing fulfills a large part of these prerequisites, and indeed, signs and drawings appear again and again that astonishingly approach the idea of an oracle. Some participants of our seminars have showed a high sensitivity and talent in this direction. In 1999 we started a group with some highly gifted people, to experiment with automatic drawings and automatically written texts to get answers to asked questions.

The results have been amazing. We have encountered phenomena that make many people think. Some of the results are shown on the following pages.

They point out that the creativity of the unconscious has access to areas of perception that are barred to us in our everyday mode.

Just as amazing as the drawn results have been the interpretations given. Both image and image perception/interpretation are obviously inseparable.

Subsequently, automatic drawings as oracles for the coming months have been generated monthly and sent to interested participants by e-mail, with the request for interpretation and comment. This oracle project continues today and reaches many participants worldwide.

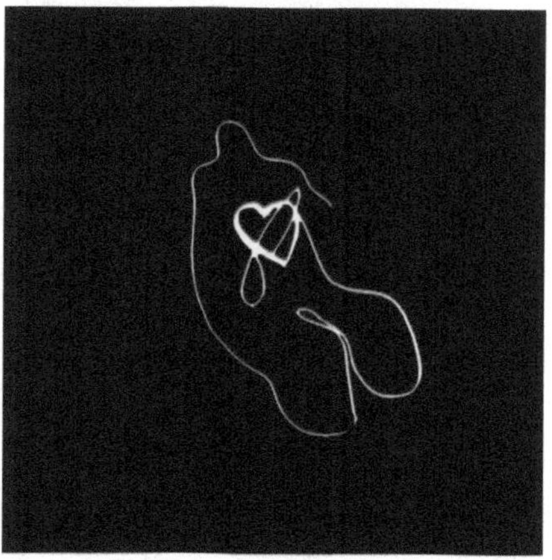

Automatic drawing, generated 20 days before a heart attack.

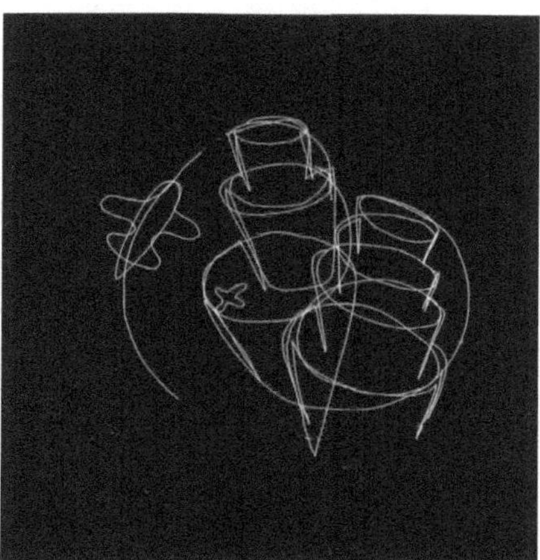

Automatic drawing to the question Important Event? 1985 Feb. (published as projection, Documenta 8, Kassel 1986)

Q: what am I waiting for?

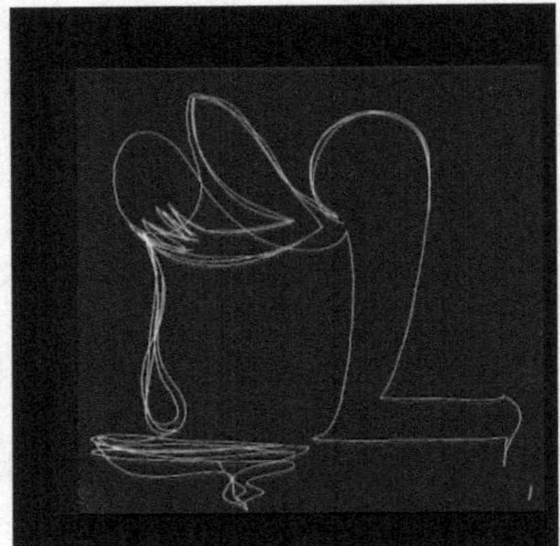

Q: 2002?

Q: what is the best moment?

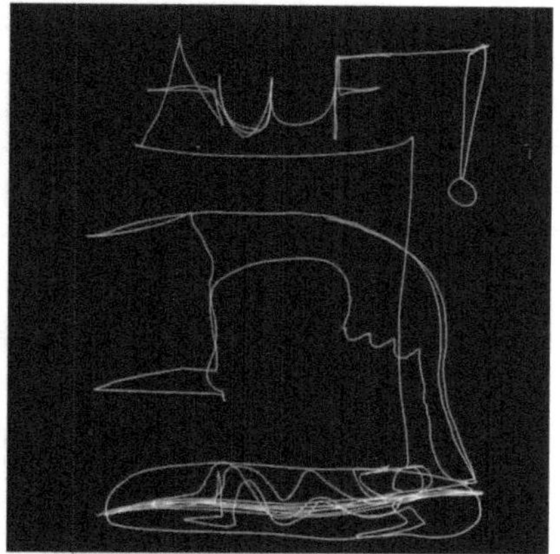

Q: What must be done?

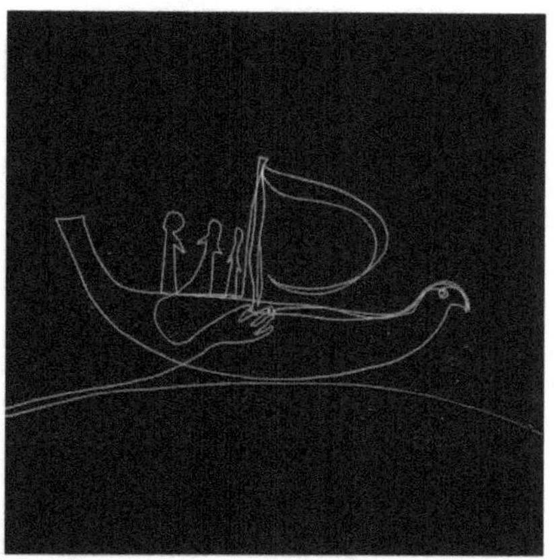

ORAcle for the year 2015 (sent out December 2014)

ORAcle March 2019

ORAcle April 2019

ORAcle May 2019

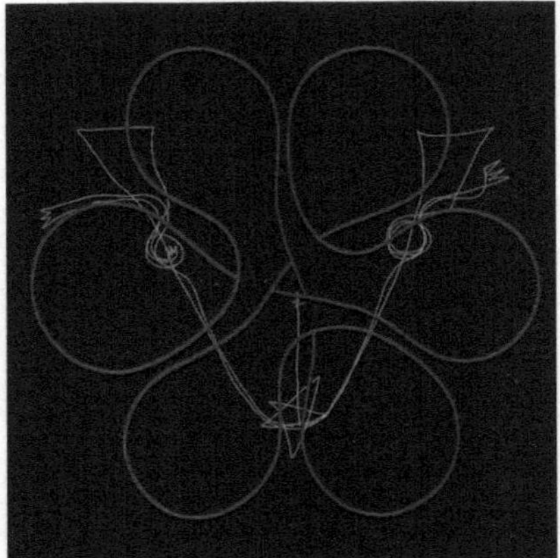

ORAcle June 2019

Introduction/welcome to Schloss Brunnenburg, and Ezra Pound, Joseph Ennemoser and "Animal Magnetism"

Siegfried de Rachewiltz

I've been given the dubious privilege of actually taking up two sessions. It's not something one necessarily wants, but the first part will consist simply in trying to explain a little bit about where we are, and why you are here, ultimately. In the second part I will read from my paper on Ennemoser.

For many years, twenty-one to be exact, I was the director of the Schloss Tirol Museum, which I had the privilege of actually building and constructing; literally as a history or cultural history museum, which was something that was actually missing from our landscape. In 1972, Schloss Tirol and the cradle of this geopolitical entity known as Tirol, was transferred from the Italian government to the local authorities, the "Autonome Provinz Bozen." As usual, the politicians had no idea really what to do with it. They had clamored for it, and they wanted it back and so on, but once they had it, they really didn't know what to do with it. They tried to make a kind of a "mixed bag": put in some archaeology, put in some contemporary art, and so on. In 1991, I was sort of commandeered from the Denkmal Amt, the Department of the preservation of monuments here in the local province. I had a big ally, because that very same year, Ötzi decided to emerge from the ice.[1] He was my greatest ally, to the extent that it suddenly became clear that Schloss Tirol was not suitable for an archeology museum in the classical sense. Because it would mean that one would have to go back to prehistory, to periods that preceded the building, and preceded the Middle Ages; not forgetting the whole technical question that something like that needs to be in an urban context, with all the technology that is available.

I do believe in Hermes, in the lucky find. The local Fire Department came to me because there had been some fires at Buckingham Palace, etc, etc. And they said, "Look, we don't have enough water here at Schloss Tirol in case of a fire, so you must build a reservoir." We started digging, but of course, anywhere where you started digging around Schloss Tirol, all kinds of things started to come to the surface, which meant, "no, you can't dig here, you can't dig here." So we kept going further south, down into the vineyards. Finally I thought we were going to be safe, because it was all vineyards. And sure enough, for about two and a half meters,

---

1 "Ötzi", the name given to a man living in the Südtirol region approx 3300 BC. He was preserved in masses of ice, and was eventually discovered in 1991.

there was nice humus earth, and so on. Then at the three meters level, suddenly a circle apeared, a semi circle… Obviously, what seemed to be the axis of a little chapel. Well, alright, everything stopped. Hand digging ensued for two years just scraping away at it. In the end, what it turned out to be was not a little chapel; it was actually one of the earliest Christian churches that we know of in South Tirol; meaning fourth, fifth century AD. Quite a spectacular find, because nobody knew of the existence of such a church at that place. There was no written record, no oral tradition, nothing. It left us again with all kinds of open question marks. But we then also saw that the church had later been expanded in Carolingian times and had existed up until, more or less, the year 1000 AD. Then it suddenly disappeared, or at least great parts of the walls were taken off. And that coincided with the building of Schloss Tirol, which is a different story altogether, and I won't go into that.

The reason I've mentioned these two things – Ötzi and the Paleo-Christian church – is that whenever I would stand in front of the castle and try to explain to my visitors where we are and why this place is so important, it wasn't just a matter of the strategic importance of the fact that the Roman road used to cross the mountains here, and that you could sort of imagine these Roman troops, and probably then the first missionaries, coming along these roads, and then the wine trade coming through, crossing the Alps, all of that… But much before that, this whole area must have been a holy precinct, because we found menhirs just at the foot of Schloss Tirol; these two big really extraordinary remains of what must have been once a very large, megalithic culture right here, which was to a large extent, of course, destroyed by the new religion coming in. Some of these menhirs were found in Vinschgau upside down, and used as an altar plate. So the message was quite clear. We did have all kinds of records of these missionaries coming here and saying that the people here still insist on venerating stone idols, and things like that. So, whether we go back to the Bronze Age, to which these menhirs belong, or whether you were to take a long hike up to the seven lakes which lie behind these mountains here, we actually have something that with some exaggeration, but not too much, one could call the "Stonehenge of the Alps." The fact is that it is a very, very large expanse, but tourists fortunately just walk over it and don't really realize what they're walking over because it's just a big field of cup stones. And these cup stones are distributed over a very large area. Archaeologists do tend to make a big detour around such things that they cannot explain. This is one of them. But the most serious and really not that original observation is that this must have been used as an astronomical observatory, because it was obvious that they were watching the phases of the moon; it was a calendar. Like Hesiod's, the way it works with the days in a Farmers' Almanac. Of course, the Farmers' Almanac contains other things as well: when is the right day to take your cows to the bull? When is the right day to sow? You have this mixture of folk tales in the Tirolian tradition, where it's always "die Saligen," these fairy women, that will come and tell the farmer: "Farmer, go out and sow because there is a wind blowing from Paradise." Which was this ancient notion that the doors of Paradise sometimes just open just a little bit and when that air comes, that wind which comes through is a positive wind, a fertile wind, that will bring growth.

So anyway, all of this simply to indicate that throughout these many centuries, there has been a continuity of human presence on these sunny terraces. Schloss Brunnenburg has its own stories that indicate perhaps a cult of the house snake. I've collected so many stories here in this particular region, that one could do an interesting comparison, for example, with Lithuania, where the cult of the house snake was still very alive, even some thirty years ago. Here it's the story of a young shepherdess standing in front of Brunnenburg, looking after her goats: a shepherdess, a goat herdess. A little snake comes by, and every day she gives her a little bit of milk, which is pretty much the same story at the beginning of Virgil's *Aenid*. There is an offering made with milk, and the house snake comes and drinks of it. Something similar must have gone on here: the little snake is grateful for the milk she gets, and beckons the girl to follow her. There is a cave and the little girl goes inside the cave, and finds great treasures. She's alright for the rest of her life. There are variations of this story, which are a little bit more moralizing.

Up at Schloss Tirol was found a statue of Isis Fortuna, which is a clear indication that in Roman times, there was probably some higher official stationed up there to make sure that the tolls would be be collected and other things. Administrative things, but as a being belonging to a certain higher class, he was a follower of Isis. We know that the Isis cult was reserved to a certain level of class. And we have the Mithras Stone, right across there. Quite a few indications that Jove was venerated in the mountain passes here, and we also have a Diana statue fragment. This entire area here essentially has always been used for some form of cult, for some form of prayer, religion, whatever. And that, in my mind, makes it particularly interesting to be here, and to talk about things that may have to do with spiritualism, and mystical traditions and so on.

Another legend says that there is a golden calf buried under Schloss Brunnenburg. The golden calf motif, by the way, recurs in a number of Tirolian folktales. And it is only on one night, on the Johannesnacht,[2] that this golden calf will actually appear, but it is guarded by two giants. If you are scared, the treasure will disappear. My father thought that he would dig at the bottom. The idea was to actually to see if there was anything to it. Every castle has the tradition that there is an underground passage connecting it to the other castle, which of course geologically is totally out of the question here. But these are things that one does. And it's great fun for children to be able to partake in such treasure hunts.

On a more serious note, my father Boris de Rachewiltz was actually himself quite interested in esoteric teachings. As an Egyptologist, he mostly wrote books about Egyptian magic. And this comes into play into the *Cantos*, because when Pound arrived here in 1958, he had in my father a conversation partner, who would actually talk about such things and who would be able to tell Pound something new about a mythology that he had not at that point known that well; namely

---

2 Johannesnacht: the night of the summer solstice.

ancient Egyptian mythology. My father invited people like Marius Schneider, who for musicologists is a particularly interesting name because Marius Schneider wrote *Singende Steine*. He basically discovered a kind of a hidden musical code in the architecture of certain Spanish Romanesque buildings and made connections between the medieval musical symbolism of these cloisters with actual ancient Indian musicological symbology. And Elémire Zolla is another name that perhaps is known to some of you anyway; a founder of the *Studie Religiosi*, one of the few serious Italian reviews. He translated *The Teachings of Don Juan*, introduced a lot of the Mesoamericans, Mexicans, Indians. Pound too, was very interested in Native American folk tales. In fact, one of the first things he had me do while he was back here was to translate Jaime de Angulo. Again, a fascinating character to be rediscovered because he has unfortunately been largely ignored, especially in his native California. Alright, so here were just a few very sundry connections from the Brunnenburg, as if it were a visitors' book. I hope you will all sign the visitors' book before you leave this evening.

Ezra Pound, Joseph Ennemoser and "Animal Magnetism"

A few years ago, up at Schloss Tirol, we did an exhibition called "Für Freiheit, Wahrheit und Recht: Joseph Ennemoser and Jakob Philipp Fallmerayer." These two characters, Fallmerayer and Ennemoser, really represent some of the most fascinating intellectuals that have come out of this region. But as you can well imagine, they were not popular at all during their time. In fact, they were regarded as Public Enemies, as traitors, etc., because they did not fit into that clerical conservative power mesh, which said that Tirol was a Catholic fortress and it was to remain as such, and no Protestants should ever set foot here or get to own a piece of land here. No Jew, no other believer should ever taint this immaculate region. There were three things here: one was Schloss Tirol, of course, as the Palladium of this country. Then there was the birth house of Andreas Hofer, the freedom fighter. And the third was Maria von Mörl. She was a young lady from Kaltern, who had received the stigmata. She was, as it were, turned into an icon of this Catholic Tirol that would not change. The Kaiser was making concessions to religious tolerance and so on, but not in Tirol. Things have changed a little bit since then. But... This is about Ennemoser and Pound, and Yeats. What connects these three very different characters?

In November 1913, William Butler Yeats was getting ready to spend a few months in a small country house about an hour south of London, in Stone Cottage, far from the "maddening crowd." He hoped to find new inspiration, catch up on some reading, and work on some esoteric projects: the "Elucidations," and Lady Gregory's "Visions and Beliefs in the West of Ireland,"[3] and two essays, "Witches and Wizards and Irish folklore," and "Swedenborg, Mediums and the

---

3 *Visions and Beliefs in the West of Ireland Collected and Arranged by Lady Gregory: With Two Essays and Notes by W.B. Yeats* (1920)

Desolate Places." For conversation and secretarial functions, he had invited a young American colleague who had caused quite a splash with his iconoclastic ideas on art and poetry. He was one of the many admirers of the Irish Bard, even though he did not share Yeats's fascination with spiritism and the occult at that time. Since Yeats's eyesight was bad Ezra Pound was asked to read out aloud to him in the evenings from books that Yeats had brought along, including some from his vast esoterica collection.

Pound had first feared that the dealings with the occult would take up much of their time. But as it turned out, these secret things coincided with his own interests much more than he had expected. At Stone Cottage, Pound had planned to translate some Japanese Noh plays, sent to him by Ernest Fenollosa's widow. These medieval plays revolve around the apparition of ghosts and otherworldly beings from Japanese mythology. Obviously, this kind of material appealed greatly to Yeats as well, but neither of them could have foreseen that the Noh plays would help Yeats find a new dramatic voice and influence all his subsequent work, causing that creative breakthrough which later led to his success and renown, and to the Nobel Prize in 1923. Among the books brought along were Henri de Montfaucon de Villars's *Le Comte de Gabalis*, Robert Kirk's *The Secret Commonwealth of Elves, Fauns, and Fairies*, and Joseph Ennemoser's *The History of Magic...* 1670, 1691, 1854 respectively. Many years later, near Pisa, Pound would reminisce about those quiet days in Sussex, and about Joseph Ennemoser:

> at Stone Cottage in Sussex
> by the waste more
> (or whatever) and the holly bush
> who would not eat ham for dinner
> because peasants eat ham for dinner
> despite the excellent quality
> and the pleasure of having it hot
> well those days are gone forever
> and the travelling rug with the coon-skin tabs
> and his hearing nearly all Wordsworth
> for the sake of his conscience but
> preferring Ennemoser on Witches.[4]

This is Pound remembering his somewhat snobbish friend disdaining peasant food, listening to nearly all of Wordsworth, out of a sense of duty, yet really much more interested in Ennemoser's *History of Magic*, as it deals profusely with prophecy, witchcraft, and the persecution of witches and wizards. Ennemoser's thousand-and-one page book appeared in Leipzig in 1844. And ten years later in William Howitt's English translation. William Howitt and his wife Mary Botham deserve a footnote here, as they offer us a glimpse of a particular brand of British esotericism.

---

4 Canto 83

They both started out as Quakers. William published *A Popular History of Priestcraft in all Ages and Nations* (1833). Mary translated Hans Christian Andersen. After a period spent in Germany where they probably got acquainted with Ennemoser's work, they returned to England and devoted themselves more or more and more to Mesmerism and to the occult in general. They consorted with the Rosettis, Dante Gabriel and his sister Christina, with Alfred Lord Tennyson, and with Robert and Elizabeth Barrett Browning, and corresponded with Dickens and Wordsworth. In 1852, William Howitt set sail for Australia, in the wake of the Gold Rush there. On board he translated *The History of Magic*, and later sent the manuscript to Mary for proofreading. She did more than that; she added a lengthy appendix "of the most remarkable and best authenticated stories of apparitions, dreams, second sights on ambulation predictions, divinations, witchcraft, vampires, table turning and spirit rapping." Upon his return, William organized seances with Daniel Douglas Home, a famous medium, and the Howitts spent their latter days actually here in Tirol, curiously enough, not far from Giess. Mary Howitt is still remembered for a famous children's poem, "The Spider and the Fly." So much for Ennemoser's translators.

Although Pound could not muster up much enthusiasm for popular forms of spiritism and the occult, he had begun to apply some fundamental ideas of medieval mysticism, alchemy, and even of mesmerism and magnetism to his own poetics, as shown in a number of poems predating Stone Cottage. In "Mesmerism," written in 1909, he addresses Robert Browning as "ye old mesmerizer" and pays tribute to his ability to summon the souls of great men and having them speak in his dramatic monologues. In "Paracelsus In Excelsis," 1911, the sidereal spirit rises to the eternal peace of celestial bodies as an unchangeable fluid: "And we that are grown formless, rise above-, Fluids intangible that have been men." Pound finally became an alchemist and necromancer himself; the alchemist attempting to conjure up all the lost beauty through the magic of language. At this time he was forging a new poetical credo, which was to rid poetry of the blurred and trite language of the late Romantics. Through clarity and precision, poetry would regain the liberating force and healing power of a divine epiphany, which it had with Dante and the troubadours. The Noh plays and the readings in Stone Cottage played an important role in this process. And so it came that the Tirolian physician and natural philosopher Joseph Ennemoser was indirectly godfather to the birth of the first poetical avant-garde movement of the 20th century. It was probably Ennemoser's clear ethical stance, his fearless, intellectual curiosity, and his deep respect for the clairvoyance – the clearer vision of the pagans, the "Helleseenden Heiden" – which appealed to Pound. Otherwise, he would not have recommended the *The History of Magic* to his fiancée, when trying to explain to her, "The profounder sense of symbolism." In that same letter, he tells her, that, "A symbol appearing in a vision has a certain richness and power of energizing joy." Something similar to what Ennemoser intends, when he speaks of the positive imminent vital force of symbols. He and Pound both shared the notion that myths arise out of the attempt to communicate through symbols, otherwise unexplainable, visionary experiences.

The points in common are many. Ennemoser's "A hospital should be like a place of worship, for only then will we be able to regain the healing priesthood of earlier days. Everybody carries in himself the power to magnetize. One needs power combined with wisdom in order to apply it." For Pound it is the artist who embodies both visionary and healing powers, seen as the antenna of the human race. "Because he associates with Gods, the poet is responsible for other human beings."

Brancusi, Saint and alchemist: "Perhaps every artist, at one time or another, believes in a sort of elixir or Philosopher's Stone, produced by the sheer perfection of his art by the alchemical sublimation of the medium." The problem that has to be confronted is desensitization. Loss of perception. Ennemoser: "Everything merely superficial is unpoetic and irreligious." Pound, in Canto 34, derides the superficial trivialization of animal magnetism by the American middle class. It was something very "in" in those days, in the 1850s. He himself on the other hand resorts to magnetic imagery only when trying to convey the utmost intensity of perception, as in the image of the rose in the steel dust in Canto 74:

> This liquid is certainly a
> property of the mind
> nec accidens est but an element
> in the mind's make-up
> est agens and functions dust to a fountain pan otherwise
> Hast 'ou seen the rose in the steel dust
> (or swansdown ever?)
> so light is the urging, so ordered the dark petals of iron
> we who have passed over Lethe.

Pound's world unchanging, the world of fine animal life, the world of pure form. What the Neo-platonists sometimes called the "Anima Mundi." Ennemoser, referring to Plotinus and Porphyry, writes, "What the ancients called Anima Mundi is what we call magnetism, a universal cosmic force of nature." As a Christian, and Neo-platonist, he adds, "An inner secret poet leads humanity with an unfailing thread, through the labyrinth of space and time. In our breast, lie hidden the eternal messengers of Heaven and Hell." And later, "God is within us, not outside of us," to which Pound echoes, "All is within us, purgatory and Hell." Again, what matters is the quality of perception, the ability to perceive "the radiant world, where one thought cuts through another with clean edge, a world of moving energies, magnetisms that take form, that border the visible, the matter of Dante's Paradiso, the glass underwater." That's from the *Literary Essays*.

This leads to the tradition of undivided light, to the genealogy of light to Plotinus, and to Bacon. Ennemoser quoting Plotinus: "The eye would never see the sun, if it were not of the nature of the sun." Plotinus is described as a great healer, who has "command over images, shapes and spirits that flow unceasingly from

God's eternal fountain of life." Again, Ennemoser. And in Canto 91, Pound writes: "In the green deep of an eye, crystal waves weaving together towards the great healing." And Ennemoser again in *The History of Magic*: "Procreation is more than just symbolically a projection of light into the darkness of night." Pound in Canto 87: "In nature, there are signatures, needing no verbal tradition, oak leaf, never plane leaf." This is from John Haydon's *English Physician's Guide or a Holy Guide* (1667) which was among the books in Yeats' library. Haydon took the doctrine of divine signatures in plants and minerals from Paracelsus. It's God placing signatures on plants and minerals in order to signal their healing properties to the adepts. Ennemoser got it via Jacob Boehme, another favorite of Yeats's. In order to see God and to recognize the signatures in nature, they have to become nothing to themselves and poorer than a bird. Finally, a common rejection of all form of religious and non-religious fanaticism. Pound chastises: "The asceticism that is anti-flesh, followed by the asceticism that is anti-intelligence." In *The History of Magic*, Ennemoser condemns any form of witch-hunting and diabolization, which includes the persecution of so called heretics, like the Templars. He dared stand up against the religious fanaticism of his own time, which wanted to preserve Tirol as a pure Catholic fortress against the rest of the world. For this, he was accused of treason.

So, who was Jospeh Ennemoser? He was born in 1787, in a remote hamlet here in Tirol, where he spent his childhood as a shepherd and cowherd. His father, a subsistence farmer, died when he was two, and so the boy was raised by his grandfather. Being a bright kid, the village priest encouraged him to continue his studies beyond elementary school. In 1809, Ennemoser was 22 years old, and he enrolled to study medicine at the University of Innsbruck. Andreas Hofer, the leader of the Tirolian farmers that kept Napoleon's troops at bay for almost eight months, made him his adjutant. He fought bravely and, as we know, in vain, as the Habsburgs surrendered to Napoleon and left the Tirolians standing in the rain. Andreas Hofer was executed in 1810. Soon his fame spread all over Europe. Wordsworth even dedicated sonnets to him.

Ennemoser wanted to continue his medical studies and landed in Berlin, where he immediately was enrolled or made contact with anti-Napoleonic circles. In 1812, he was sent on a secret mission to Britain to seek aid for the resistors as an officer with Major Lützow's *Freikorps* of volunteers. He led a company of Tirolian sharpshooters and was later awarded the Iron Cross for his bravery. In 1816, he completed his doctorate with a dissertation on the influence of mountains on human health. He knew something about that... He got increasingly interested in the possibilities of curing patients with the help of animal magnetism. One of his mentors was the Jewish physician David Ferdinand Koreff, a personal doctor of the Prussian Chancellor and a follower of Anton Mesmer and his theories. In 1819, Ennemoser published his first book, and that same year he was appointed professor of magnetism at the newly founded University of Bonn. From 1819-37, he ran a medical practice. He cured famous patients, married, had two daughters, battled on many fronts for a more humane treatment of the mentally ill.

After initial enthusiasms, mesmerism and animal magnetism came under increasing attack. Ennemoser became the target of vicious academic intrigues, and decided to leave University and return to Tirol, where he hoped to make a living as a private practitioner. During one of his visits, he had expressed skepticism towards the widespread phenomenon of the so called ecstatic virgins, who claimed to have visions, fall into trances, and who were regarded as saints by a large segment of the population. While Ennemoser maintained that there are enough miracles in nature, he believed the leaders of the clerical conservative forces claimed the ecstatic virgins were messengers sent by God to manifest the intention that Tirol should remain a pure Catholic fortress. Ennemoser had made himself some powerful enemies, and when he moved to Innsbruck with his family in 1847, his enemies did everything they could to make life difficult for him. He co-founded and became secretary of the Tirolian agricultural society and their newsletter. He made many suggestions on how to improve soil fertility and grow more resistant crops. For example, he encouraged farmers to grow more resistant potato crops and different kinds of cereals, and warned them that the future of viticulture lay in quality and not in quantity, and suggested varieties of grapes to grow. But most of all, he tried to convince them not to waste natural resources. For that purpose, he designed a new, more efficient kind of stove, which would enable families to save on wood. But all these activities did not generate an income. Every time he tried to launch himself into some new venture like curing patients with salt baths, invisible bureaucratic barriers would suddenly pop up and obstruct his project. He finally had to come to terms with the fact that the authorities and whoever was behind them was not going to let him make a living in Tirol. So reluctantly, in 1841, he retreated to Munich, where he could count on a larger pool of patients.

But in 1848, all of continental Europe was rocked by revolutions. All the many despots, beginning with the Austro-Hungarian Emperor, and down to the myriad of little Counts and Dukes of Germany had to make significant concessions. One of them was an elected parliament that convened in Frankfurt to work on a new German constitution. The other one was freedom of the press. Ennemoser didn't think twice; he rushed back to Tirol, and with his own personal funds, founded the *Innsbrucker Zeitung*, a newspaper, through which he and a few like-minded friends valiantly tried to propound the notion of civil rights, religious tolerance, and freedom of speech in a society which considered all of these as threats to the authority of the Emperor and of the Church. We know all too well how the story ended. In June 1849, what remained of the Frankfurt Parliament, of which also Fallmerayer was a member, was disbanded militarily. Ennemoser's newspaper was forced to close down by the reinstated censorship authority in 1852.

In 1854, the English translation of *The History of Magic* appeared. It is doubtful that Ennemoser ever got to see a copy of it. He had started on his own autobiography, but managed only to write one first magnificent chapter on his childhood in the Tirolian mountains. He died September 19th, in Egern on Lake

Tegernsee in Bavaria, where his tomb is still looked after today. In the years that followed, Ennemoser was deliberately forgotten. The few encyclopedias where his name appeared ridiculed him as a quack. His archive was partly destroyed, and partly scattered over Germany and Austria. In 1921, a young medical student wrote his inaugural dissertation on Ennemoser. He was able to talk to the last surviving descendants and to transcribe some documents, which then went up in flames during World War II.

Ironically, it was William Butler Yeats' interest in *The History of Magic*, and the fact that Ezra Pound remembered it in Pisa, that led to a rediscovery of Ennemoser in his own homeland. In 2009, as part of the bicentennial celebration, the South Tirolian History Museum of Schloss Tirol inaugurated an extensive special exhibit on Ennemoser and his times entitled "For freedom, truth and justice," the motto of Ennemoser's short-lived newspaper. A catalog appeared, a symposium was held, and in the course of three years, we were able to locate the scattered remains of Ennemoser's archive in over a dozen different collections and libraries, and his native village has just named a square after him. All because of these tantalizing lines in Canto 83: "…preferring Ennemoser on witches." Thank you.

Pound's Occultism: The Development of Automatic Writing and Occult Philosophy in the Pisan Cantos

Katrina Makkouk

Despite being written some thirty years later, *The Pisan Cantos* are in part a product of the occult education Ezra Pound received in London between 1909 and 1916. One of the most influential occult figures in Pound's developing occultism was W.B. Yeats. During the Stone Cottage winters between 1913 and 1916, Pound served as secretary for Yeats and often accompanied him to various occultist meetings in London. Despite his fierce admiration for his mentor, Pound approached occult study and experimentation with a fair amount of reserve for what did not seem to him an altogether practical pursuit. Nevertheless because of his exposure to Yeats and the London occultists, Pound's writing shows obvious occult characteristics such as his inherent exclusivity, personalized form of automatic writing, and invocation of the dead. The purpose of this article is to examine how occultism became a part of Pound's writing *The Pisan Cantos* by focusing on the lifelong impact of Yeats's occult mentorship. Under Yeats's guidance, Pound's academic pursuit of occultism influenced his writing and became a theme to which he often returned.

Occult study has the regrettable problem of bestowing a sense of eccentricity to any author or artist within its broad societal affiliations. In general usage, the definition of occultism encompasses the practice of magic for the purpose of gaining supernatural insight. For a scholarly interpretation, Demetres Tryphonopoulos defines the term, "…to mean the whole body of speculative, heterodox religious thought which lies outside all religious orthodoxies. As well, occultism involves the belief in the possibility of gnosis or direct awareness of the Divine" ("Occult Education" 74). Yeats's lifelong interest in occult study gave him connections between his strong sense of spiritualism, Irish nationalism, and religious upbringing. After establishing his friendship with Yeats, Pound began to develop his own interest in the occult through a less romantic perspective than his mentor, preferring a more academic point of view. Pound cultivated his occult ideas based upon what Tryphonopoulos calls the "celestial tradition." This celestial tradition combines the pursuit of supernatural wisdom with the mythology of the ancient classics. The works of Dante, Homer, and other canonical writers provide Pound with recurring themes in his epic *Cantos* as well as his *Pisans*. This proves his involvement with the occult movement in London is a largely unaccredited influence in his *Cantos*. By employing the occult as a tool for scholarship rather than a zeitgeist in modern literature, the negative connotations it carries can be dispelled.

Fascination with the occult had swept quickly across the literary landscape of Europe prior to Pound's 1908 arrival in London, where Yeats had already become an established practitioner of the occult. Yeats's curiosity about magic and all manner of occult subjects led him to join Madame Blavatsky's Theosophical Society in 1897. The group's central doctrines were built around "…Eastern religions, from European occultism, mysticism, philosophy, and when it served their purpose, from science" (Ellmann 62). When his committee failed to produce a single magical result despite Yeats's enthusiastic experimentation and research, he resigned and promptly joined the Hermetic Order of the Golden Dawn. Ever unsatisfied with his work, Yeats became determined to find a method to combine his literary interests with the supernatural knowledge he so desperately sought. Yeats's innate desire to maintain exclusivity in his work found fulfillment within the Golden Dawn's stringent levels of authority and rituals of initiation required to access occult secrets. The rituals Yeats took part in as a member of the Golden Dawn led to "visions." The visions are a precursor to Yeats's attempts at automatic writing. These meditations were meant for mediums to use "their imaginations to dwell on ancient divinities, who would often obligingly seem to take definite shape and to enlighten them on various aspects of the other world" (Ellmann 126). As a result of these visions Yeats began to keep a diary for his occult studies, testament to the level of sincerity with which he approached these practices. His continued research and experimentation only solidified his belief in the possibility of gaining knowledge from the spirits. Yeats's search for supernatural wisdom and enlightenment were well advanced by the time Pound attempted to make the acquaintance of the respected older poet.

Being initiated into Yeats's exclusive inner circle brought Pound a step closer to achieving his goal of modernizing poetry. In Pound's opinion, Yeats possessed the talent and connections he needed to introduce new life into the old and unfashionable modes of Victorian poetry. Pound made his rounds through meetings such as the Poet's Club and the Irish Literary Society in an effort to establish himself as one of London's literati and claim a much desired invitation to Yeats's Monday Evenings. After gaining an invitation to join this elite circle of artists and writers Pound still felt as if he had not yet reached his full potential. Inspired by Yeats's earlier Rhymer's Club, Pound organized his own exclusive two man group which he dubbed the Order of the Brothers Minor. The two-member group, consisting of only himself and Yeats, significantly raised his status as one of London's newly distinguished modern poets.

However, Yeats's fascination with the supernatural did not coincide with what Pound deemed necessary study for modernizing poetry. In an effort to please Yeats, Pound initially assumed the role of "interested and informed outsider" (Occult Education 77). Nevertheless, Pound went to occult meetings with an open mind and concentrated on finding ideas to share with Yeats such as his theories on symbolism and aesthetics. As Yeats's involvement with the occult became more dedicated, his Monday Evenings developed into mostly a gathering of his closest occult associates including G.R.S. Mead, A.R. Orage, Allen Upward, the

Shakespears, and Laurence Binyon. These meetings spanned all the major occult groups such as the Theosophical Society, the Golden Dawn, the Quest Society, and minor groups whose roots grew from the Freemasons and the Rosicrucians. After Yeats introduced Pound to this diverse group, the young poet began his occult education. Occultism gave Pound the resources and vision to bring a fresh perspective to modern poetry.

Although much of Pound's early career was spent amongst these occult groups, Pound's occultism is largely overlooked by scholars and widely undervalued as a theme in his poetry. Pound's budding occultism began to thrive after he had been exposed to Yeats's research and occult acquaintances. Pound may have favored his occult connections because of the exclusivity these groups created amongst themselves. After his acceptance to London's "occult milieu," Pound developed an enduring interest in myth and initiation rituals. These subjects quickly became recurring themes within his poetry. For the literary community in London, occultism aided in the development of modernism. Because of a correlation to literature and art, studies of the occult began to transform into more serious scholarly pursuits rather than a vogue pastime. Pound's many collaborations with his colleagues provide a strong argument for his occultism through the evidence of his literary contributions to occult scholarship.

Pound succeeded in linking his occult and non-occult interests by fostering an attitude of exclusivity created with Yeats through their mutual desire to modernize literature. A particularly apt summary from James Longenbach attributes their bond to a shared "impulse to insult the world" with harsh criticism and similar arrogant attitudes. Pound's arrogance results from having Yeats as one of his primary influences (73). Pound's need to promote exclusivity within his work gave him a certain amount of dominance over his literary peers despite his inexperience and youth. He gleaned this approach from Yeats, whose desire for exclusivity in his work found fulfillment within the Golden Dawn's rites of initiation and levels of authority which granted access to occult secrets. After undergoing his own initiation, Pound adopted the occultist method of sharing selected or secret knowledge as a tool for exclusivity to compose his poetry. Pound's understanding of occult exclusivity and select knowledge originate from an interest in historicism based on his readings of Dante, Homer, and tomes of the classic philosophers. These studies supplied Pound a natural accompaniment to Yeats's occultism.

Pound's *Cantos* are notoriously full of bits and pieces of news, language, and references which the average reader might find challenging. By combining myth, history, and secret knowledge in his writing, Pound constructs an environment of initiation into which he can bring his readers. He believed that to gain comprehensive understanding of a people or culture resulted directly from the initiation of the reader. Pound defends his choice of difficult material and the lack of understanding amongst his readers by saying, "YOU WILL NEVER KNOW either why I chose them, or why they were worth choosing, or why you approve or disapprove my choice, until you go to the TEXTS, the originals" (*ABC of Reading* 45). In his poems, Pound recreates the occult perspective that once a reader is initiated, then true understanding of the material will follow. Pound intended for his poems to provide illumination for the unenlightened. By hinting at secret histories and select knowledge, Pound serves the initiator of secrets to his readers in mimicry of Yeats who was Pound's initiator into the occult.

Just as *The Pisan Cantos* are designed to fit into the larger schema of *The Cantos* epic, Pound's occult initiation ritual for his audience continues from one canto to the next. In the *Pisans*, Pound returns to his theme from Canto I where Odysseus' descent and journey towards *gnosis* which is symbolic of Pound's own *katabasis*, or descent to the underworld, as he writes his own epic. In *The Pisan Cantos*, Pound utilizes a form of automatic script to describe his visions and séance, the very essence of a journey to the underworld. This re-emphasizes the influence of his occult education and legacy of his relationship with Yeats during his London years. However, Pound's journey into the underworld was of his own making. From 1940 to 1943, Pound had a bi-weekly radio broadcast supporting Mussolini's regime. Deemed an American traitor, Pound was arrested in 1945 and sent the American Disciplinary Training Center in Pisa. While incarcerated Pound composed ten poems which he fatalistically perceived to be his final work. Since fear of death and uncertainty consumed Pound, he turns to a type of automatic script in which to house his calling forth of ghosts, spirits, and gods to witness his perdition as an American traitor and disgraced poet. These poems were published as T*he Pisan Cantos* in 1948.

—⁂— —⁂— —⁂—

Analysis of *The Pisan Cantos* reveals Pound's unique form of automatic writing as evident through his séances, spirit guides, and invocation of the dead. For automatic writing to occur, the medium or writer must be receptive to creative and supernatural influences. In an automatic writing session, the primary goal of the medium is to produce writing inspired by supernatural or spiritual influence. Automatic writing can assume several formats including free-hand drawings, abbreviated phrases, and even multi-lingual composition. Automatic writing is defined as, "Writing performed without conscious thought or deliberation, typically by means of spontaneous free association or as a medium for spirits or psychic forces" (OAHD). The primary objective is to discern a subconscious or spiritual meaning from thought processes not always fully understood or accessible to the writer. During his London years, Pound became familiar with occult experimentation including automatic writing, its connection to the medium's identity, and potentially autobiographical nature. On more than one occasion he witnessed Yeats and his fellow occultists hold séances and practice automatic writing for the purpose of divination or prophesy. The perspective of many self-proclaimed occultists concerning automatic writing is that the practice is more parlor trick than serious research.

During the Stone Cottage years with Yeats, Pound generally held himself aloof from the many occult practices Yeats undertook. Although he gained familiarity with its purpose as Yeats grew more deeply involved in his studies. Per Richard Ellmann, one of Yeats's ongoing tests with automatic writing took him more than two years to complete, beginning in 1912. In this experiment, Yeats endeavored to ask questions by method of telepathic communication and have them answered by one of his automatic writing participants. He became unfailingly convinced that "a living mind could serve as a medium for departed spirits" (198). This test is among many that Yeats conducted while sharing a close association with Pound in London. Pound recalls his Stone Cottage studies in *The Pisan Cantos* when he thinks of "Uncle William / downstairs composing" (83.165-166). He writes regretfully:

> well those days are gone forever
> > and the travelling rug with the coon-skin tabs
> and his hearing nearly all Wordsworth
> > for the sake of his conscience but
> preferring Ennemoser on Witches (83.184-188)

As Yeats's secretary, Pound's duties included reading aloud to the elder poet. There is little surprise that Yeats preferred Ennemoser's text over the Romantic Wordsworth. Ennemoser's book includes investigation into animal magnetism and occult science, which would have been a primer for Yeats and Pound who were "scientifically illiterate" (Surette 150). Pound took an interest in reading those occult texts alongside Yeats and developed a more latent occultism which was exposed in his *Cantos*. The occult education Pound underwent more than thirty years prior to his imprisonment in 1945 is an important factor in his composition of *The Pisan Cantos*. The occult overtones of the *Pisans* are generally ignored in favor of discussing Pound's politics and autobiography. However, Pound wrote *The Cantos* based upon secret histories while weaving *The Odyssey* into its fabric to complete the formula for his epic. Yeats once said that Pound's epic ambition was "'constantly interrupted, broken, twisted into nothing by its direct opposite, nervous obsession nightmare, stammering confusion...'" (Longenbach 172). Yeats's analysis of Pound's work offers a deeper understanding of the poet who has relinquished himself to become a medium for his ghosts and the unerring dream of leaving behind an epic legacy within the Pisans should they indeed be his final writings.

The ghosts who haunt *The Pisan Cantos* guide Pound from the road to hell and onto the path towards a meditative state as the poet becomes possessed by the Odyssean spirit as he believes death is imminent. He begins Canto 80 with an adamant plea against his imprisonment as he channels the conversation of his fellow inmates:

Ain' committed no federal crime,
jes a slight misdemeanor" (80.1-2)

Pound never apologizes for his controversial stance concerning fascism and carried this loyalty with him through *The Pisan Cantos* and into his stay at St. Elizabeths Hospital after his release from the DTC.[1] From this point onward the canto carries Pound's "death-chill" (80.33) into automatic script while conjuring the ghost of friends and colleagues who:

…as Santayana has said:
They just died   They died because they
just couldn't stand it (80.86-87)

George Santayana is resurrected here because Pound must have been familiar with his theories concerning metaphysical naturalism and may have possibly read his *Realms of Being*. Pound steps beyond Santayana to wail his grief as he finds that he is unable to peacefully accept his own looming execution. He admits to approaching the end of his wits at "the gates of death" (80.660-661). With no hope of escape from mental and physical duress, Pound allows his occultism to emerge as sources of strength and inspiration through his full immersion into the use of automatic writing.

From an academic or scientific perspective, automatic writing is more than just a tool to contact the spirits or to gain supernatural knowledge and guidance. For example, Dr. Anita Muhl's work as a psychoanalyst led her to study the practice of automatic writing as a therapeutic tool. Muhl thought that automatic writing could be utilized as a way to clear the mind; the practice is influenced by the writer's personality, experiences, and memories. In opposition to Muhl's scientific use of automatic writing is the perception that it may be practiced by a mentally unstable individual. In *An Encyclopaedia of Occultism*, Lewis Spence says that automatic writing can be produced as a result of "a slight disturbance in the nerve centres occasioned by excitement or fatigue to hystero-epilepsy or actual insanity" (56). Spence's analysis of automatic writing as a symptom of fatigue is applicable to Pound as he suffers through imprisonment. This perspective assumes that only mental or emotional instability would influence someone to undertake automatic writing. However, Muhl presented the idea that automatic writing can actually combat and heal emotional stress by providing the medium an outlet for expression. This would provide a much more charitable explanation for the belief that Pound must have suffered from insanity and his emotionally charged Pisan poems are the result.

In my personal efforts to understand the automatic writing, I created a project built on the idea that automatic writing can be used in the therapeutic sense to support my argument that Pound uses automatic writing in his *Pisans*. Pound's fusion of therapy and the writing of poetry is intriguing. I asked ten people to

---

1 DTC: A military detention camp/disciplinary training center.

follow the basic rules Muhl outlines in her text to identify the purpose behind practicing automatic writing. The participants were asked to sit quietly for ten to twenty minutes, clear their minds, and simply write or draw what they felt. Summarily, all the participants said they felt a sense of emotional release from stress. Several of the results included pictures, phrases, and nonsensical sentences one participant said was the inspiration for a new story he intended to write. The effect of automatic writing is difficult to execute for those who were self-described as "stressed out" and "too tired to think." Overall the clinical applications of Muhl's automatic writing analysis proves to be applicable to Pound's situation as he sat under the burden of emotion caused by his imprisonment. As I discovered as a result of my project, automatic writing takes a great deal of silence and concentration to be used effectively. This supports my argument for Pound's use of automatic writing as the results of my exercise produced pages that are remarkably similar to Pound's method of composition for *The Pisan Cantos*. One example is Pound's use of memory and myth in Canto 82 as a tool to deal with the stresses of the prison environment. In keeping with Muhl's perspective, it is evident how Pound's automatic writing as a therapeutic tool helps him retain the memories he so feared to lose. Automatic writing is useful in revealing a writer's previous experiences in a safe and therapeutic manner.

Additionally, Pound's contribution to the scholarly argument surrounding occultism is based largely on how he approaches the practice of automatic writing. While writing *The Pisan Cantos* Pound uses automatic writing as a therapeutic tool for channeling a séance. The seemingly nonsensical jumble of subjects in the *Pisans* assume a more coherent structure when viewed through the lens of automatism. Automatic writing can function as a way to dispel personal fears since the act of automatic writing is the tool for releasing emotional energy. Spence writes, "As a rule automatic speech and writing display nothing more than a revivifying of faded mental imagery, thoughts, conjectures, and impressions which never come to birth in the upper consciousness" (56). With this method a writer can access hidden feelings or memories which give an autobiographical or narrative focus to their sessions. In her analysis of automatic writing from a medical academic perspective, Muhl explains some of its uses, "In obtaining quickly the subject's own explanation of delusions, fears, obsessions, and hallucinations. As a means of bringing phantasy into actual expression. As a means of recalling forgotten incidents. To explain and elaborate other visual imagery" (38). Pound's automatic writing enables him to come to terms with his fears and state of exhaustion. Physically and emotionally fatigued, Pound scrambles to write another chapter for his epic and to support his brief attempt at an autobiography. Pound drafts his poems as quickly as he can in an effort to preserve his memories. He applies the emotional distress from his imprisonment to create a set of poems so unique with his automatic writing style that they were given the Bollingen Prize for poetry.

After being taken to the DTC, Pound begins keeping a "diary-like notebook" of his thoughts. At first he "laments a world in ruins and seeks consolation in a landscape suffused with Greek and Confucian presences" (Bush 171). These presences are a few of the spirit guides and ghosts we encounter throughout Pound's Pisan journey. His ever increasing fear of memory loss and death leads him to hold a séance of ghosts and continual "testimonials to the dead" (Bush 197). He establishes himself as the medium for a personal séance filled with friends who have passed away and Pound looks to them for hope of his much sought-after Paradiso and release from hell. By attempting to retain his memories, Pound's mnemonic exercise becomes "like a mantra that sidesteps physic resistance and discovers sympathetic powers beyond the ego" (197). Pound imagines himself seeing guiding goddesses:

> "With us there is no deceit"
>> said the moon nymph   immacolata
>> give back my cloak, hagaromo.
>> had I the clouds of heaven
>>> as the nautile born ashore
>> in their holocaust
>>> as wisteria floating shoreward (80.260-266)

Taken from one of Pound's earlier Noh plays, hagaromo refers to the cloak lost by an "aerial spirit" or the moon nymph (Sieburth 146). Pound also sees Venus as born ashore perhaps in reference to Pound's longing for the safety of home and the love of a woman. Pound immerses himself in his visions of a possible Paradise, aware of these goddesses in addition to the ghosts of long-dead friends watching over him. As Pound learned from his occult education, one objective for an automatic writing session is to reveal supernatural visions outside of the medium's physical reality. Pound believes in Paradise but questions:

> I don't know how humanity stands it
>> with a painted paradise at the end of it
>> without a painted paradise at the end of it
> the dwarf morning-glory twines round the grass blade
> magna NOX animae with Barabbas and 2 thieves beside me,
>>> the wards like a slave ship, (74.389-394)

Within a few weeks of his imprisonment, Pound loses his hope of freedom and his thoughts turn towards the possibility of death. In these lines he falters between faith in the "painted paradise" beyond his prison walls and the damnation of hell. His vision of heaven becomes connected to his loss of freedom in the DTC.

Automatic writing guides his hand throughout his imprisonment in the DTC. The visual text of the *Pisans* themselves are at times wild, unpredictable, and haunting. As he searches for solace in the midst of his *nekyia*, Pound resumes the occult consideration of life after death and its tenuous connection to humanity.

Pound's automatic writing is continually driven by the ghosts and spirits he raises throughout his Pisan séance. He seeks guidance from his goddesses and hope for the afterlife from the specters of friends and acquaintances from days long past. Pound had at first only hoped to hold on to his memories through the comforting practice of putting pen to paper, but what makes the *Pisans* one of the most memorable parts of his epic *Cantos* is the use of automatic writing and the influence of Yeats's unfailing belief in magic and séances. Pound's occult education marks these poems with wisps of ghosts and a writer immersed in the depths of his mind, where memories live. Dove sta memoria.

Works Cited

—⁓— "Automatic Writing." Def. 1. Online American Heritage Dictionary Online. American Heritage, n.d. Web. 12 Dec. 2012. <http://americanheritage.yourdictionary.com/automatic-writing>.

—⁓— Baumann, Walter. *The Rose in the Steel Dust: An Examination of the Cantos of Ezra Pound*. Coral Gables: University of Miami Press, 1970. Print.

—⁓— Bush, Ronald. 'Quiet, Not Scornful'? The Composition of *The Pisan Cantos*." In Lawrence S. Rainey (ed). *A Poem Containing History: Textual Studies* in The Cantos.

—⁓— Ellmann, Richard. *W.B. Yeats: The Man and the Masks*. New York: W.W. Norton, 1999.

—⁓— Harper, George Mills. "Unbelievers In The House": Yeats's Automatic Script." *Studies in The Literary Imagination* 14.1 (1981): 1. *Academic Search Premier*. Web. 14 Jan. 2012.

—⁓— Harper, Margaret Mills. *Wisdom of Two: The Spiritual and Literary Collaboration of George and W.B. Yeats*. Oxford: Oxford UP, 2006.

—⁓— Kenner, Hugh. *The Pound Era*. Berkeley: University of California Press, 1971. Print.

—⁓— Lady, Lee. "Reading Ezra Pound's *Cantos*." Web. 10 Nov. 2010. <www2.hawaii.edu/~lady/ramblings/ABC.html>.

—⁓— Longenbach, James. *Stone Cottage*. Oxford: Oxford UP, 1991.

—⁓— Muhl, Anita. *Automatic Writing*. Washington: Kessenger Publishing, 2003.

—⁓— Mussolini, Benito. *The Doctrines of Fascism*. New York: Howard Fertig Publisher, 2006.

—⁓— Nally, Claire V. "Leo Africanus As Irishman?." *Irish Studies Review* 14.1 (2006): 57-67. Academic Search Premier. Web. 14 Jan. 2012.

—⁓— Pound, Ezra. *ABC of Reading*. New York: New Directions: 1960. Print.

---. *Selected Prose 1909-1965*. Ed. William Cookson. New York: New Directions: 1973. Print.

---. *The Cantos of Ezra Pound*. New York: New Directions: 1971. Print.

---. *The Pisan Cantos*. Ed. Richard Sieburth. New York: New Directions: 2003. Print.

—- Sieburth, Richard. Introduction. *The Pisan Cantos*. By Ezra Pound. New York: New Directions: 2003. Print.

—- Spence, Lewis. *Encyclopaedia of Occultism*. Mineola: Dover Publications, 2003.

—- Surette, Leon. *The Birth of Modernism*. Montreal: McGill-Queen's UP, 1993.

—- Tryphonopulos, Demetres. *The Celestial Tradition*. Ontario: Wilfrid Laurier UP, 1992.

---. "Ezra Pound's Occult Education." *Journal of Modern Literature* 17.1 (1990): 73. *Academic Search Premier*. Web. 14 Jan. 2012.

—- Woodward, Anthony. *Ezra Pound and the Pisan Cantos*. London: Routledge and Kegan Paul Ltd., 1980. Print.

THE COLONIAL CRUSADE AGAINST MAGICAL THINKING

Vanessa Sinclair

By this point in time, many if not most academics understand that European colonization of other continents from the early 15th century onwards has resulted in widespread systematic racism, misogyny, oppression and a vastly uneven distribution of wealth worldwide. This colonial violence continues to impact our society in a variety of ways to this day. But colonization occurs not only in the land grab of physical terrain, resources, and slave labor, but also through the colonization of the mind. Western European values are held as the standard by which all others are measured. And while this portion of the population is a small minority compared to the billions of people on the planet, it considers itself to be the norm, and considers all other cultures to be just that: "others." This point of view is of course, quite infantile, simplistic and narcissistic to say the least.

As mentioned, at this point most academics seem to understand this and are working towards an understanding of the ramifications of colonization worldwide. However, there seems to be a sort of blind spot or denial about the ways in which colonization has impacted the way we think about mental health, the field of psychiatry and psychology in general, and the "symptom" of magical thinking in particular. Despite "magical thinking" not being clearly defined in the DSM,[1] it is nevertheless indicative of such serious diagnoses as Schizophrenia and Schizotypal Personality Disorder. Simply described as "odd beliefs or magical thinking that influences behavior and is inconsistent with cultural norms (e.g., superstitiousness, belief in clairvoyance, telepathy, or 'sixth sense')." The online version of the DSM links to a definition of magical thinking at BehaveNet which states that magical thinking is a "primitive thought disorder characterized by content which suggests that the patient believes that his thoughts can produce actions (may be normal in children)." And *Encyclopedia Britannica* defines magical thinking as "the belief that one's ideas, thoughts, actions, words, or use of symbols can influence the course of events in the material world."

The reason I am focusing on magical thinking in particular as an important area to address at this time, is that it is something that most people seem to have internalized as true. That magical thinking is a small sign of a much larger issue: the first step on a slippery slope, a "royal road" to psychosis, a life-long, chronic and incurable medical condition. And people are warned of this at a young age, often in adolescence, when they are taught they must shed these "primitive," "childlike" ideas and "grow up."

---

1 DSM: "Diagnostic and Statistical Manual of Mental Disorders"

This prohibition on magical thinking in Western European society has been internalized by individuals and can effect them on a daily basis. And as it is less severe that overt psychotic symptoms, this implicit pathologization of it is also quite insidious, as it erodes individuals' ability to trust their own personal experience, encouraging them to abandon their own perceptions to adhere to societal norms. A great many aspects of human life and experience have been pathologized, and overly so, as individuals are continually coerced into fitting into smaller and smaller boxes to maintain the status quo and appear "normal." People's autonomy and sense of agency has been stripped away from them bit by bit in a variety of overt and more covert ways over time.

As a clinician, I can say that almost every patient that has come through my office has at one time or another stated, "I know this sounds crazy but..." or "I don't want you to think I'm crazy but..." Usually what comes after this "but" is either a synchronicity they've noticed – a moment when the outside world and their internal experience seem to connect or reflect in a meaningful way. Or when a person has experienced a vision or encounter with a deceased loved one, whether through a dream or other kind of dream-like state, a time when the analysand felt their ancestor or loved one communicated with them in some way. The fact that patients feel they will be seen as "crazy" or that they have to justify themselves or their experience when they feel an intimate connection or communication with a deceased loved one or ancestor is tragic... The fact that people are made to feel pathological, desperate, "primitive" or regressed for experiencing such a moment is an absolute shame. Humans have been holding space for and venerating our ancestors for millennia, as well we should. We should not forget the trials and tribulations of those that came before us, their perseverance, strength and determination. This is how each and every one of us came to be, why we are here today. Perhaps the perpetuation of such a worldview that belittles and disregards the memory of and connection to our ancestors has contributed to phenomena such as trans-generational transmission of trauma and the clear need we have now as a global society for recognition of the past, of our collective history. The evangelism of the colonists and crusaders, who "carried the cross in one hand and a sword in the other," forced people of a variety of cultures to give up long held traditions of respecting and venerating their own ancestors in order to adopt someone else's; These saints as "foreign ancestors," to quote MJ Maher.

There is a reason black magic is called black magic. It is no coincidence and has everything to do with race and colonization; the oppressors belittling the practices of the occupied Native peoples and Africans they used as slave labor. To quote Nicholaj Frisvold, "Macumba was the tool used by the people of the streets, the outcasts, the slaves, free-born slaves and all strata of society that suffered under oppression" (2011, p. 2). Fortunately, people are innovative and the colonized found ways to continue to practice their rituals and traditions by merging them with the iconography of the Catholic oppressors. The Orishas of Yoruba become the saints of Santeria, wearing the ornamentation of Catholicism as a means of survival, evolving and forming new iterations of old religions. Altars and rituals are created for Exus and Pomba Giras, the Virgin Mary and Santa Barbara, alike.

In the White Western European standard, even traditions that have histories thousands of years older than western medicine, which is really, really relatively new, are deemed to be "alternative." Traditions that work with the cycles of nature, meridians of energy, herbs, earth, land or direction, including Chinese medicine and Ayurveda, are seen as New Age, hocus pocus, something fun or relaxing but not anything to be taken seriously.

As for the first part that I mentioned, the making of meaning in one's life through the "noticing" of or even "creation" of synchronicities... People make meaning in their lives all the time. If the main argument against synchronicity is that there cannot possibly be an "actual" connection between inner experience and external reality, and therefore the individual is inventing meaning where there is none, well then I don't really see that as much of an argument. People make meaning in their lives all the time. Implying that someone's personal experience is not valid because it does not conform to socially normative ways of making meaning in one's life is not useful and in my experience does more harm than good.

Oftentimes the anxiety an individual has around the fear of being "crazy" or "going crazy" does more harm than anything else. If making meaning in one's life through the noting of synchronicities gives a person a sense of security in the world, a feeling that they are on the right track, then what's the problem? If someone is Christian and they say that God sent them a sign, then it's socially acceptable to "have faith." But if someone speaks of synchronicities, then they've fallen into the realm of the "magical" or "occult;" they've lost the plot and are seen as New Age, flaky, or Jungian. These are all ways to belittle, judge, write-off, and condescend the personal experiences of others. Another way to colonize the mind.

This realm of magical thinking seems to still be taboo, even among persons that otherwise understand the widespread effects of colonization that have occurred in other areas, such as internalized racism, homophobia, misogyny and oppression. But even among the most well meaning of people, the idea of folk magic practices, coming of age rituals, and the like – at least ones that are not a part of mainstream society – still seem to be looked upon as quaint at best; something that people of an older generation believed in, your sweet grandmother, who is still quite superstitious. It may be ok for someone who lives rurally, or in some other exotic culture, or country where they "still" think like that. But certainly not for someone in an urban setting, among the educated, academic or elite. And that's at best. In many parts of the world, indigenous or folk magic practitioners are still persecuted as witches and ostracized or even killed. It wasn't that long ago, in the 1980s and early 90s in fact, that Satanic panic spread across the United States, resulting in the imprisonment and incarceration of adolescents and young adults accused of Satanism and witchcraft. Several of whom were just finally acquitted and released in recent years, like the West Memphis 3, who were released in 2011, cleared of all charges after DNA testing showed they were not at the scene of the crime. After sitting on death row for nearly 20 years… And they are the lucky ones, whose case was publicized by celebrities. Imagine all those who remain in prison, on death row, or have already died. Even more recently the case of Amanda Knox, an American exchange student in Perugia, who was accused of being some sort of hysteric harlot involved in the supposed ritual cult killing of her roommate, and held in an Italian prison for 4 years before finally being released and acquitted in 2015. And even this year, in 2019, the Pope continues to blame Satan for the systemic abuses and pedophilia that continues to pervade the Church. These are very real events that have affected many people's lives, and continue to do so. It is not a joke, and it is still happening today. Christian missionaries continue to make their way across Africa, Latin America and other parts of the world, in an effort to convert under the guise of bringing aid, and somehow we're supposed to see this as a noble and honorable endeavor.

Having worked with many university students, I have found that what is surprisingly under-addressed is that between the ages of 18-22, when people are often heading off to college, is also the time when many individuals begin to experience more severe symptoms of stress and anxiety than they ever have before, and sometimes even psychotic breaks. This makes sense as this is the time when adolescents are often leaving their home of origin for the first time to head off on their own, a time when they must learn to support themselves in their day to day lives in ways that hadn't had to before, and if they are at university or in a full-time job, they may well be experiencing higher levels of pressure and stress than ever before.

Unfortunately, when these young adults seek help from the authority figures and medical doctors, they are often told they are experiencing symptoms of psychosis, are borderline or bipolar, that they have a chronic medical condition that is biologically based and has no known cure or reliable form of treatment, that there is something fundamentally wrong with them, biochemically, biologically, or genetically, and that they will likely be on prescription medication for the rest of their lives. Now, how does this help anyone? This only adds anxiety and despair, helplessness and hopelessness to a young person who has just been given a life sentence at such an early stage in their life. This can only serve to exacerbate their symptoms.

What if, instead, we let them know that actually many people experience intense symptoms at this transitional time in their lives, that this makes sense given the stressors they are enduring, that stress often manifests itself in these types of symptoms, including physical and somatic symptoms, and that with the work of analysis or talk therapy and a support system in place, they can learn to understand what's going on with themselves, work through these symptoms, and go on to live productive, fulfilling lives.

Whereas other cultures have provided rituals and models for marking these transitions in life, particularly from childhood to adolescence and adolescence to adulthood, the current Western European colonial social structure is lacking in this area, as well as in ways the community can hold or make space for times of crisis that may occur when individuals are making these transitions. Over the decades, there have been a variety of books written addressing the lack of resources available during these times and offering alternate ways of thinking about and understanding symptoms of psychosis than our current paradigm. Many of these books are written by persons who have experienced such a crisis themselves or by someone close to them, such as *My Mysterious Son* (2014) by Dick Russell or the recent, *The Collected Schizophrenias* (2019) by Esme Wang. Still others have been written by psychiatrists and other mental health clinicians, such as *Spiritual Emergency: When Personal Transformation Becomes a Crisis* (1989), a collection including articles by Stanislav Grof and RD Laing. Many of these contributions include discussions of different ways about thinking about mental illness that deviate from the standard accepted view of Western medicine, and how the Western European social structure, as opposed to many other cultures, lacks a socially delineated system to approach, address, work through and provide space for a person experiencing symptoms of crisis, emotional or behavioral duress, including hallucinations, delusions and other symptoms of psychosis.

Unfortunately, the standard of care has become psycho-pharmaceutical and very rarely is any other method of treatment, like talk therapy, implemented, even concurrently. It has become all about symptom suppression or management and not about rehabilitation, understanding and treatment.

In his book *What is Madness?* (2011), Darian Leader notes that when we think of madness and treating psychosis, what we are really concerned with is returning patients back to what is considered to be the societal norm. In this book, he gives an example of a patient he was working with that seemed no different than many of his friends. He was thoughtful and engaging, studied philosophy and psychology. When Darian asked the staff why this person was interned in a long-term mental health care facility, the staff seemed to look at him like he hadn't learned the secret yet. Eventually, in one of their sessions, the patient began talking about some other planet he lived on that was not Earth. The patient's affect didn't change, he was not distressed. He spoke about this place like it was any other fact of life. While Leader understood that this discrepancy between the patient's personal reality and the agreed upon consensus reality of society meant this patient had a "delusion," he didn't seem to think it warranted someone having to live in an inpatient facility the rest of their lives.

I had a similar such experience with a patient I worked with at a government run HIV+ clinic in New York City. We'll call him Mr. Gatsby.

I vividly remember the first day I met the great Mr. Gatsby. Working in an outpatient HIV+ clinic in Brooklyn, our waiting room tended to be chaotic. People speaking loudly, often yelling at one another, yelling at the staff or the television. Others talking to themselves, pacing about the room. In the midst of all of this waits the great Mr. Gatsby, quietly, patiently gazing ahead with hands folded in his lap. A 60 year old African American man born and raised in NYC, Mr. Gatsby always dressed in the same clothes, a kind of uniform of navy blue pants and blue nylon jacket with black shoes. Naturally a thin man, even more so due to his condition, and tall, standing at 6'3".

He enjoyed playing basketball and had the physique for it, but unfortunately, Mr. Gatsby was not able to play basketball recently, as he had contracted a viral infection during a hospital stay some years back. The virus affected his brain, leaving his right side semi-paralyzed. So now Mr. Gatsby walks with a limp, slowly and deliberately swinging his right leg forward in such a way that he has developed a sort of stride. Refusing to use a cane or walker, he never allowed me to hold the door for him. A soft-spoken intelligent man, his large brown eyes possessed a sense of wonder, as well as a hint of mischief as if he had a secret that no one else knew. And in fact he did. Mr. Gatsby reported his mission was to bring clean energy to the world through the development of technology that would harness the energy of the tides of the ocean. Too dependent on fossil fuels, Mr. Gatsby worried that humans were destroying the Earth as well as themselves. He wanted to help address the Earth's energy crisis, and felt the solution was tidal energy.

As the year 2012 was approaching, Mr. Gatsby spoke of the end of the Mayan calendar and the coming apocalypse. He explained that the Mayans saw the whole world lit up and assumed it was engulfed in flames, and that this meant the end of the world. But they were mistaken. "It wasn't flames they saw," he explained, "it was electricity." Because once we implement tidal energy, we can bring electricity to every corner of the globe. Even children in the most rural areas will have access to electricity and with it, clean water.

Mr. Gatsby expressed great concern for the children of the world, hoping future generations would not have to grow up in such a polluted environment. He explained a system for raising children that he felt was superior to ours. "Children shouldn't necessarily be raised by their biological parents. Biological parents aren't always the best ones for the job. In Star Fleet Academy, the children live together in group homes. They'll all be treated the same, so there will be no class system. They live, play and work together. It's a much better way, you'll see."

Mr. Gatsby grew up in a family of Jehovah's Witnesses with very strict religious beliefs. Celebrations of any kind were forbidden and conventional medical care was not routine. He had several siblings but really only spoke of one older brother whom he seemed to admire but hadn't seen in years. Mr. Gatsby hadn't had any contact with his family for decades. He assumed they continued to reside in the city but stated they wanted nothing to do with him because he was gay.

Mr. Gatsby was diagnosed in the early 1980's before HIV+ had a name. Now, 30 years later, he'd beaten the odds. He'd tried several different HIV+ medications over the years but was rarely 100% adherent. Most of the time he chose to abstain from medications of any kind. He enjoyed smoking marijuana every day but didn't drink alcohol. "Don't get me wrong, I was wild back in the day. Partying in the city in the 1970s – those were the days. I used to go to dance clubs every night. I knew all the spots. I sure was a wild one, but not anymore. Now, I just smoke weed and surf the internet."

Mr. Gatsby had been working diligently at a hospital in NYC for over 20 years, as an accountant. He went to work every day, sat quietly at his desk and attended to his responsibilities. A quiet man, he kept to himself but always shared a smile on his way into the office and wished everyone a good evening on his way out. His coworkers found him to be pleasant. He rarely took a day off of work for illness or holiday – the ideal employee. Until one day it came time to share his special knowledge with the world. You see, Mr. Gatsby wrote everything I just explained about tidal energy, Star Fleet Academy and him being in "tribe homosexual" in an email and sent it to his colleagues at the hospital.

And the following day, Mr. Gatsby went to work. As usual, he greeted everyone and sat down at his desk, but soon he was surrounded by hospital police – for those of you that may not know, the hospital system in NYC as its own police department, and all the city hospitals have police stations on site, often in the basement of the facility. Hospital police immediately escorted him to the inpatient psychiatric unit of his own hospital – which was quite a prominent one, the name of which is often a signifier for psychiatric institutions – where he was held for several weeks. He initially refused psychiatric medication but eventually relented as he realized being compliant was the only way he would ever be set free. He was eventually released but in this process lost his job and had been unemployed ever since. That was 5-6 years ago.

As soon as he was home, he stopped taking all prescribed medications. He was placed on public assistance and disability. Part of his release plan included attending outpatient psychotherapy sessions at a nearby clinic, so he met with a psychologist weekly and psychiatrist monthly but continued to refuse medication. After a couple of years, he tired of treatment. He felt the mental health professionals weren't really listening to him and were only concerned with "treatment adherence." "Every session they'd asked me why I didn't want to take my medications, both the HIV+ and psychiatric ones. I've never believed in taking medication. And how can I trust the government after what they did to me? I worked for them for 20 years, and this is how they repay me? I think their medications are poison. It's those medications that are making people sick." He eventually stopped attending sessions and ceased to answer their phone calls. Case managers showed up at his home, and after asking them to leave him alone on several occasions, he stopped answering the door. He rarely left his house, afraid of even going out for groceries, fearing he'd be ambushed, terrified they'd lock him up again.

Then one day, his nightmare became true. After exhausting efforts to reengage Mr. Gatsby in treatment, his case managers called in Mobile Crisis. Mobile Crisis is a team of psychologists, psychiatrists and social workers that travel into the community to patients' homes, often accompanied by the police, with the hope of bringing patients back into treatment. They assess the patient's risk of harm to self or others and if deemed to be at risk, the patient is removed from his home and brought to the hospital. In Mr. Gatsby's case, he wasn't actively threatening suicide or homicide, but because he was HIV+ and refusing to take medication, he was deemed to be "passively suicidal," a danger to himself, and due to "psychotic thought processes" was felt to be without the capacity to make his own medical decisions.

It was at this time Mr. Gatsby was taken to the hospital where he incurred the viral infection that affected his brain, leaving him with hemiparesis. He was suffering from pneumonia, which was able to be treated at the hospital, but as he'd contracted this virus that left him semi-paralyzed during his stay there, he felt he would have been better off had he never been forced into treatment. As soon as he returned home, he discontinued all prescription medications again, left the clinic altogether, and never returned.

He became increasingly isolated. With no family support or friends, Mr. Gatsby spent most of his time locked in his room, smoking pot, working on his blog and chatting with other "conspiracy theorists" (his words, not mine).

After more than a year, he was feeling lonely and decided to seek out treatment again. It was at this time he came to our clinic. Mr. Gatsby agreed to see the psychiatrist for an evaluation but refused any medications offered. He was referred to me for individual psychotherapy and agreed to meet weekly for 45 minutes. He also agreed to continue to meet with the psychiatrist once a month even though he refused medication.

I met weekly with the director of mental health at our clinic, as he liked to stay abreast of the progress of patients, being sure to address any high-risk patient issues. As I discussed Mr. Gatsby with my supervisor, he insisted that I address treatment adherence issues with the patient every session, and insisted I write, "Patient continues to refuse HIV+ and psychiatric medications" at the end of every note to ensure the hospital was free from any liability. I consulted with other clinicians as well, as I was worried about this liability and wanted to ensure I was doing the right thing. But the overall consensus was that Mr. Gatsby was treatment compliant. He attended our sessions every week, never missed, and had the same Primary Care Physician (PCP) for over 10 years. What else could we do? If he refused to take the recommended medication, it was his right to do so. He was also what is known as a slow progressor. This means that although he had been HIV+ for over 30 years, his T-cell count had never fallen below the 200 range, which means he never had AIDS. So he had the HIV+ virus, but was not in critical condition with respect to that. I was able to be in touch with his PCP, who also had a good rapport with him, said he never missed an appointment, and that he had always refused medications.

The interesting thing is that once I related the patient's history to my supervisor, and that he was raised a Jehovah's Witness, then suddenly all of the concern of liability and the pressure to focus on treatment adherence was dropped. In other words, when the patient refused medication because he didn't personally believe in it, didn't feel he needed it, or when he thought medication was poison and didn't trust the government, it was not ok, but now that he was raised as a Jehovah's Witness, even though he was non-practicing, now it was ok, because it was his religious right.

Nothing changed in Mr. Gatsby's mind. It was just this piece of information imparted to my supervisor that changed everything from the hospital's point of view. And while I'm sure that Mr. Gatsby's religious upbringing did affect his current beliefs about medical intervention and prescription medication, that was always present, no matter who was or was not aware of it. So why wasn't Mr. Gatsby to make his own decisions regarding his care, from the beginning, as an adult? And would he even have been treated this way at all, if he were a straight white man instead of a gay black man?

We continued on in much the same way, for a couple of years, until one day Mr. Gatsby came in for his regularly scheduled appointment but wasn't feeling too well. He was walking more slowly than usual, feeling a little dizzy, but still refused to use a cane. Instead he steadied himself with the handrail that runs the length of the hall, and this time he allowed me to hold the door open for him. He spoke of the usual plans to implement tidal energy and save mankind but was speaking more slowly and quietly than usual. I asked him how he was feeling and suggested we let a clinic doctor take a look at him. He insisted he was fine. I knew he had a good rapport with the psychiatrist, so I asked if I could call him in. He agreed, and the psychiatrist came to my office to evaluate him. Mr. Gatsby had experienced these dizzy spells before, saying they began after he contracted the viral infection that affected his brain. He insisted that he just needed to go home to rest and refused to see another medical provider. We were able to persuade him to allow the hospital ambulette service to drive him home, instead of taking the bus when he wasn't feeling well. The psychiatrist escorted him to the exit, ensuring that he safely boarded the hospital van. As the two were leaving my office, Mr. Gatsby turned to me and said, "Thank you for all you've done."

As you may have guessed, this was the last time I saw the great Mr. Gatsby. He missed the next two appointments, which had never happened before. I called and left voicemail messages. Then, finally I received a call. The woman on the line explained she was Mr. Gatsby's landlord. She hadn't seen him in a while and had become worried. She liked to keep an eye on him because he didn't have any family or friends around. Sometimes she'd bring him some soup or a plate of dinner. When she hadn't seen him in a few days, she decided to knock on his door, and when he didn't answer, she went in to have a look. "I found him laying in his bed. He'd passed away. But the good thing is he looked peaceful, like he'd died in his sleep. I called you because yours was the first number in his phone. And I just thought someone should know."

REFERENCES

Frisvold, N. (2011). *Pomba Gira & the Quimbanda of Mbùmba Nzila*. London: Scarlet Imprint.

—⁓— Grof, S. & C. (1989). *Spiritual Emergency: When Personal Transformation Becomes a Crisis*. Los Angeles: TarcherPerigee.
—⁓— Leader, D. (2011). *What is Madness?* London: Penguin.
—⁓— Maher, MJ. (2012) *Racism and Cultural Diversity: Cultivating Racial Harmony through Counseling, Group Analysis, and Psychotherapy*. London: Karnac.
—⁓— Russell, D. (2014). *My Mysterious Son: a Life Changing Passage between Schizophrenia and Shamanism*. New York: Skyhorse Publishing.
—⁓— Wang, E. (2019). *The Collected Schizophrenias*. Minneapolis: Graywolf Press.

The Roots of Modern Satanism,
from John Milton to Mickey Katz

Blanche Barton

Many of you may know little about Satanism. I will introduce it with this endorsement: Our foundational document, *The Satanic Bible* by Anton LaVey, is probably the book most often stolen from bookstores and libraries in the United States. They can't keep it on the shelves. It sells well and has been in continual print since it was first published as an original paperback exactly 50 years ago. But people steal it. Either they are attracted to what it has to say, almost in a fetishistic way, like a secret vice. Or they might want to steal it in order to take this dangerous heresy off the shelves so it can't corrupt their children. Maybe they take it home and burn it. I can't say. But it disappears off the shelves. People read it and they either throw it across the room in disgust or fear, or they embrace it, remarking, "Well, that's simple. That makes sense. What's the big deal?"

What thinking human would not agree? Wild indulgence tempered with personal responsibility, groundbreaking creative and scientific heresy, defiance of large faceless oppressive entities, sensual and intellectual excitement—where's the problem? But I'm damned, so perhaps a bit prejudiced. I've been a Satanist since I was 12 years old—old enough to see that, as a girl, I was already cursed and disdained by an absent God. But I was in good company in my child-brain, because it seemed animals didn't get much sympathy from the Almighty either— and I got along great with most animals, better than I did with most humans. I was drawn to the magic and ancient mysteries of what was then broadly termed "the occult" which included everything from witches and vampires to UFOs, time travel and pyramid power. So when I read about this mysterious Anton LaVey in San Francisco who was not only exploring ritual magic in new ways but who also advocated for women's power, sexual freedom, who loved animals and was proudly standing forth to give due credit to the ultimate rebel—Satan himself—I was all in, and have been an enthusiastic blasphemer ever since. Drawing on these decades of defiance and hellish delight, and 13 years spent with our founding High Priest, I'll take this time to provide some perspective on where Anton LaVey got the ideas he brought together to form the philosophy of Satanism and the Church of Satan.

Anton LaVey invented Satanism in 1966. While we have ties to wide-reaching traditions and philosophies, there was no significant, organized group that propounded Satanic allegiance as a religion before LaVey founded the Church of Satan. All reports of Satanic practices before then were formed as accusations cast upon two extremes of society, either against those of wealth and authority, or against the poor and marginalized. There have been isolated magicians through the ages who can rightly be called diabolists, and perhaps a few groups who practiced devil worship, but this was done within a Christian (often more specifically a Catholic) context, simply inverting the rubrics of worship to create a Pageant of Perversity. This apocryphal Satanism stood as a protest against the chokehold of the Catholic Church, or as a path to power by alignment with what the Church had constructed as its greatest enemy. There were even some who performed presumed Satanic horrors for paying audiences, and, in the early eighteenth century, indulgent, wealthy young men across Europe were immersing themselves in Hellfire Clubs which offered blasphemy and diabolical debauchery.

It is most definitely not a religion based in revelation; LaVey never claimed to be in direct contact with Lucifer, or that such a being even exists. Anton was fundamentally influenced by the same writers and thinkers that have shaped contemporary society, blasting away the rigor mortis of Christianity and dogmatism. From Enlightenment thinkers like Voltaire who rallied around the motto "Sapere aude!" (urging people to "Have the courage to use one's own reason!"), through the Surrealists and Decadents which LaVey followed in his own art, to the Romantic poets (especially Shelley, Byron and Keats), to the heavy influence of Existentialist philosophers like Nietzsche, Jean-Paul Sartre and Dostoevsky, LaVey was deeply inspired by their courage and creative will. Anton gave credit to the Founders of America, as well, particularly Thomas Paine, Benjamin Franklin and Thomas Jefferson, who were Deists, at best.

When looking for a personification of what many of these rebels and reprobates represented, many of them would point to the strength of one character in one particular poem, published in 1665. John Milton portrayed Satan as the proud, defiant, favored angel who dared to assert himself as God's equal. It can be argued that Milton did too good a job of fashioning his villain, allowing him to dominate the stage in the opening chapters of *Paradise Lost*. Though Milton was a devout Christian and most of his writings reflected the rigors of prayer and holy contemplation, the lines that have come to define the Miltonian anti-hero are majestic Satan's speech after he and his rebellious angels have been cast into the Pit: "The mind is its own place, and in itself can make a Heav'n of Hell, a Hell of Heav'n….Here we may reign secure, and in my choice to reign is worth ambition, though in Hell; Better to reign in Hell, than serve in Heav'n." (*Paradise Lost*, Book I, lines 254-263)

LaVey also gained wisdom from men of unholy mystery and power he admired: Grigori Rasputin, Niccolo Machiavelli, Anton Mesmer, Count Cagliostro, Basil Zaharoff…men who held royalty in thrall to their hypnotic, disreputable machinations. LaVey was strongly inspired by Sir Francis Dashwood's Medmenham Hellfire group, as well as more recent writers such as Mark Twain, H.L. Mencken, Jack London, Oscar Wilde, Ben Hecht, H.P. Lovecraft, Somerset Maugham, and Cornell Woolrich. Many of these acerbic and blasphemous authors were given due credit in LaVey's original dedication pages for both *The Satanic Bible* and *The*

Satanic Rituals, as well as the bibliography for *The Compleat Witch*, which LaVey intended as reading lists to provide the intrepid Satanist with direction for further study.

Of particular interest to this historic gathering here at Brunnenburg Castle would be the influence Anton acknowledged from Sigmund Freud. LaVey was learning a great deal from his study of psychiatry and basic human psychology, gravitating to the writings of Freud and his ideas concerning sexual repression, the id, dream interpretation and the importance of early sexual explorations. Though Freud has been demonized over the years, much of what we understand and practice as basic psychology now was originally formulated by Freud. LaVey's concept of ECI is directly Freudian; our libido, our sexual awakening, our kundalini, sustains and inspires us throughout our lives. As icing on the cake, Anton discovered a 1919 essay by Freud titled, "The Uncanny", which was an early exploration of the psychological roots of aesthetics, fictional narrative and creative drive. LaVey conceptualized his form of ritual as effective and useful psychodrama.

Anton also toyed with concepts from Carl Jung such as eternal recurrence (from Nietzsche), universal archetypes, collective unconscious, synchronicity, his fearless embrace of man's Shadow self, anima/animus interplay, and his openness in attempting to place psychic phenomena, UFOs, alchemy and the tarot in some psychological context. Where Freud was ostensibly anti-religious (despite his secret Kabbalistic readings), it seems Jung saw the uses of more impressionistic experience. LaVey entertained notions of metempsychosis or blood (genetic) memory, engrams (not the Dianetics kind), atavistic responses, and other ideas associated with fringe theories of the mind derived from Jung.

Anton was equally intrigued by the concepts of psychoanalyst Wilhelm Reich and made many references to his insights concerning character analysis, mass psychology, muscular armoring, the function of the orgasm, orgone accumulators, cosmic superimposition and rainmaking with his cloudbusters. Reich is credited as the main architect of the sexual revolution. His thoughts on "orgone energy" seem to view this substance as akin to the chi, ba, qi and universal life force of other cultures, but more directly sexual. Reich claimed he had isolated it and could use it for healing psychological and physical maladies. He became known as much for the outrageous suppression of his work by the U.S. government as for his influence on later therapists and writers. Though long regarded as psychologically unbalanced, his theories dismissed as pseudoscience, Reich has been somewhat redeemed since the examination of his unpublished papers. He had left instructions that his work be sealed for 50 years after his death, which expired in 2007, and some have judged Reich's work to be significantly more valuable than it was regarded during his own lifetime.

LaVey referred to William James' work as well, who certainly betrayed a sense of the Satanic when he wrote: "Passive happiness is slack and insipid, and soon grows mawkish and intolerable. Some austerity and wintry negativity, some roughness, danger, stringency, and effort, some 'no! no!' must be mixed in to produce the sense of an existence with character and texture and power."

As you can see, LaVey's acknowledged influences were extensive and wide-ranging. He wasn't offended when journalist Walt Harrington called him a "junkyard philosopher" in the *Washington Post* magazine section in 1986. Anton was a Renaissance man—musician, painter, photographer, carny, animal trainer, philosopher. But his ideas were shaped as much from his own personal experience and observations—and, significantly, from fiction he found inspiring—as they were by any specific strain of thought. He didn't fit himself into a legacy of Existentialism or position himself in relation to a particular esoteric lineage. On the contrary, he found little worth in many of the magical groups he examined on his way to founding Satanism.

Since our time is short, instead of giving you a litany of Satanic roots you can easily track down from LaVey's own writings, I'd like to concentrate on an overview of what innovations Anton LaVey brought to magical and esoteric studies. Our proud Satanic heritage rightly stretches back to Pythagoras, Epicurus, the Knights Templar and the Yazidi in the Middle East. LaVey wrote in *The Satanic Rituals* that Satanic Ritual is, "...a blend of Gnostic, Cabbalistic, Hermetic and Masonic elements, incorporating nomenclature and vibratory words of power from virtually every mythos." Throughout his lifetime, LaVey became an avid collector of ancient magical manuscripts from throughout Europe and the Middle East, deciphering secrets purposely hidden there by powerful adepts and alchemists.

But Anton drew as much from psychology, psychiatry and common sense as he did from esoteric studies—and that is as it should be. This is where true magic lies, within the human mind. LaVey knew the power of myths. Much esoteric scholarship gets bound up with vaguely scientific secrets, becoming distanced from the passion and imagination that brings us to esotericism in the first place, such studies instead growing sterile and self-referential. Empty memorization rather misses the point; as has been said of Christian rituals, the acolytes might as well be reciting nursery rhymes for all the conviction or enthusiasm they convey. LaVey moved boldly beyond dry recitations, rote gestures and belly-button gazing. He evoked blood, sex, lust, life, and real results from his magical practices. He wasn't content just studying Enochian keys or Sumerian mythology—he was seeking methods for the active application of ancient principles. LaVey looked for grains of truth in the legends, guided by passion, spontaneity, and instinct.

As I quoted LaVey regarding ritual work in my 1990 *Church of Satan* book: "Your ritual chamber is your fantasy world: harnessing the potent wattage of your emotions, you psychically extend yourself to shape the world beyond the surrounding walls. You impose your magical will, using the metaphors or images you feel most aligned with. You aren't limited to Judeo-Christian myths—though we call our religion by the name of the antagonistic Judeo-Christian deity, Satan, because the majority of Western culture is still Christian. Unlike those who depend on dogma, a blind faith, you can choose your fictions to live by. Rather than having archetypes and idols thrust upon you…you have dozens of neglected gods and demons to conjure forth. Rather than depending on mass mindlessness to dictate fashions to you, you choose, even create, your own Master." (p. 96)

Since esotericism is our broad topic at hand, I see seven significant elements Anton LaVey added to his distinctly diabolical brand:

1) Humor—I place this first because Anton said on more than one occasion that a magician without a sense of humor is worthless. He abhorred pretentiousness and made it our second deadly sin, right behind stupidity. That's why I included the comic musician from 1950s America—Mickey Katz—in the title of our little talk. Katz, for LaVey, expressed not only some very funny musical jibes, but he was consistently riffing off of his Jewish heritage, something which might have been considered more of a liability at the time. This attitude informed LaVey's sound counsel to turn what others might perceive as a negative into an advantage. The High Priest himself was surprisingly self-deprecating. Whenever the conversation became too focused on him or became bogged down in Satanic minutia, he would insert an instructive joke. We jested with each other that he used jokes like Jesus supposedly used parables, and that he should compile a book of Satanic parables that he regularly repeated—that it would be much more fun and instructive than the Nazarene's stories, and would probably sell well.

2) Anton introduced The Beast—Everything before LaVey was either rainbows, faeries and healing, or intellectually masturbatory, dogmatic initiatory rubrics of ceremonial magic. With unflinching Satanic hubris, LaVey flung wide the ritual chamber doors, brazenly inviting the chaos and animal musk of immortal demons and infernal destroyers into his domain—without mitigation or protection from a Magic Circle. Greet me as your Brother and Friend—that is the path set forth in *The Satanic Bible* and turns out it works surprisingly well for the human spirit. LaVey grew up steeped in the horror and madness of Arthur Machen, Edgar Allan Poe, H.P. Lovecraft, Clark Ashton Smith, Seabury Quinn, A. Merritt, and other *Weird Tales* writers.

A definition of horror from *Psychology Today* (February 2017) is offered: "Horror is the initially familiar becoming increasingly unfamiliar." Horror writer Andy Peloquin elaborated that "horror is about tapping into the subconscious fears and bringing them to life on the page." He listed fear of the unknown, fear of darkness, fear of higher predators, fear of being alone, fear of being forced to make life and death decisions as primal fears horror writers draw from.

LaVey created a religion that draws from these fears and invites us into the ritual chamber to explore, exploit and delight in them, furthering our own self-enchantment, concretizing our creative visualizations in a powerful way, so that fiction blends into reality, and we walk out of the ritual chamber purged of debilitating doubt and distraction, charged with power, and focused on our specific goals.

In his *Satanic Rituals*, LaVey drew deeply from poetry in "Le Messe Noir" and fiction in his Lovecraft mythos ceremonies, presented alongside and interwoven with remnants of ancient black magical rites. In LaVey's religion, each are just as valid, as his goal is emotional potency. In his *Devil's Notebook*, LaVey wrote, "Bertrand Russell has equated logic with mathematics. I equate the brain and its potential with the thing called 'soul' or 'spirit'." (p. 145) For Anton, music, special effects, and dramatic evocations that happened in the ritual chamber were all intended to unleash the power within us.

Satanism is grounded in true esoteric traditions, with a devilish twist. In the 1940s and '50s, young Anton LaVey eagerly researched, read, networked wherever he caught a vague whiff of something occult or magical, anything he hoped might harbor true secrets. He tracked down all he could, and found it all rather flaccid, lacking in authentic perspective or power. He was searching for the *Necronomicon*, the ancient unholy book (much like Jung's *Red Book*, exploring the Shadow Self, the Beast which is man), the tome that can only be written in blood. Finding none, LaVey invented his own secret society to explore, encourage and ignite those frightening hellfires within us.

3) Connected to this point, but significantly different is the idea that, in acknowledging that we create our own gods, LaVey realized that gods were no longer being created and sustained in churches and synagogues, but in the huge, elaborate temples of the movie palaces that he grew up with. He drew much of Satanism from films—from the German Expressionist films he saw in immediate post-war Germany, and in the film noir that followed them. Anton was inspired by narrative storylines about misunderstood anti-heroes or unreliable madmen emerging from individuals the audience was led to believe were perfectly acceptable and sane. There were also the maddening angles of surrealistic sets that LaVey found riveting. Visuals, music, the interplay of darkness and light—all these informed LaVey as he synthesized Satanism into the force it is today. Films are where our most potent myth-making occurs in popular culture today, not in churches. We no longer have breathtaking pagan mystery festivals dedicated to Dionysus or Demeter to influence our culture. Even the Christian myths are being broadly overshadowed by the myth-cycles of Skywalker and Vader, Harry Potter and Severus Snape, and the grand presence of the reptile god, Gojira (only now gaining acknowledgement as the anti-hero we always knew Godzilla to be).

In his *Satanic Rituals*, LaVey unapologetically included rituals tied to beings he knew to be fictions, created by Lovecraft and others in his circle (many of which LaVey counted among his friends). In doing this, Anton made a defining statement of what religion really is. We have joyous power to create myths that satisfy and empower us, and are not constrained by myths imposed on us. We should not take these somber characters from fables as absolutes, capable of mercilessly judging or rewarding us.

4) Reason—in keeping with the true roots of Esotericism, LaVey demanded that Satanism maintain intellectual rigor from an atheistic posture. The ceremonial magic we inherited from the ancient Egyptians, passed through the Greek mystery traditions, emerging in Renaissance Europe as alchemy and Hermeticism was science-based. We are all grasping for truth, whether in the context of psychology

or science. Esoteric studies benefit from a Satanic posture. Our skepticism, our disdain for murky thinking and self-deceit is tempered with our openness to novel ideas and an insistence on a third-side approach, along with a general playful enthusiasm for creativity and life. We keep magical studies on a productive path—not wandering off in the weeds but rewarding deep scholarship.

5) Application—Anton LaVey loved secrets, codes, ciphers, and musty corners of fringe knowledge, but wanted to see how it worked. He resented the game he saw with most esoteric traditions available to him in the 1940s and 50s that demanded payment for lengthy study along a complicated and ill-defined initiatory path, which (in true P.T. Barnum fashion) seemed to lead (after picking your pockets) to a fancy sign over the exit at the back door saying, "This way to the egress!". LaVey wanted to change that, bringing esotericism, ceremonial magic, and the Black Arts into a circle of heady experimentation and practical application. Again, as with personifying the fictional, bringing dark magical principles into the light seemed productive and important to him. As an example, a young, brash Anton was seriously cautioned against publishing the Enochian Keys. These were considered too dark to be widely revealed to an unprepared public. The thinking generally ran thus: "You don't know what you will be unleashing on an unsuspecting world to put these damned revelations in such easy access of untrained minds, rather like giving nuclear weapons to hot-headed children." So, of course, as the defining Satanist, that made LaVey all the more determined to include them in his immortal Black Book, which he did when *The Satanic Bible* was published in 1969.

From his earliest magical explorations, LaVey had little patience for occultniks who pursued vacuous hermetic puzzles, while never making the leap to the possible real-world applications. He felt it became a bit of a circle jerk; that magic doesn't go anywhere and remains an empty vessel, unless robustly exercised. The High Priest of Hell certainly saw a use for antiquated references when used as arcane soil to spur the dark imagination (à la Lovecraft and the *Necronomicon*)—but otherwise, he found so much of what scholars studied as presumably "significant" was simply more crypto-Christian meandering and gobbledygook if taken seriously as an end it itself. Anton LaVey moved us past that.

Rather than spending years in isolated contemplation and dedicated memorization (or manufacturing some vague protestations of witchcraft skills inherited from your great-grandmother), LaVey felt the principles of magic could be applied fruitfully and immediately. Satanists take an experimental approach, always testing and creating in our "intellectual decompression chambers", our ritual chambers. These are our laboratories, developing methods of both Lesser and Greater Magic that are refined specifically for our own goals and godhood. These might be our art studios, writing spaces, outside groves or actual science labs—where our creativity and concentration are most potent. Science may not be able to fully quantify, reproduce and name these forces yet (much like Victorian parlor exhibitions with electricity), but that won't prevent us from applying our methods to accomplish our intentions.

6) Anton LaVey defused guilt. He had help on this one, obviously, but there is no other religion devised that vigorously and aggressively discards this cancer that has been imposed on us for millennia. Guilt is not the exclusive purview of the dominant Abrahamic religions; shame, hatred of life, and denial of attachment to the flesh, seem to be common and inescapable themes. This is, needless to say, crushingly inhibiting and stifling. In this narrative, we are born in sin and must work a lifetime to achieve some level of forgiveness or redemption. Abrahamic myths also seep into our culture in a wider sense, teaching that, as humans, we dominate all other creatures on this planet, killing and exploiting in the name of Manifest Destiny, polluting the planet to the brink of our own extinction. Even within esoteric paths these insidious concepts communicate guilt with their lengthy, purposely intimidating and convoluted systems of study, designed to make any sincere initiate feel that he or she is not worthy. LaVey threw a big Johnson Smith stink bomb into the whole enterprise. Satanism is deliciously liberating. Which leads us to the final, and perhaps most important element that LaVey brought to his new religion.

7) SEX! Satanism is the only religion that puts sex front and center, as well it should be. This rather brings us back full circle to our themes of psychiatry and healthy reinvention. Satanic sex is raw, naked lust, not shrouded in the traditional magical symbolism of inserting the dagger into the chalice, or metaphors about awakening the kundalini. LaVey wrote frankly about sex in his *Satanic Bible*, reveled in little boy glee, naughtiness and abandon, and saw the interplay between masculine and feminine elements as completely natural and—wow!—fun! We proudly worship at a breathing nude altar, and express ourselves as lustful Satanic witches and warlocks, celebrating our honest libidinous natures. Talk about productive energy exchange! The history of Satanism is one of decadence and hedonism, from the Hellfire Clubs to present day. LaVey frequently lectured at the Sexual Freedom League in his early days, and though I seldom speculate on what Anton would think of modern societal or technological directions, I think it's safe to say the High Priest of Satan would caper with joy at the sexual and gender identity options increasingly open to us today.

Because the general populace has moved along parallel lines, influenced by the Enlightenment and recognizing organized religions for the harmful scams they often are, all this adds to a feeling of familiarity with the diabolical in our contemporary secular humanist society. Satanism is accessible, funny, welcoming, strengthening, and obvious. In the years since the Church of Satan's founding, we have seen LaVey's stated agendas and goals progressing in the realms of atheism, productive nondogmatic ritualizing, Artificial Human Companions, virtual reality development, total environments, sexual freedom, along with LGBTQ and gender identity rights. Larger society is definitely catching on to the uninhibited joy of dancing to the Devil's tunes. But LaVey didn't want to create a popular philosophy or a political movement. We will always work in the shadows, and our iconography will always be off-putting to most people. In this way, Satanism will remain self-selecting and self-regulating. That's as our original High Priest intended, and the way Satanism works best.

There is so much to study within the larger umbrella of Satanism in the realms of visual arts, literature, philosophy, psychology and psychiatry, Freud and DeSade, ECI, the misuses of religion, music, comparative religion, ethics and applications of power in the real world, stage magic, theatre arts, rhetoric and classical languages, mass psychology and fascism, environmentalism, nutrition and health, vegan cooking and ethics, Western Esotericism and symbology, consciousness, emerging technology and scientific theory, and psychic exploration are just some paths that come immediately to mind.

An entire undergraduate liberal arts education awaits within Satanism. That's why it has survived so well after our founder's passing in 1997. Anton LaVey pointed us to his foundations so that the Church of Satan would never stultify as a mere personality cult. He ensured that we would be well armed to develop his concepts, moving ever forward to shape societal and scientific horizons. Our current High Priest, Peter Gilmore, and High Priestess, Peggy Nadramia, fully embrace and personify the myriad facets of the Satanic, savoring their opportunities to combat complacency and ignorance, whether the occasion requires a feather touch or a smack across the face with a wet mackerel.

Outside of the Church, there are now bold researchers and scholars contextualizing Satanism within the wider counterculture movement in which it began, as well as within the Western esoteric heritage we can perceive as a driving force behind much of the philosophical and even scientific vigor of the early 21st century.

I hope this has been a useful, if cursory, glimpse at the esoteric and, more importantly, the human roots of Satanism. Dr. LaVey certainly studied esotericism and any magical strains he could find. But his brilliance was in drawing from his musical and artistic/photographic knowledge, from *Weird Tales* and horror, from photographer William Mortensen, Freud and Jung, as well as adding a healthy dollop of humor and earthy lustiness. Satanism moved religion out of the darkness of belief and revelation. LaVey applied human psychology and ritual needs, placing the strength and majesty of the fallen Dark Prince firmly at the center of human experience, where he rightly belongs. Integrating these magical elements consciously, with awareness, Anton LaVey created a bridge from empty, rote Gnostic mutterings into the stimulating light of true human poetry, music, grandeur, and genius. Satan guides us in our most painful decisions. We need the Devil, our own devils, our demons, to challenge, inspire and demand more than we think we can achieve.

As poet Arthur O'Shaughnessy reminds us, "We are the music makers, and we are the dreamers of dreams." We create the magic of our own destinies, as individuals and as brothers and sisters of our fellow untamed beasts on this magnificent planet. This intricate, intimate dance of interconnected threads pulses and weaves around all of us right now. The esoteric will never be confined to musty tomes. It is a vibrant and phantasmic presence within and without, whispering intoxicating temptations and spurring us ever forward into the delights of the darkness just beyond our grasp.

Literchoor, Kulchur, and a damned fine friendship – On the symbiosis of Ezra Pound & James Laughlin

Carl Abrahamsson

Looking at the relationship between Ezra Pound and his principal publisher James Laughlin not only gives us an interesting insight about their specific relationship, but also one about the cultural environment they were both in, and became key players in. There is something of the magical in this, both thematically and dynamically. We have a relationship that is at first imbued with the dynamic of master and apprentice, but that later changes into a more concrete working relationship and constructions of mutual creative universes and careers. The master also roams freely through religious, philosophical, mythic and magical spheres, and disseminates enlightening symbols or fragments through his vibrant poetic mind, both in his work proper but also in correspondence with the disciple, who realizes already from the very beginning what a privileged situation he is in.

This fundament was laid out already in 1933, when 18 year old Laughlin wrote to 48 year old Pound, then situated in Rapallo in Italy. Pound welcomed students and friends to come join him in what was called the "Ezuversity" – Ezra's University. If you simply stayed around, you got to hang out with one of the world's most famous modernist poets, and you could try to integrate as much or as little learning or inspiration as you saw fit. No other curriculum necessary – or even existing.

Pound at this time gave teaching as such a lot of thought, and had plans to eventually set up an Academy based on quality minds and quality source material; yet always within a non-restrictive framework. In his text "The Teacher's Mission," Pound stated didactically what the important things were: "All teaching of literature should be performed by the presentation and juxtaposition of specimens of writing and NOT by discussion of some other discusser's opinion about the general standing of a poet or author."[1]

In the same text, Pound elaborates on what seemed to be of equal importance to him at the time: teaching culture as a kind of sacred mission: "Artists are the antennae of the race. If this statement is incomprehensible and if its corollaries need any explanation, let me put it that a nation's writers are the voltometers and steam-gauges of that nations's intellectual life. They are the registering instruments, and if they falsify their reports there is no measure to the harm that they do."[2]

Recommended to go see Pound by a friend and teacher at Harvard, Dudley Fitts,

---

1 Ezra Pound, *Literary Essays of Ezra Pound*, New Directions, New York, 1968, p 60
2 Ibid, p 58

Laughlin was one of the hungrier students at the Ezuversity. After having arrived, Laughlin got a dose of Pound's acerbic yet probably well meaning advice, along the lines of: "Your poetry is no good, why don't you start a publishing company instead? I'll help you find authors that matter." Had Laughlin been a pathological poet, he would of course have stormed out in anger. But he was more insightful than that and actually heeded his master's advice. The publishing company New Directions began humbly but was supported by Laughlin's father and an aunt. Upon graduating from Harvard in 1939, Laughlin's father (a steel industrialist heir) endowed him with $100.000. Laughlin was smart, as he didn't invest all the money in the publishing but in his other passion: skiing. He opened up a skiing resort in Utah, which soon turned a profit. These profits were invested in championing modernist icons like Pound, and the result is still with us through New Directions; still a heavy duty player when it comes to fine literature and poetry. And each title still has the same line on the impressum page: "New Directions Books are published for James Laughlin." One could argue that during the first decade of their friendship, the books were to an equal degree "published for Ezra Pound."

Laughlin knew the value of the Pound (pardon the pun!). But more so in the poetic sense than the commercial one. His mind was set already from the get-go of New Directions to always keep Pound in print, as a kind of religious devotion to a poet so brilliant and important that Laughlin owed it to the world. That makes you think: what if…? What if this young entrepreneur hadn't had this unconventionally devotional attitude? Where would Pound's legacy be today?

> These days ND is abubble with a frenetic roil of switched wires and tangled gargles as we struggle to get out a lot of new books. Ruin hangs like a large garbage pail over the Halloween doorway because costs are way up and sales are way down. But who knows, who ever knows, who does? Important and gratifying: keeping all the books of Pound and William Carlos Williams in print, which I could do because I inherited money. A normal commercial publisher would have had to remainder many books ND keeps in print.[3]

Pound's own publishing history that far had been a mixed and often paradoxical bag, which very much reflected the overall modernist environment. Radical authors and poets like Pound, Joyce and Eliot were mostly published in small literary magazines, and quite often the authors themselves were part of the editorial boards of these and other magazines. There existed a rich cultural climate if we look at the "signal" and personal engagement. But then, as now, peer-produced media didn't really have a strong and wide outreach. The esoteric dynamic of preaching to the already converted needed to be overcome, and Pound was good at this, as his books also started coming out on bigger publishing companies.

This, however, was not an easy situation for Pound and the others. They shared a sentiment that the really powerful publishers were "commercial" and hence

---

3 James Laughlin, *The Way It Wasn't*, New Directions, New York, 2006, p 219

infected somehow by a kind of base "unseriousness" and lack of comprehension of what these modernists were trying to achieve. More often than not, this can be ascribed more to narcissistic neurosis than anything else. In fact, there were many publishing companies who were interested in what these new pioneers were doing, but the poor sales discouraged them from carrying on at the same pace as these wild, formal experimentalists. So that mix between small literary journal freedom, and unwillingly willingly trying to secure better publishing deals, was a normal situation at this time. One could complain in vitriolic rants to fellow poets about the corruption and inefficiency of big publishing companies but at the same time gladly accept invitations from these same environments.

How perfect then for Pound that here comes a really smart and potentially wealthy young one. A poet at heart who is soon washed clean of those aspirations by an elder with many ulterior motives. But Laughlin didn't mind. Not at all. He understood the dynamics well right from the start. Not only would this mean an incorporation of an already existing and inspiring friendship but also access to a very strong network of the very best poets and writers of the era. Let's not forget that Pound had at this time already for decades defined and refined both others' works and authorships proper. TS Eliot dedicated *The Waste Land* to Pound, who had edited the masterpiece into full glory. Eliot wrote "For Ezra Pound, Il miglior fabbro," which means "the better craftsman."

For Laughlin, hosting Pound's authorship also meant hosting Pound's mind, and friends. Already in 1934, Pound put Laughlin in touch with William Carlos Williams and Louis Zukofsky, who both became solid literary worker horses in his stable. Pound also made sure Laughlin became the literary editor of Gorham Munson's "Social Credit" magazine *New Democracy*. The literary page was called "New Directions," and that set a snowball in motion that is still rolling today.

While the two were working on editions of Pound's already overwhelming oeuvre – focusing mainly on the many variants and developments of the *Cantos* – the correspondence soon integrated other topics, dealing with the most important things in life. That is, "Literchoor" and "Kulchur." But it became clear as time passed by, and Laughlin in many ways individuated himself out of the pure acolyte stage, that he was well aware of a situation of gratitude vis-à-vis Pound – they both were – but that Laughlin was also his own. As Pound's radical economic reform ideas merged with literally classical forms of anti-semitism, Laughlin objected and said straight out he'd publish none of that.

In a way, there was a streak of a Christic archetype in Pound. His work in itself was not enough, it seems. It needed to be contextualized in perhaps unnecessarily complex ideas and marketed to the world, but with himself as a clearly visible instigator. The economic reform ideas are one such example, and one that was actually already actively taken care of by other instigators at the time. When these economic ideas were padded in anti-semitic clothing, it's another Christic Gestalt taking form – that of Golgotha, and of Pound as not only a poet-thinker but also a martyr. After the war, back in the US and interned at St Elizabeths hospital in Washington DC, Pound's work on an utopian Academy that would define a certain Poundean learning, and also way of learning, could be seen as an example of the same phenomenon: Pound's mind was so advanced and lofty that he probably couldn't see that these structural issues or constructions actually hampered his strictly poetic flow – not to mention his career. In the context of his books like *ABC of Reading* and *Guide to Kulchur* there is a strong didactic, pedagogic streak, but even here, when the teacher disseminates his wisdoms to us, there is also lofty poetry at work and in motion, and aphorisms that still stick:

> It doesn't matter which leg of your table you make first, so long as the table has four legs and will stand up solidly when you have finished it.[4]

> Literature is news that STAYS news.[5]

> Without gods, no culture. Without gods, something is lacking. Some Stoics must have known this, and considered logic a mere shell outside the egg. (*Kulchur*, p 126)[6]

> A civilized man is one who will give a serious answer to a serious question. Civilization itself is a certain sane balance of values. (*Kulchur*, p137)[7]

Basically, when Pound's ideas leave the lofty arena of poetry, developed during a lifetime of advanced learning and creative association, and drift into pseudo-political demagogia and a perhaps compensatory need for majestic structures, they lose their mythic and inspirational value. Laughlin saw this very clearly, and could therefore be adamant about saying no to certain works. Laughlin saw the value and brilliance of the *Cantos* – as did many, many others already early on – in that it included an entire universe, perhaps even more, of thoughts, ideas and emotions; of past, present and future; of experimental theory and pragmatic poetic practice. To stretch beyond the experimental perfection of Pound's poetry (and, by all means, also prose) was simply not necessary, according to Laughlin.

Even if he had wanted to, Pound would have had a hard time de-contextualizing his own approaches. It was simply one cluster of attitudes and ideas in which everything was connected and relevant, and it seemed impossible for the Maestro to untangle personal poetic perspectives from a general Nietzschean legacy that so often seeped through. In 1918 Pound stated, in a piece about Henry James:

> The whole of great art is a struggle for communication. All things that oppose this are evil, whether they be silly scoffing or obstructive tariffs. And this communication is not a leveling, it is not an elimination of differences.

---

4 Ezra Pound, *ABC of Reading*, Faber and Faber, London, 1991, p 62
5 Ibid, p 29
6 Ezra Pound, *Guide to Kulchur*, Peter Owen, London, 1952, p 126
7 Ibid, p 137

> It is a recognition of differences, of the right of differences to exist, of interest in findings things different. Kultur is an abomination; philology is an abomination, all repressive uniforming education is an evil.[8]

Even a literary overview of an admired author apparently couldn't be spared from general demagogia! If we are kind and diplomatic today, we could call this attitude "passionate." But it is also an example of Pound's recurring tendency to drift from the poetic or descriptive center to his own web of strained associations and almost justifying ideas, although, essentially, no justifications are necessary. In literary criticism this was fine, as a kind of highbrow seasoning in a heady soup that a fair chunk of western intellectuals ate with a great appetite and also found nutritious. But when one group or culture was targeted in similarly eloquent flows that could never be read as anything *but* political, having severed all ties to any literary, poetic or even general cultural contexts, the situation naturally became more problematic. As Laughlin was preparing for new editions of the ever swelling *Cantos* in 1940, he and Pound wrote back and forth about clauses in their contract that would release New Directions from any litigations stemming from anti-semitism, or perhaps to even have an introduction in the new edition, explaining and perhaps even justifying some of Pound's ideas. Laughlin:

> I think that I ought to write a preface, or something, to these new CANTOS, explaining what is what: I mean, linking them up with what has gone before and giving a summary of the earlier ones. You see the attitude over here is that the CANTOS are incomprehensible.[9]

To this Pound was strongly opposed but at the same time more than willing to suggest various improvements to appease Laughlin's publishing conundrum. Thereby in some ways admitting, if not guilt, then at least awareness of the controversial sticks of dynamite they were tossing back and forth; Laughlin respectfully striving for avoidance of headaches and disaster; Pound striving for an almost gleeful pushing of the boundaries. Pound:

> I don't mind affirming in contract, so long as I am not expected to alter text. You can put it this way. The author affirms that in no passage should the text be interpreted to mean that he condemns any innocent man or woman for another's guilt, and that no degree of relationship, familial of racial shall be taken to imply such condemnation. – – – But no group national or ethical can expect immunity not accorded to other groups.[10]

And so on and so forth, back and forth, and in minute detail. In 1941, Laughlin

8 Ezra Pound, *Literary Essays of Ezra Pound*, New Directions, New York, 1968, p 298
9 David Gordon (ed), *Ezra Pound and James Laughlin: Selected Letters*, Norton, New York, 1994, p 113
10 Ibid, p 114

hears of Pound's radio broadcasts from Italy. Laughlin:

> You are pretty much disliked for your orations. Your name in general might be said to aspire but not attain to the dignity of mud. I would rather fill this unfortunate interim with fairly uncontroversial things like cantyers/Cantos selection and the Cavalcanti…[11]

Pound wrote back:

> No use your saying I am disliked. I want to know HOW, and by whom. Details welcome. What you need is a little trip to Europe as refresher.[12]

As the US entered into the second world war in 1942, that little refresher trip literally wasn't on the map for Laughlin. The two remained in touch sporadically during the war to keep business going, but Pound's destiny now seemed as sealed as Italy's, as well as that of the axis powers in general, and this in a very Wagnerian sense: Götterdämmerung is real, so let's stoke the funeral pyre! Pound's insistence, eloquence and stamina, and his active integration of not so symbolic anti-Roosevelt orations, eventually led to his arrest, and to being placed at first in a cage and then later in a hospital tent in Pisa. A Jewish chaplain provided him with writing materials so he could write his classic *Pisan Cantos*; a strange twist of destiny for Pound, I'm sure.

Laughlin wrote to Pound in September 1945:

> I'm afraid that things are going to be kind of tough for you here, but rest assured that though you have many spiteful enemies, you also have a few friends left who will do their best to help you. No one takes your side, of course, in the political sense, but many feel that the bonds of friendship and the values of literature can transcend a great deal.[13]

In many ways, their correspondence both during the war and then afterwards, as Pound was interned in the US, is endearing and genuine but also in many ways "pussyfooting." There is no straight out clarity, and especially not when it comes to problematic issues that could inflict damage on both men's careers. I think this stems back to the very first communications in the early 1930s, when, on the surface, there was mutual admiration for energy and zest but underneath the surface a mutual reckoning and evaluation going on. The poet saw a young publisher who could keep his old and new works in print and develop a career on American soil while he himself enjoyed Italy and was, at least before the war, out of reach of tangible hostilities. Laughlin saw a mentor and a source of inspiration,

---

11 Ibid, p 134
12 Ibid, p 135
13 Gregory Barnhisel, *James Laughlin, New Directions and the Remaking of Ezra Pound*, University of Massachusetts Press, Amherst, 2005, p 15

but also an open door to a pretty vast network of authors and poets that he could exploit under the umbrella of "mutual benefits." And since the formula worked so well from basically day one, no-one wanted to rock this boat.

As Pound grew more and more infirm during the 1960s, Laughlin stepped forward and took on more of the role of literary agent. He helped set up deals of recordings, editions with other publishers, translations etc. Their correspondence was never really personal or emotional but rather continuous eruptions of wit and puns, of agreements and disagreements. When Pound was back in Europe, and living right here where we are assembled today, this position of Laughlin's became even clearer. He was at a vital 50 in 1965 whereas Pound was at a dwindling 80. The power dynamic had changed quite diametrically but there was still plenty of loyalty both ways.

In a letter from May 22 1965, Pound wrote Laughlin: "I hope you will find some way to print something that will remedy past errors. If you do that I will sign it 200 times."[14]

At this time, Pound was depressed and often questioned his own value as a poet. Laughlin did his very best to inform Pound that the world looked at him differently. There was a strong upsurge of editions and translations in the final decade of Pound's life. With a few exceptions like certain people wanting to publish Pound's clearly pro-fascist radio broadcasts, he could actually enjoy his autumn years knowing Laughlin was still out there and pushing his poetic genius onwards; if not to the masses then at least to new generations of intelligentsia. This was certainly, again, to both men's advantage, and with age the relationship graduated from epiphytic to actually symbiotic. There is in many ways, symbolically at least, a big difference between "living off one another" and "feeding each other."

In the times of hardship, it was Laughlin who brought forces together to make things easier for Pound. Whether to reach out to old friends like Ernest Hemingway for money for Pound's attorneys, or to make sure he had reading and writing materials at St Elizabeths, or any other important things, Laughlin was the great facilitator that went well beyond the expected. This also included continually feeding the American intellectual environment with plenty of Pound. This also led to many co-champions appearing, who saw beyond (or simply neglected) the politics and preferred the poetry. One of these champions was Allen Ginsberg, who in many ways became a poet laureate of sorts of the American underground, just like Pound had been in the 1910s and 20s. In a conversation in the Pound studies journal *Paideuma* in 1974, Ginsberg sums up the attitude of, I think, many younger American intellectuals at the time, many of whom were Jewish:

> Pound told me that he felt that the *Cantos* were 'stupidity and ignorance
> all the way through,' and were a failure and a 'mess', and that his 'greatest
> stupidity was stupid suburban anti-Semitic prejudice,' he thought – as of
> 1967, when I talked to him. So I told him I thought that since the *Cantos*

---

14 David Gordon (ed), *Ezra Pound and James Laughlin: Selected Letters*, Norton, New York, 1994, p 283

were for the first time a single person registering over the course of a lifetime all of his major obsessions and thoughts and the entire rainbow are his images and clingings and attachments and discoveries and perceptions, that they were an accurate representation of his mind and so couldn't be thought of in terms of success or failure, but only in terms of the actuality of their representation, and that since for the first time a human being had taken the whole spiritual world of thought through fifty years and followed the thoughts out to the end – so that he built a model of his consciousness over a fifty-year time span – that they were a great human achievement.[15]

Whether Pound appreciated Ginsberg's comments I don't know. But I think it's a valid perspective. Although Pound was absolutely correct when he claimed that artists are the antennae of the race, these antennae need to stick to a mythic language – whether written, visual, musical, whatever – or else they will be painted into a corner that will be very hard to get out of. This period of history is filled with examples of genuine artists, genuine antennae, who were far too easily flattered and cajoled into being poster boys or girls for devious people and movements going on around the fairly well insulated antennae. Pound's good fortune was his network of family and very loyal friends, and it's to them we owe the gratitude for the preservation and re-packaging of Pound as our modernist genius and master, who opened the floodgates to the subconscious – his own and that of our culture – in a much more powerful way than esthetically accessible, psychedelic surrealists of the same era. Pound drew from the source of the classics of many regions and eras, filtered it all as a scholar and expressed it as a truly unique artist; thereby bridging not only spaces and times but also his inner sanctity and the outer chaos of 20th century Europe. In that sense, a shamanic archetype that freely roams and shares his findings, although unsure of who actually understands them. In that sense also a don Quixotic paraphrase, in which James Laughlin played the part of Sancho Panza – ever willing to make sense of a confusing world to the pure and good-hearted romantic knight; and vice versa.

---

15 Allen Ginsberg, "Allen Verbatim," in *Paideuma*, vol 3, no 2, Maine, 1974, p 268

Contributors

Carlos Abler is an artist, researcher, and digital media expert. His career includes dance and physical theater, puppetry, mask work, spoken word, and digital media. He has performed and taught internationally. As a lifelong researcher into the history of religions, cultural theory, and how humans work and make meaning in general, his craft and workshops manifests as an alchemy of global anthropological and cross-disciplinary approaches. He draws from multiple performative traditions such as modern mime, Butoh, and Noh theater; from physically based psycho-therapeutic interventions, such as yogic techniques, Reichian influenced approaches, hypno-mimetic trance-logics; and a highly synthetic and paralogical approach to a hermeneutics of the cosmos that continuously questions the boundaries of where the human individual begins and the universe ends. As a digital strategy and media practitioner Carlos specializes in content-driven applications and experiences that deliver both societal and business impact, and works with businesses, non-profits, and NGOs in support of digital transformation and to make the most of the Internet. His favorite digital work has a cultural and human empowerment emphasis, clients for which include The Smithsonian, and History Channel. Carlos enjoys helping radical culture creators become more business-savvy so as to help them have a stronger hand in shaping the world, as well as in helping giant corporations become more socially sustainable so as to help them not destroy it.

Carl Abrahamsson is the editor and publisher of *The Fenris Wolf*, and the founder of the Institute of Comparative Magico-anthropology. Among his books are *Anton LaVey and the Church of Satan* (2022), *Genesis Breyer P-Orridge: Sacred Intent – Conversations with Carl Abrahamsson 1986-2019* (2020), *Occulture – The unseen forces that drive culture forward* (2018), *Reasonances* (2014), and the novels *The Devil's Footprint* (2020) and *Mother, Have A Safe Trip* (2013). More information can be found at: www.patreon.com/vanessa23carl and www.carlabrahamsson.com

Tom Banger: In 1986, punk promoter Tom Headbanger confounded the Denver scene by founding the Temple ov Psychick Youth North America. Over the next four odd years, he wrote numerous texts on contemporary magick and shamanism under the name Coyote *2 and helped facilitate the coming together of an unprecedented collaborative network of artists, magicians, shamans, and charlatans. During this time, TOPYUS published more than a thousand pages of original occult research, including Television Magick and the first two editions of EsoTerrorist by Genesis P-Orridge. Banger stopped coordinating TOPYUS in 1990 in order to focus on his interest in engineering and technology. He is now a full-time cybersecurity expert and father, and has decided it is time to come out of the shadows and share some stories and perspective.

BLANCHE BARTON: Blanche Barton's first words were "Hermes Trismegistus," which certainly perplexed her parents. She was born in San Diego, California, where she loved to explore old missions and commune with Leviathan at the beach, drawn inexorably to all things arcane and sinister. She received her B.A. from Johnston (a hippie college on the campus of the University of Redlands) emphasizing writing and literature. In 1984, she relocated to San Francisco to work directly with Anton LaVey, remaining with him as demonic cohort and lover until his death. Barton has been a leader and representative of the Church of Satan for most of her life, serving as High Priestess for 12 years and now as the Magistra Templi Rex. She has written the biography of Anton LaVey, and *We Are Satanists: The History and Future of the Church of Satan*.

KATY BOHINC grew up in the outskirts of Cleveland and graduated from Georgetown with degrees in Pure Mathematics and Comparative Literature, leaving her studies for a time to work in Beijing with the Chinese Urgent Action Working Group, a human rights organization. Now living in New York City, she works as a data scientist and marketer. Since 2013 she has collaborated with Lee Ann Brown in directing Tender Buttons Press, a distinguished publisher of experimental women's poetry for which she edited *Tender Omnibus: The First Twenty-Five Years of Tender Buttons Press* (2015) and *Please Add To This List: A Guide To Teaching Bernadette Mayer's Sonnets and Experiments* (2014). Bohinc is the author of *Dear Alain* (Tender Buttons, 2014), letters to the French philosopher Alain Badiou about poetry, philosophy, and love, and a book of poems about the divine feminine, *Trinity Star Trinity* (Scarlet Imprint, 2017). *Publisher's Weekly* describes her most recent title, *Scorpio* (Miami University Press, 2018) as "an astute, witty, feminist collection."

UGO DOSSI: "Art is a tool of telepathy and drawings can be magical objects. Just the fact that a few lines on any surface have the power to bring memories, emotions and inner attitudes to life in the viewer, is magic" (2002). The art of Ugo Dossi revolves around the creativity of the unconscious; the sensual and the supersensual. It plays with archetypal and collective images, with automatic drawings, with topological models, and with paranormal phenomena. Typical of his work is his handling of forms that represent the boundless; which lead into the perception of the infinite and incomprehensible behind everything. His installations have been shown twice at Documenta (Documenta 6 and Documenta 8), at the Venice Biennial (1986 and 2011), Paris Biennal (1975), and Buenos Aires Biennal (2000), as well as in numerous solo exhibitions in international museums and art institutes. www.ugodossi.com

PER MAGNUS JOHANSSON is a licensed psychologist, psychoanalyst, PhD and

Associate professor in the History of Ideas at the University of Gothenburg (GU). He teaches psychoanalytic theory, psychoanalytic psychotherapy and Foucauldian discourse analysis, and many other topics. He is also in private practice in Gothenburg. His research mainly concerns the history of psychoanalysis, psychotherapy and psychiatry.

HAUKUR INGI JÓNASSON is an assistant professor in leadership, management and organization behavior in the School of Technology at Reykjavik University. He is the director of the Masters in Project Management (MPM) of the university. He holds a Cand. Theol. degree from the University of Iceland, and a PhD degree in Psychiatry and Religion from Union Theological Seminary in New York and has clinical certifications in pastoral counseling from The HealthCare Chaplaincy Inc. and in psychoanalysis from the Harlem Family Institute in New York. Mr. Jonasson has also pursued education at the Indiana University School of Business, the Heriot-Watt, Edinburgh Business School and Stanford. He is the co-founder of the Nordica Consulting Group and a research affiliate at the Cooper Union for the Advancement of the Sciences and the Arts. Haukur is the author of twelve books, including five that have been published by Routledge/Taylor and Francis in the UK/USA.

KADMUS is a practicing ceremonial magician. He has written extensively for the website "Gods and Radicals" and recently published the book *True to the Earth: Pagan Political Theology* through Gods and Radicals Press, presented his paper "True to the Earth and a Pagan Conception of the Self" at the conference *Re-writing the Future: 100 Years of Esoteric Modernism and Psychoanalysis*, and taught two classes at the 2020 Salem Summer Symposium on "Pagan Approaches to Goetia" and "Learning from Legendary Practitioners: Circe".

KOSHKA is a Colorado native. She was active in the Denver punk scene in the mid to late eighties and began collaboration with Thee Temple ov Psychick Youth in 1988. She helped with answering mail, printing and distributing books and essays as well as coordinating campouts. In 1990 she moved to Texas and helped run the T.O.P.Y. access point there until 1992. She completed her degree in Anthropology after an archaeology field school in Belize focussing on Mayan studies. She went on to do several tours with the band Crash Worship in the U.S. and Europe. Her extensive collection of personal journals and photographs, along with the bulk of surviving T.O.P.Y. documents are among her archives. She currently resides in Denver, Colorado and travels to Belize whenever possible.

SIMON MAGUS BSc (Hons) MB BS MA PhD is a psychiatrist with a special interest in Early Intervention Psychosis. He studied medicine in London at Charing Cross and Westminster Medical School, now part of the Imperial College of Science, Technology and Medicine. After qualifying, he taught Anatomy as the Royal

College Prosector to the Royal College of Physicians and Surgeons of Glasgow, and as an associate lecturer in Anatomy and Embryology at the University of Glasgow. After initially following a surgical path, he changed to psychiatry in 1996. Simon's interest in esotericism predates his medical studies by a number of years. He completed an MA in Western Esotericism at EXESESO (The Exeter Centre for the Study of Esotericism), The University of Exeter in 2008/9. His thesis was entitled *Austin Osman Spare and the Conquest of the Imaginal: Paranoia, Metanoia and Phronesis of the Magical Mind*. He is interested in the interplay of descriptive psychopathology and the phenomenology of magical praxis, and spirituality and psychosis. During his MA studies he developed broad perspectives in esotericism on subjects including alchemy and its transmission to the Latin West, Alexandrian Hermetism and Renaissance Kabbalah. His specialist field of enquiry currently centres on Victorian and Edwardian literary expressions of occultism, having completed a PhD at Exeter with the thesis *Rider Haggard and the Imperial Occult: Hermetic Discourse and Romantic Contiguity*. He is a member of the European Society for the Study of Western Esotericism.

KATRINA MAKKOUK is a graduate of Clemson University where she earned her Master's degree in English. She moved from South Carolina to the West Coast in 2010 where she still pursues her love of literature through poetry and writing. Her primary research interests are modernism and how occult philosophy and methodology are applied in literature. She published her study on the occultist elements seen within the works of Ezra Pound—most notably focusing on The *Pisan Cantos*.

STEPHANIE MORAN is an artist and researcher. She is an AHRC-funded PhD candidate in Transtechnology Research at the University of Plymouth, and has an MFA in Fine Art. Recent talks include Coding the Digital Occult at Occulture, Berlin (publication forthcoming, in the Pomegranate International Journal of Pagan Studies) and Symbiont Encounters, for the Shaping of a Message symposium at Goldsmiths, London. Her research interests include interwar Dionysian nature cults; divination and nonlinear phase space in hypertext fictions; hyperstition; and occult numerological ontologies. She is currently working on producing a UK-US Digital Occult survey exhibition.

KASPER OPSTRUP is a writer and researcher based in Copenhagen. He is the Danish translator of, among others, Alexander Trocchi and William Burroughs and is currently finishing a monograph with the tentative title *An Imaginary Kingdon in the Wastelands of the Real: On Art, Esotericism and the Politics of Hope*. His most recent book is *The Way Out: Invisible Insurrections and Radical Imaginaries in the UK Underground from 1961 to 1991* (Minor Compositions, 2017).

ELISABETH PUNZI is a licensed psychologist, PhD and a lecturer at the Department of Psychology at Gothenburg University (GU). She leads a project concerning heritage and health at the Centre for Critical Heritage Studies, GU and teaches psychoanalytic theory, psychology of religion and qualitative research methods, and many other topics. Her research concerns clinical practice, critical psychology/psychiatry, the importance of expressive arts for health and recovery as well as Jewish identity, heritage and congregational life.

SIEGFRIED DE RACHEWILTZ is an author and ethnologist, and also the grandson of American poet Ezra Pound. He has been responsible for the inventarisation of historical farms and material culture, Landesdenkmalamt, Autonome Provinz Bozen-Südtirol, 1980-1990. He has also been the director of the Schloss Tirol Museum of History, Autonome Provinz Bozen-Südtirol, 1991-2013, and is the founder and director of the Brunnenburg Agricultural Museum and International Study Center.

CHARLOTTE RODGERS is an animist and magickian who lives in Somerset, England. Author of various books including *P is for Prostitution* and *The Sky is a Gateway Not a Ceiling*, Charlotte has also contributed to many magazines and anthologies. She is also an artist who creates sculptures from remnants of death and discarded objects. Her art has been exhibited widely and she has spoken about various aspects her work at Edinburgh and Leicester University, numerous conferences, and the Museum of Morbid Anatomy in New York. www.perdurabu.com/

ANNA SEBASTIAN is an artist exploring the intersection of occultism, art and psychoanalysis. She is interested in the utilisation of symbols by painters and how, in image making, networks forgotten, unseen, or unspoken might be revealed. Her artistic research examines how images made can become a key to the collective unconscious and the sacred, and their capacity to reveal the destructive and banal relationships modern cultures have with objects and images. Sebastian has a BA in Fine Art from Goldsmiths, University of London, and exhibits in London and internationally. Recent exhibitions include the Ghetto Biennale, Port au prince, and DOX Gallery, Prague. She is currently involved in a project at the Philadelphia Association, London, investigating the nine mystical gates through a series of themed lectures.

VANESSA SINCLAIR, Psy.D. is a psychoanalyst based in Sweden, who sees clients internationally. Her books include *Switching Mirrors* (Trapart Books, 2016), *The Fenris Wolf 9* (Trapart Books, 2017) co-edited with Carl Abrahamsson, *On Psychoanalysis and Violence: Contemporary Lacanian Perspectives* (Routledge, 2018) co-edited with Manya Steinkoler, and *Scansion in Psychoanalysis and Art: the Cut in Creation* (Routledge, 2020). Dr. Sinclair is also a founding member of Das Unbehagen: A Free Association for Psychoanalysis. She hosts conferences and events internationally, and is the host of the Rendering Unconscious Podcast. For more information, please visit: www.drvanessasinclair.net.

HANS-PETER SÖDER is an intellectual historian at the department of Modern and Classical Languages, Literatures and Cultures at Wayne State University (Detroit, USA). He has a joint appointment as the resident director of the Junior Year in Munich at the University of Munich. He is member of the executive board of The International Society for the Study of European Ideas (ISSEI) and an advisory editor of The European Legacy. Editor of the cultural journal *Wendepunk.t* he has elsewhere published widely in the area of technology, philosophy, and culture. His most recent monograph *Metalogicon: Eine Liebeserklärung an die Philosophie* appeared in 2016 and his most current publication "Pain is Good: Warburg`s and Heidegger`s Iconological Struggle Against Technological Modernity" will appear in IKON in 2019.

a Māori Mental Health Service in New Zealand, Elliott Edge – *An Occult Reading of PAO! Imagining in the Dark with Our Vestigial Shamanism in a Shade, Shadow, Wide*, Charlotte Rodgers – *Stripped to the Core: Animistic Art Action and Magickal Revelation*, Alkistis Dimech – *Dynamics of the Occulted Body*, Fred Yee – *Cut-Up As Egregore, Oracle and Flirtation Device*, Robert Ansell – *Androgyny, Biology and Latent Memory in the Work of Austin Osman Spare*, Ray O Neill – *Double, Double, Toil and Trouble: Psychoanalysis Burn and Surrealism Bubble*, Derek M Elmore – *Dreams and the Neither-Neither*, Julio Mendes Rodrigo – *Rebis, the Double Being*, Eve Watson – *Bowie's Non-Human Effect: Alien/Alienation in The Man Who Fell to Earth (1976) and The Hunger (1983)*, Carl Abrahamsson – *Formulating the Desired: Some similarities between ritual magic and the psychoanalytic process*

THE FENRIS WOLF 8 (2016)

Carl Abrahamsson – *Editor's Introduction*, Vanessa Sinclair – *Polymorphous Perversity and Pandrogeny*, Charles Stansfield Jones (Frater Achad) – *Alchymia*, Tim O'Neill: *Black Lodge/White Lodge*, Nina Antonia – *Bosie & The Beast*, Aki Cederberg – *Festivals of Spring*, Michael Moynihan – *Friedrich Hielscher's Vision of the Real Powers*, Friedrich Hielscher – *The Real Powers*, Orryelle Defenestrate Bascule – *Ear Horn: Shamanic Perspectives and Multi-Sensory Inversion*, Zbigniew Lagos – *The Figure of the Polish Magician: Czesław Czynski (1858-1932)*, Gary Lachman – *Rejected Knowledge: A Look At Our Other Way of Knowing*, Carl Abrahamsson – *Intuition as a State of Grace*, Bishop T Omphalos – *The Golden Thread: Soteriological Aspects of the Gnostic Catholicism in E.G.C.*, Kendell Geers – *iMagus*, Johan Nilsson – *Defending Paper Gods: Aleister Crowley and the Reception of Daoism in Early 20th Century Esotericism*, Gordan Djurdjevic – *The Birth of the New Aeon: Magick and Mysticism of Thelema from the Perspective of Postmodern A/Theology*, Tim O'Neill – *The Derleth Error*, Antti P Balk – *Greek Mysteries*, Carl Abrahamsson – *The Economy of Magic*, Stephen Sennitt – *The Book of the Sentient Night: 23 Nails*, Henrik Dahl – *We Ate the Acid: A Note on Psychedelic Imagery*, Jason Louv – *Robert Anton Wilson's Cosmic Trigger and the Psychedelic Interstellar Future we need*, Carey Hodges & Chad Hensley – *New Orleans Voodoo: An Oddity Unto Itself*, Alexander Nym – *Kabbalah references in contemporary culture*, Zaheer Gulamhusein – *Standing in Line*, Carl Abrahamsson – *As the Wolf Lies Down to Rest*, Vanessa Sinclair & Ingo Lambrecht – *Ritual and Psychoanalytical Spaces as Transitional, featuring Sangoma Trance States*, Hagen von Julien – *Listening to the Voice of Silence: A Contemporary Perspective on the Fraternities Saturni*, Erik Davis – *Infectious Hoax: Robert Anton Wilson reads H.P. Lovecraft*, N – *II. Land*, Cadmus – *Neo-Chthonia*, Kadmus – *A Fragment of Heart: A contribution to the Mega-Golem*, Stojan Nikolic – *The One True Church of the Dark Age of Scientism*, Miguel Marques – *The Labors of Seeing: A Journey Through the Works of Peter Whitehead*, Renata Wieczorek – *The Conception of Number According to Aleister Crowley*, Orryelle Defenestrate Bascule – *Fragments of Fact*, Derek Seagrief – *Conscious ExIt*, Kasper Opstrup – *By This, That: A spin on Lea Porsager's Spin*, and Genesis Breyer P-Orridge – *Greyhounds of the future*.

Inauguration of Kenneth Anger, Carl Abrahamsson – *An Interview with Genesis P-Orridge*, William S Burroughs – *Points of Distinction between Sedative and Consciousness-Expanding Drugs*, Carl Abrahamsson – *Jayne Mansfield: Satanist*, TOPYUS – *Television Magick*, Anton LaVey – *Evangelists vs The New God*

THE FENRIS WOLF 2 (1990)
Lionel Snell – *The Satan Game*, Carl Abrahamsson – *In Defence of Satanism*, Anton LaVey – *The Horns of Dilemma*, Genesis P-Orridge – *Beyond thee Valley ov Acid*, Phauss – *Photographs*, Jack Stevenson – *15 Voices from God*, Jack Stevenson – *18 Fatal Arguments*, Tim O'Neill – *Art On the Edge of Life*, Terence Sellers – *To Achieve Death*, Stein Jarving – *Choice and Process*, Tim O'Neill – *Under the Sign of Gemini*, 93/696 – *The Forgotten Ones In Magick*, Tim O'Neill – *The Mechanics of Maya*, Coyote 12 – *The Thin Line*, Genesis P-Orridge – *Thee Only Language Is Light*, Jack Stevenson – *Porno on Film*, Carl Abrahamsson – *An Interview with Kenneth Anger*

THE FENRIS WOLF 3 (1993)
Jack Stevenson – *Vandals, Vikings and Nazis*, von Hausswolff & Elggren – *Inauguration of two new Kingdoms*, Tim O'Neill – *A Flame in the Holy Mountain*, Frater Tigris – *A Preliminary Vision*, Carl Abrahamsson – *The Demonic Glamour of Cinema*, William Heidrick – *Some Crowley Sources*, Peter H Gilmore – *The Rite of Ragnarök*, ONA – *The Left-Handed Path*, Zbigniew Karkowski – *The Method Is Science...*, Fetish 23 – *Demonic Poetry*, Ben Kadosh – *Lucifer-Hiram*, Freya Aswynn – *The Northern Magical Tradition*, Anton LaVey – *Tests*, Austin Osman Spare – *Anathema of Zos*, Rodney Orpheus – *Thelemic Morality*, Nemo – *Recognizing Pseudo-Satanism*, Philip Marsh – *Pythagoras, Plato and the Hellenes*, Terence Sellers – *A Few Acid Writings*, Hymenæus Beta – *Harry Smith 1923-1991*, Andrew M McKenzie – *Outofinto*, Beatrice Eggers – *Nature: Now, Then and Never*

GENESIS BREYER P-ORRIDGE: SACRED INTENT
– CONVERSATIONS WITH CARL ABRAHAMSSON 1986-2019

Sacred Intent gathers conversations between artist Genesis Breyer P-Orridge and longtime friend and collaborator, the Swedish author Carl Abrahamsson. From the first 1986 fanzine interview about current projects, over philosophical insights, magical workings, international travels, art theory and gender revolutions, to 2019's thoughts on life and death in the the shadow of battling leukaemia, *Sacred Intent* is a unique journey in which the art of conversation blooms.

With (in)famous projects like C.O.U.M. Transmissions, Throbbing Gristle, Psychic TV, Thee Temple Ov Psychick Youth (TOPY) and Pandrogeny, Breyer P-Orridge has consistently thwarted preconceived ideas and transformed disciplines such as performance art, music, collage, poetry and social criticism; always cutting up the building blocks to dismantle control structures and authority. But underneath the socially conscious and pathologically rebellious spirit, there has always been a devout respect for a holistic, spiritual, magical worldview – one of "sacred intent."

Sacred Intent is a must read for anyone interested in contemporary art, deconstructed identity, gender evolution, and magical philosophy. The book not only celebrates an intimate friendship, but also the work and ideas of an artist who has never ceased to amaze and provoke. Also included are photographic portraits of Breyer P-Orridge taken by Carl Abrahamsson, transcripts of key lectures, and an interview with Jacqueline "Lady Jaye" Breyer P-Orridge from 2004.

GENESIS BREYER P-ORRIDGE: BRION GYSIN – HIS NAME WAS MASTER

Brion Gysin (1916–86) has been an incredibly influential artist and iconoclast: his development of the "cut-up" technique with William S. Burroughs has inspired generations of writers, artists and musicians. Gysin was also a skilled networker and revered expat: together with his friend Paul Bowles, he more or less constructed the post-beatnik romanticism for life and magic in Morocco, and was also a protagonist in an international gay culture with inspirational reaches in both America and Europe. Not surprisingly, Gysin has become something of a cult figure.

One of the artists he inspired is Genesis Breyer P-Orridge, who collaborated with both Gysin and Burroughs in the 1970s, during his work with Throbbing Gristle and C.O.U.M. Transmissions. The interviews made by P-Orridge have since become part of a New Wave/Industrial mythos. This volume presents them in their entirety alongside three texts on Gysin by P-Orridge, plus an introduction. This book is an exclusive insight into the mind of a man P-Orridge describes as "a kind of Leonardo da Vinci of the last century," and a fantastic complement to existing biographies and monographs.

NINA ANTONIA: DANCING WITH SALOMÉ
– COURTING THE UNCANNY WITH OSCAR WILDE & FRIENDS

Dancing with Salomé unmasks the occult aspects of Oscar Wilde's celebrated tome The Picture of Dorian Gray, whilst exploring how the unseen manifested not just in the famous author's life but in that of his love interest, Lord Alfred Douglas. The gilded backdrop to their ill-fated liaison was the Decadent movement, a literary and artistic feast of the divine and debauched which redefined the lines of male beauty. Curiously, Aubrey Beardsley, the most renowned illustrator of the Decadents, refused to keep any of Oscar Wilde's books in his home, as he believed, like many of his friends, that the playwright was accursed. Beardsley's theory is not as far-fetched as it seems if one takes into account the doomed lineages from which both Oscar and Lord Alfred Douglas were descended. Through a series of interlinking essays, Nina Antonia takes us to meet the Decadent demi-monde of the 1890's with whom Wilde and Douglas mingled. Whilst eroticism and mysticism were key themes of the Decadents, there was also a surge of interest in ritual magic, enabled by the flowering of the "Golden Dawn" – the most significant esoteric order in England's history. Wilde's wife, Constance, was a member, as was W.B. Yeats, alongside Aleister Crowley and Arthur Machen. All would play a part, directly or indirectly, in the drama of Oscar Wilde's enchanted & accursed life.

Steven Cline: Amok!

In this collection of recent texts, American surrealist artist Steven Cline has opened the floodgates to his inner worlds, demanding that we take a look. When we do, we are irrevocably drawn in further by a force that resembles our very own curiosity. Is this a mirror or a windowpane? Are these mesmerising thoughts and short essays catapulted from an overarching Zeitgeist or from a very talented writer who desires to express himself? Or both? No matter what, once you have begun reading, you are in it for a thrill ride. Steven Cline is a compelling author, weaving surreal and sensual spells until all resistance is futile... You might as well step right in!

Carl Abrahamsson (ed): The Trapartisan Review I

The Trapartisan Review welcomes you to enjoy unique works of art created by a number of highly talented contemporary and international painters, writers, photographers, poets, performance- and collage artists, etc, jointly assembling a strong and elegant bouquet of timeless expressions for your pleasure and inspiration. This first issue contains contributions by Jason Atomic, Hector Domiane, Val Denham, Johan Hamrin, Billy Chainsaw, Andreas Kalliaridis, Jordi Valls, Peter Köhler, Nicolas Ballet, Carl Michael von Hausswolff, Carl Abrahamsson, Anna Sebastian, Gabriella Eriksson, Karl Max Fredriksson, Vanessa Sinclair, Susana Vico Valero, Jake Kobrin, Tom Banger, Tim Pewe, Gunner Wright, Sean Bonner, Charlotte Rodgers, Annsofie Jonsson, Jason Haaf, Hazel Cline, Ruby Ray, Lars Sundestrand, Åsa Ersmark, Nestor Povarnin, Hannah Haddix, Sergey Martyn, Gustaf Broms, MV Carbon, Steven Cline, Paul Bee Hampshire, Christopher Mealie, Gabriela Herstik, and Tom Benson.

Carl Abrahamsson: The Devil's Footprint

God proposes the challenge of the millennium: if Satan sorts out the ever growing human mess on Earth, God will lovingly take him back to Heaven as his favorite Archangel. Satan accepts, and sets out on a massive operation to balance out over-population, pollution, corruption, and other severely Satanic headaches – many of which he originally helped create... Easier said than done! Satan's love of the ambitiously mischievous humans is challenged as his own "Team Apocalypse" fervently sets to work. But as the world begins to change quickly and dramatically for the better, a new question arises: can God and his suspicious Archangels really be trusted in this cataclysmic, cosmic undertaking?

CARL ABRAHAMSSON: MOTHER, HAVE A SAFE TRIP

Unearthed plans and designs stemming from radical inventor Nikola Tesla could solve the world's energy problems. These plans suddenly generate a vortex of interest from various powers. Thrown into this maelstrom of international intrigue is Victor Ritterstadt – a soul searching magician with a mysterious and troubled past. From Berlin, over Macedonia, and all the way to Nepal, Ritterstadt sets out on an outer as well as inner quest. Espionage, love, UFOs, magic, telepathy, conspiracies, LSD, and more in this shocking story of a world about to be changed forever…

"It's a thrilling roller coaster ride through psychedelic adventures, juicy romantic interludes, metaphoric dreamscapes, high Himalayan yoga enclaves, telepathic portals, 60's flashbacks, magical constructs, secret government pursuits and many more twists that kept all three of my eyes open. It's a story that you'll definitely want to keep non-stop reading, which I enthusiastically recommend."
– George Douvris, Links by George

"*Mother, Have A Safe Trip* is a highly entertaining and thought-provoking novel. Chock-full of psychedelia, the book is also a much welcome addition to the far too few fictional works published dealing with psychedelic culture."
– Henrik Dahl, Psychedelic Press

"The dialogues are great. But it's too short. I wanted more."
– Genesis Breyer P-Orridge, Artist

"It's a wonderful read. A lovely book."
– June Newton/Alice Springs, Photographer

CARL ABRAHAMSSON: DIFFERENT PEOPLE

Different People is an anthology of interviews by Swedish author Carl Abrahamsson, focusing on art, life and the creative process. Included are in-depth conversations with Conrad Rooks, Malcolm McLaren, Stelarc, John Duncan, Charles Gatewood, Mark McCloud, Ralph Metzner, Peter Beard, Bill Landis, Ralph Gibson, Maja Elliott, Michael Bowen, Bob Colacello, Dian Hanson, Anton Corbijn, June Newton, Kendell Geers, Simeon Coxe III (Silver Apples), Vicki Bennett (People Like Us), and Brian Williams (Lustmord). These groundbreaking artists, writers, musicians, photographers, filmmakers, editors and psychedelic researchers have all helped shape the culture we live in. But what makes them do what they do? Which are their driving forces and their inspirations; their joys and fears?

CARL ABRAHAMSSON (ED):
THE MEGA GOLEM – A WOMANUAL FOR ALL TIMES AND SPACES

An anthology volume celebrating a decade of occult mischief by the "Mega Golem." Originally conceived by Swedish author Carl Abrahamsson as a "quantum quilt" project that artists and magicians can contribute to, the Mega Golem now has a life of its own. Whether its parts and abilities are known and tangible or secret and ethereal, the impact of its presence is undeniable. It weaves a special kind of magic for the 21st century, in and through art and talismanic approaches. Is this being invisible? Indivisible? Invincible? Intangible? Whose desires and dreams are incorporated in the sinews and cells of this benign mutation of our inertly causal culture? The Mega Golem is the poetic transcendence of expected transgression, and as such a psychosexual embrace from behind the front-lines. Free for all, and dreams made flesh! This first Mega Golem book collects ideas, theories and artworks that all constitute its first incarnation. This book is therefore nothing less than a Magical Womanual for any and all who are willing to believe wholeheartedly in the disbelief of psychic prestidigitation and its many emotional pitfalls. With contributions by Carl Abrahamsson, Vanessa Sinclair, Kadmus Herschel, Gabriel McCaughry and others.

VANESSA SINCLAIR & ELISABETH PUNZI (EDS):
OUTSIDER INPATIENT – REFLECTIONS ON ART AS THERAPY

Outsider Inpatient is an anthology of perspectives about the value of art and creativity within psychiatric environments. It specifically shines the light on experiences at Lillhagen Hospital in Gothenburg, Sweden, where inpatients were allowed to paint and decorate the entire walls of long corridors in the basements of the hospital. Also included are valuable thoughts about creativity in general from clinicians, art historians, psychoanalysts, and artists. What constitutes "outsider" art? How can creativity be used in the treatment of (in)patients? Why do certain artists create the way they do, and how does it affect them? *Outsider Inpatient* is an informative study about a topic that has created as much controversy and criticism as it has support and adherents, in environments as diverse as clinical psychiatry and psychology, art theory, social sciences, psychoanalysis and philosophy. This book has been produced in cooperation with the Center for Critical Heritage Studies and the University of Gothenburg, and contains texts by Elisabeth Punzi, Per Magnus Johansson, Johannes Nordholm, Inez Edström, Christian Munthe, Carl Abrahamsson, Vanessa Sinclair, and Val Denham.

VANESSA SINCLAIR & CARL ABRAHAMSSON:
IT'S MAGIC MONDAY EVERY DAY OF THE WEEK

In 2020, psychoanalyst-artist Vanessa Sinclair & author Carl Abrahamsson decided to create an online presence specifically for their magical practice & philosophy. This led to a weekly transmission aptly called "Magic Monday." This book sums up the first year of these writings, photos, poems, collages, and cut-ups. In an inspiring tour-de-force for all senses, Sinclair & Abrahamsson touch upon ritual, runes, psychedelics, sex, tarot, individuation, ancestor worship, talismania, the third mind method of Brion Gysin & William S Burroughs, creating sigils, shamanism, the Mega Golem, necromancy & glitchcraft, dealing with death & loss, making charged art, time travel, biospheric morals, and much more... The book also contains more than one hundred colour photographs and collages. *It's Magic Monday Every Day of the Week* is a book that will keep intriguing and inspiring you to experiment freely, and to develop as a human being. With an attitude of cutting up and rearranging the givens – of disrupting the narrative – you can change more things in life than you've ever dreamt of. Sinclair & Abrahamsson share their own intimate, magical experiences and show you how easy it can actually be to take charge and write your own story.

Vanessa Sinclair: Switching Mirrors

Switching Mirrors is an amazing collection of cut-ups and mind-expanding poetry by Vanessa Sinclair. Delving into the unconscious and actively utilising the "third mind" as developed by William S Burroughs and Brion Gysin, Sinclair roams through suggestive vistas of magic, witchcraft, dreams, psychoanalysis, sex and sexuality (and more). Causal apprehensions are disrupted by a flow of impressions that open up the mind of the reader. What's behind language and our use of it? What happens when random factors and the unconscious are given free reign in poetic form? *Switching Mirrors* is what happens.

Vanessa Sinclair: The Pathways of the Heart

Vanessa Sinclair's new collection of poems and collages is rooted in the dark earth of death, but to an equal degree it also celebrates the vibrant life-force that grows inside this eternal darkness, and the transformation, love and magic we all need to live. The constant interplay of motion and emotion filters fragments of questions we try so hard to avoid but always fail to. *The Pathways to the Heart* are many but they need to be trodden lightly, with love and deep appreciation. Once there, you can assemble the fragments of your life and see what they say – the poetry of an existence that is inevitable until it is not.

Vanessa Sinclair (ed.): Rendering Unconscious
– Psychoanalytic Perspectives, Politics & Poetry

In times of crisis, one needs to stop and ask, "How did we get here?" Our contemporary chaos is the result of a society built upon pervasive systems of oppression, discrimination and violence that run deeper and reach further than most understand or care to realize. These draconian systems have been fundamental to many aspects of our lives, and we seem to have gradually allowed them more power. However, our foundation is not solid; it is fractured and collapsing – if we allow that. We need to start applying new models of interpretation and analysis to the deep-rooted problems at hand.

Rendering Unconscious brings together international scholars, psychoanalysts, psychologists, philosophers, researchers, writers and poets; reflecting on current events, politics, the state of mental health care, the arts, literature, mythology, and the cultural climate; thoughtfully evaluating this moment of crisis, its implications, wide-ranging effects, and the social structures that have brought us to this point of urgency.

Hate speech, Internet stalking, virtual violence, the horde mentality of the alt-right, systematic racism, the psychology of rioting, the theater of violence, fake news, the power of disability, erotic transference and counter-transference, the economics of libido, Eros and the death drive, fascist narratives, psychoanalytic formation as resistance, surrealism and sexuality, traversing genders, and colonial counterviolence are but a few of the topics addressed in this thought-provoking and inspiring volume.

Contributions by Vanessa Sinclair, Gavriel Reisner, Alison Annunziata, Kendalle Aubra, Gerald Sand, Tanya White-Davis & Anu Kotay, Luce deLire, Jason Haaf, Simon Critchley & Brad Evans, Marc Strauss, Chiara Bottici, Manya Steinkoler, Emma Lieber, Damien Patrick Williams, Shara Hardeson, Jill Gentile, Angelo Villa, Gabriela Costardi, Jamieson Webster, Sergio Benvenuto, Craig Slee, Álvaro D. Moreira, David Lichtenstein, Julie Fotheringham, John Dall'aglio, Matthew Oyer, Jessica Datema, Olga Cox Cameron, Katie Ebbitt, Juliana Portilho, Trevor Pederson, Elisabeth Punzi & Per-Magnus Johansson, Meredith Friedson, Steven Reisner, Léa Silveira, Patrick Scanlon, Júlio Mendes Rodrigo, Daniel Deweese, Julie Futrell, Gregory J. Stevens, Benjamin Y. Fong, Katy Bohinc, Wayne Wapeemukwa, Patricia Gherovici & Cassandra Seltman, Marie Brown, Buffy Cain, Claire-Madeline Culkin, Andrew Daul, Germ Lynn, Adel Souto, and paul aster stonetsao.

More information can be found at our web site: www.trapart.net